Practical Strategies for the Teaching of Thinking

Practical Strategies
for the
Teaching of Thinking

Barry K. Beyer
George Mason University

ALLYN AND BACON, INC.

Boston   London   Sydney   Toronto

Library of Congress Cataloging-in-Publication Data

Beyer, Barry K., 1931–
  Practical strategies for the teaching of thinking.

  Bibliography: p.
  Includes index.
  1. Thought and thinking.   2. Thought and thinking—
Study and teaching.   I. Title.
LB1590.3.B49   1987   370.15′2   87-1780
ISBN 0-205-10544-0

Printed in the United States of America

10 9 8 7 6 5 4 3 2   92 91 90 89 88 87

for GREG

and all his generation
and those to follow

Contents

Foreword

D. N. Perkins

Is this book an opportunity or an irrelevancy? To answer the question, let me expand on a favorite metaphor of mine that Barry Beyer is kind enough to quote a few pages from here: thinking as walking. The skeptic, who believes that the words sandwiched between these covers are pretty irrelevant, might urge instead that thinking is as natural as walking. Every normal child learns to walk in the course of growing up. Crawling leads to the first teetering baby steps, these to bolder excursions from the couch all the way to the window ledge, these in the course of years to such extensions of walking as running, skipping, and jumping. No one has to worry much about making it happen. It simply happens. In many ways, the same story can be told for thinking. We all learn to think. We all start with baby steps of thought that, to an adult, can seem pretty naive. And almost all of us grow into competent adults who can think quite well enough to maintain a job, cast a vote, buy a car, raise a family of our own. If thinking is as natural as walking, why all the fuss about *teaching* thinking?

The question gets even more interesting when we recognize that we quite legitimately *want* thinking to be as natural as walking. There is not much lure in the image of thinking as a matter of constant studied caculation, and not much of a match with what our intuitive experience suggests good thinking should be like. Oh sure, we recognize that there will be hard problems that call for hard thinking, just as there are occasional rough terrains that call for hard walking. But our everyday experiences of good thinking should be no more troublesome than walking across the street to borrow a cup of sugar.

Of course, there is one obvious difference between thinking and walking: We view *good* thinking as a special achievement, while we hardly think of good walking as an achievement at all, although of course it is. But what kind of an achievement is good thinking? Most likely, the skeptic views good thinking as a spontaneous achievement, a matter of natural talent. Indeed, schooling often seems to proceed in that spirit, reflecting what you might call a "nutrient" conception of mental development. The idea is that teachers and texts should present knowledge as a kind of nutrient, so students have the opportunity and encouragement to assimilate the knowledge and think with it. How *well* they think with it is a natural consequence of their natural talents. According to this nutrient model, the educator simply nourishes the flowers and lets each bloom as bountifully as its nature allows. So what is Barry Beyer up to with the calculated instructional strategies in this book? They seem less like nutrient and more like the hooks and strings that artificially shape bonsai. Can't Beyer leave things alone?

But what an opportunity this author brings! A door opens when we recognize that good thinking perhaps is not as natural as it looks. Do most of us really just grow up into good thinkers, just as we grow up into good walkers? Is a dose of thinking instruction just for those few who need remediation? With a little pondering, it is not hard to find some reasons why thinking does not come as readily as walking after all.

First of all, while walking may be natural, riding around in vehicles such as cars, trains, and planes is not. Well, in much of our thinking we ride around in vehicles, too—the symbolic vehicles of language, mathematics, picturing. Thinking as we do it is not some kind of "raw" act of the mind performed apart from any artifice. On the contrary, we think in words, images, notes, sketches, outlines, diagrams, and whatnot. If these symbolic resources were somehow stripped away, we might be able to think in some sense, but certainly in a much impoverished sense. Moreover, attaining reasonable competence with symbolic vehicles plainly helps us to think better; for instance, we can think better about complicated messy situations if we have the skills to list, chart, or diagram the factors involved.

While symbolic vehicles are one sort of artifice, we gain from others too. For instance, we use various patterns for organizing our thoughts. Consider the many patterns of argument that serve in different fields— the hypothetical-deductive thinking of the scientist; the adversarial debate in court trials, based upon law and precedent; the formalisms of mathematical proof. At a more everyday level, consider the diverse folk sayings that urge people toward one of the most basic organizations of thought—thinking ahead to the consequences of current actions. We are told in no uncertain terms that "a stitch in time saves nine," "an ounce of prevention is worth a pound of cure," "haste makes waste," and we are therefore enjoined to "look before you leap."

Such counsel must occur for a reason. It hints that, far from being natural, good thinking often is actually counternatural. Without prompting of some sort, our thinking slips off track. For instance, it is easier *not* to look before you leap than to make the effort to forecast consequences, so often people just leap impulsively. For another example, we all know that good decision-making calls for thinking about both sides of a case. However, abundant research shows that very few people give even-handed attention to both sides of a case when exploring an issue; they quickly gravitate to a favored side and hardly explore the other side at all. For a third example, there is a strong tendency for people to think in a "solution-minded" way. When an everyday problem comes up, people almost at once start to develop particular solutions, without asking exactly what the causes of the problem are or exploring alternative ways of formulating the problem. Consequently, people miss less conventional but superior solutions. In general, good thinking does not mean "going with the flow" of natural thought, but, instead, rowing upstream.

So good thinking is full of artifice. Which is why it is not enough just to read and remember the framework for instruction that Barry Beyer has arrayed here. To really take the opportunity, we need to put it to use. The teaching and learning of thinking must be taken seriously, approached strategically, pursued diligently. This has rarely been the case in normal schooling, perhaps because of the nutrient attitude mentioned earlier. Revising that attitude means recognizing that thinking is something you have to *do* something about, and Barry Beyer offers in this volume a well-organized framework for what to do, well-grounded both in his abundant practical experience and in the technical literature.

But wait a minute. If thinking is not so natural, must it always feel unnatural? Does our status as *homo sapiens* somehow condemn us to lives of belabored cogitation if we are to live up to the potential of our species? Does this opportunity to think better come with strings attached, as so many opportunities do?

No, good thinking is not so grim at all. In fact, good thinking can be quite a bit of fun. Here it's useful to remember another kind of nature we sometimes talk about—second nature. If ordinary thinking is like ordinary walking, *good* thinking is like refined kinds of walking—the moves of a skilled hiker, jogger, or rock climber. Now for enthusiasts, hiking or jogging or rock climbing becomes second nature. In fact, anything we do a lot becomes in large part second nature—fluent, comfortable, intuitive, no matter how laborious its learning may have been. Thinking is no different. By all means let us have good thinking that feels natural. It is just the nature of good thinking not to start natural, but to come natural as it becomes our second nature. If our original nature lacks the artifice for really good thinking, let us work to make good thinking part of our second nature.

What Barry Beyer offers in the pages that follow can help us do exactly this. His analysis of the factors that shape the teaching and exercise of thinking provide a sound perspective on improving student thinking. The teaching framework and classroom strategies he outlines offer useful guidelines for day-to-day instruction aimed at the improvement of student thinking skills and abilities. Beyer's explanation of key thinking operations and his suggestions for ways to clarify and assess them will aid in accomplishing this goal.

"Remember," Thomas Edison once said, "Nothing that's good works by itself just to please you. You've got to *make* the damn thing work." For teachers whose students seem perplexed or flounder when faced with thought-provoking questions or tasks, the ideas in this book will be immediately helpful in *making* thinking work. By using these ideas conscientiously and consistently we can make good thinking happen in our classrooms and beyond.

Preface

Ever since I began teaching, some thirty years ago, I have persistently and consciously tried to teach my students how to think better than most of them were inclined to do when left on their own. During that time, I believed I was accomplishing this goal. To this end I embraced inquiry teaching, teaching reading in the content area, and using and teaching the process of writing to learn in my subject area. Indeed, I even attempted to contribute a bit to the state of the art in these areas, with the hope always of also improving student thinking. But the results—in my classroom as well as in those of my colleagues who shared similar bents—always seemed less than desirable. While students may have inquired better or read better or written better as a result of these efforts, they didn't seem to have improved much in their general thinking.

About ten years ago it became clear to me why. Up to that time, I—we—most of us—had actually been skirting the real issue. While inquiry, reading in the content areas, and frequent writing certainly stimulate and provide opportunities for student thinking—at least for those students who choose to engage in them—these and related methods simply fail to *teach* thinking. These methods get at thinking only *indirectly* and even then not very thoroughly. What is necessary *really* to improve student thinking, I surmised, is to provide instruction *directly* in what it is we seek to teach—in this case, thinking. And so I set out to find what there was in research, theory, and exemplary classroom practice relevant to this hypothesis. This book and its companion volume, *Developing a Thinking Skills Program*,* report what I found and my elaborations and applications of these findings.

---

*Boston: Allyn and Bacon, in press.

Much of what is presented here has been around for some time, scattered throughout the literature of educational and psychological research and theory as well as in isolated classroom practice. Recent research in teaching, combined with research in the relatively new fields of knowledge engineering, information processing, and cognition, has elaborated and underscored the relevance and usefulness of this research, theory, and exemplary practice for teaching thinking. Yet, this information seems to be extraordinarily slow in filtering into our teacher training programs, into the practices of elementary, secondary, and postsecondary classroom teachers, and into the textbooks and other instructional materials used in our classrooms. We now know far more about effective ways to teach thinking than we practice.

What I have thus tried to do here is to close the gap between what research, theory, and exceptional teaching practice suggest we do to teach thinking most effectively and what generally goes on in classrooms now to accomplish this task. I have attempted to bring together and elaborate the fragmented ideas and findings bearing on this task and to combine them into a coherent whole, to make explicit what has long been implicit in them, and to use the very methods being described to explicate them. By making these strategies and principles more comprehensible and accessible, by grounding them in relevant research and practice, and by illustrating them with specific examples, I seek to make them more accessible to teachers and applicable in any classroom.

If well used, the strategies, techniques, and principles presented herein give real promise of helping novices and those less experienced in thinking (older individuals as well as the young) to improve dramatically their abilities as thinkers. For teachers just beginning to teach thinking, following these specific, detailed procedures and principles may be most helpful in getting started at teaching thinking. Those more experienced in teaching thinking, perhaps will give thoughtful consideration to these strategies and principles as well as reconsider what they have been doing to teach thinking up til now. Such reflection may help make explicit what they have been doing intuitively and thus enable them henceforth to employ effective skill teaching strategies more deliberately and consistently than heretofore. Undoubtedly, experience in using these particular strategies may lead teachers to modify and adapt them to fit their particular teaching situations and talents. So long as the principles inherent in these procedures continue to be honored in these adaptations, such modifications are highly desirable.

The strategies and techniques presented on the following pages appear suitable for use at any grade level and with students of any ability level, although close examination of them may reveal some that are more applicable to certain kinds of students and certain ability levels or levels of experience than are others. But, most importantly, these teaching strategies, techniques, and principles may be used with success in any subject or content area to teach virtually any thinking operation. They are not add-ons or extras. While they require practice and getting used to, just as do any other instructional methods, these techniques and strategies can be used regularly in the context of all the other methods employed by teachers in any subject-matter class. Mastery and continuous use of these strategies and techniques and the principles from which they are derived can provide classroom teachers, instructional materials developers, and instructional supervisors and leaders with a very powerful way of helping individuals develop the full powers of their minds.

ACKNOWLEDGMENTS

I am indebted to many individuals for the opportunity to produce this volume and for much of its content. Some of these individuals I have worked closely with over the past years. Others I know only through their research and writings. Some—indeed, a great many—I do not even know by name. I owe them all heartfelt thanks for the stimulation, challenges, and suggestions that have resulted in these pages—and apologies for any errors I have made in translating, interpreting, elaborating, or responding to their ideas and recommendations.

I am particularly indebted to Dr. Ron Brandt, Executive Editor of Publications of the Association for Supervision and Curriculum Development and editor of *Educational Leadership*. His recognition of the importance of improving the thinking of American students and his tireless efforts toward bringing about such improvement have provided me innumerable opportunities and platforms for generating, testing, and elaborating the ideas and methods presented herein. The questions Ron has directed at me and the insights he has shared with me have been unusually helpful in clarifying and shaping my ideas on the teaching of thinking. This work owes much to his support and encouragement.

I am also indebted immensely to many other educators, in Virginia and throughout the nation. I wish here to acknowledge with thanks the many university scholars, classroom teachers, and curriculum supervisors whose challenging questions and perceptive suggestions have taught me so much about the teaching of thinking over the past years. Of these, Professor Arthur Costa has given me considerable encouragement and assistance. Professors Bryce Hudgins, David Perkins, Robert Ennis, Robert Sternberg, and Matthew Lipman—through their writings or counsel and encouragement—have also been especially helpful, as have Ben Sauers, Jay McTighe, Bill Lamperes, Miki Jackson, Bill Harper, Carl Stasio and the directors of the annual Northeast Regional Conference on Social Studies, and Charles Rivera, editor of *Social Education*. Helpful, too, have been hundreds of elementary and secondary school teachers from Virginia Beach, Virginia, and Lee County, Florida, to Seattle, Washington; and from Wells, Maine, to Des Moines, Iowa, and Corpus Christi, Texas. I especially appreciate the insights shared with me by faculty committees of the Mount Lebanon, Pennsylvania, and D. C. Everest, Wisconsin, public schools and by the teachers enrolled in my graduate "thinking skills" courses at George Mason University. I am also indebted to the faculty and administration of George Mason University for providing the study leave that enabled me to research and draft portions of this book. All these individuals and organizations have contributed in one way or another to these pages.

Some of my ideas developed in these pages first appeared as articles in journals such as *Phi Delta Kappan, Educational Leadership, Social Education,* and *The American Biology Teacher.* I particularly appreciate the opportunities these journals offered me to communicate these ideas in their initial forms and, by so doing, to generate feedback that has further shaped, altered, and elaborated them.

The book would not be a reality, however, were it not for the efforts of four other individuals, for whose assistance I will be forever grateful. Sheryl Asen's research abilities, teaching talents, and sharp mind stimulated and shaped many of the ideas contained in these pages; without her hard work, persistent questioning, and creative insights this entire project might never have been completed. Sue Woodfine, Sylvia Gortner, and my indefatigable wife, Judy, put my nearly undecipherable scratchings into word processor and typescript without complaint and with sometimes creative, but appropriate, interpretation. Clearly, without their patience and persistence these pages would undoubtedly still be little more than random jottings scattered among the sea oats of the Outer Banks and various offices and library carrels of George Mason University.

To all these individuals and others too numerous to mention goes my deepest appreciation for the assistance, encouragement, instruction, and constructive criticism that have made this book possible. Many, many thanks.

Barry K. Beyer
Fairfax, Virginia

The Teaching of
Thinking—A Rationale

Improving student thinking has been a recognized goal of American education for decades. Over 160 years ago, for example, a committee of Yale faculty expressed this goal by recommending concerted efforts to teach its teenage students:

> . . . the art of fixing the attention, directing the train of thought, analyzing a subject proposed for investigation; following with accurate discrimination the course of argument; balancing nicely the evidence presented to the judgment; awakening, elevating and controlling the imagination; [and] arranging, with skill, the treasures which memory gathers. . . .[1]

Reaffirmation of the teaching of these and other facets of thinking as a goal of formal schooling and concern over the extent to which this goal is accomplished have been hallmarks of American education ever since.[2]

Improving the thinking abilities of American youth has taken on more significance today than ever before. Since 1980 especially, skillful thinking has been identified as a priority of instruction in many American schools. Perhaps the importance of doing so is best underscored by the 1982 action of the Education Commission of the States in listing among its "basics for tomorrow": evaluation and analysis, critical thinking, problem solving, synthesis, application, and decision-making, all major thinking operations.[3] Since that report was issued, innumerable professional, government and business commissions, panels and studies have endorsed the teaching of these and other thinking operations as a major goal of American education.[4] Some educators, in fact, have even gone so far as to assert that the teaching of thinking ought to be "the first order of business for [any] school."[5]

WHY IS THE TEACHING OF THINKING SO IMPORTANT?

For many reasons our schools should be attending consciously and systematically to improving the thinking abilities of our students. Chief among these reasons is that, contrary to popular belief, skillful thinking does not just develop on its own. Most individuals—especially novices, beginners, and the less able—if left to their own devices do not seem to develop to the fullest the skills of thinking of which they are capable. Effective, skillful thinking is neither an incidental outcome of experience nor an automatic product of study in any particular subject area.[6]

Harvard researcher David Perkins explains why. Proficiency in thinking, he asserts, is in many ways more artificial than natural:

> Everyday thinking, like ordinary walking, is a natural performance we all pick up. But good thinking, like running the 100 yard dash or rock climbing, is a *technical* performance, full of artifice. In a number of ways good thinking goes against the natural grain. People tend not to consider the other side of a case, look beyond the first decent solution that presents itself, or ponder the problem before rushing to candidate solutions, for example.[7]

Perkins points to Rodin's sculpture of "The Thinker" to illustrate this point. The right elbow of this famous figure rests not on the right knee as might be expected but on the left knee, forcing the body into a rather uncomfortable, unnatural position. Skillful thinking, it appears, is not as natural as it is assumed to be. It requires deliberate, continuing instruction, guidance, and practice in order to develop to its full potential. Schools thus offer an appropriate setting and the expertise for instruction in those artifices of thinking that enable individuals to develop the proficiency required for success in school and in today's world.

Student survival is a second and equally important reason for the teaching of thinking in our schools. Teachers daily create situations—by asking questions, assigning writing tasks, giving tests—in which students must think and then be passed or failed on the products of their thinking. Outside the school, students repeatedly encounter situations— in purchasing goods, relating to others, completing chores at home, and, someday, joining various social and political organizations and voting—where skillful thinking is critical to their success. Unless teachers deliberately and explicitly teach *how to execute* the various thinking tasks required for academic as well as common out-of-school tasks, students' chances of success at these tasks are greatly limited.

Teaching thinking helps students survive in school in at least three ways. First, by providing explicit instruction in the various operations that constitute thinking, teachers can improve student proficiency in thinking itself.[8] Such instruction can also improve student achievement in the academic subjects where this skill instruction is provided. It should come as no surprise, for instance, to find that instruction in skills required to understand a subject produces greater achievement in subject-matter learning (as measured by end-of-course subject-matter examinations) than does instruction in the subject without attention to these skills.[9] Finally, instruction in thinking gives students a sense of conscious control over their own thinking. When this is combined with the improved academic achievement resulting from such thinking, students develop a sense of self-confidence associated with even more achievement in school as well as outside the school.[10] Teaching skillful thinking may well be one of the most worthwhile endeavors any teacher or school could undertake.

Third, teaching thinking is important for what it can do for teachers and schools. This may be especially true where state legislatures and education agencies and national testing organizations mandate instruction in thinking or use assessment programs to ensure such instruction. Vermont, for example has for over a decade mandated the teaching of thinking in certain subject areas.[11] More recently a number of states, including California, New Jersey, Connecticut, and Michigan have developed or plan statewide testing programs to assess student proficiency in thinking. Other states seem prepared to follow suit.[12] National testing agencies seem to be continuously engaged in revising or building major test instruments to include more attention than before to the more complex thinking skills. Schools can use such tests for a variety of purposes, including assessment of school productivity and teacher performance. Thus, attention to teaching thinking may be important for the survival of school systems and teachers as well as students.

The serious teaching of thinking benefits teachers and schools in other ways, too. By helping students achieve the substantive, academic goals of classroom instruction—as measured on examinations or other indices of academic achievement—such instruction enables teachers to better achieve those subject-matter teaching goals and other curriculum objectives to which they and their schools are committed. Teaching thinking also makes possible a level of classroom discourse beyond the stultifying tedium of the drill, practice, and rote memorization typical of many classrooms, thus enhancing the excitement and attraction of classroom teaching as well as of learning. Serious attention to teaching thinking can, in fact, lead to the kind of classroom interplay of ideas and a quest for knowledge that makes teaching at least as intellectually challenging and stimulating as any other profession.

Finally, changes in our world give urgency to serious attention to teaching thinking in our schools. In years past, societal change occurred ever so slowly. The answers to yesterday's questions were worth remembering because those questions and the conditions inspiring them were bound to repeat, so those answers would be directly applicable again. Such circumstances, however, rarely exist today. Decisions to produce new automobiles in one country now directly affect the livelihood of people in many other countries. Developing and using new power sources, such as nuclear energy, in one area dramatically affect the lives of people thousands of miles away. Political upheaval in one region has immediate consequences for people far removed from events in that region. The rapid, continued shrinking of our world, the scope of change, and the new challenges this poses make it necessary to invent new responses and initiatives rather than simply recall old ones.[13] Doing this requires an ability to engage in thinking operations beyond the level of simple recall.

One dimension of this change is what is commonly referred to as the "information explosion." The amount of information generated by society has been increasing at such a rate that an individual cannot master more than a tiny fraction of it. Whereas in 1970 the information available to us was doubling every ten years, it is now estimated that by the early 1990s it will be doubling every twenty months.[14] This information explosion, coupled with other changes going on around us, often invalidates or challenges much of what is accepted as knowledge. Exclusive reliance on past information and knowledge derived from it appears to be increasingly shaky as a basis for dealing with the fast changing social, political, and economic worlds in which we live.

Thinking skills, on the other hand, remain constant in their utility for processing information of whatever kind. As Yale psychologist Robert Sternberg puts it:

> Bodies of knowledge are important, of course, but they often become outdated. Thinking skills never become outdated. To the contrary, they enable us to acquire knowledge and to reason with it, regardless of the time or place or the kinds of knowledge to which they're applied.[15]

Teaching thinking thus takes on increasing importance as a survival skill for society as a whole as well as for individuals. Such teaching can equip individuals with the tools needed to deal constructively with whatever kinds of information and conditions may typify the future. By so doing, teaching thinking enhances the chances of societal as well as individual survival in our rapidly changing world.

HOW CAN WE BEST TEACH THINKING?

Many different techniques are commonly used to teach thinking. The more popular of these methods include asking students questions at levels of increasing difficulty, having students fill in multiple choice worksheets or dittoes, posing challenging assignments, engaging students in debates and discussions, and even exhorting them to: "Think," then "Think again!" and finally "Think harder!" In spite of the best of teacher intentions, however, these techniques by themselves or in any combination, actually fail to *teach* thinking. That is, they do not show students how to execute any better than they can do on their own the various operations they need for various thinking procedures or tasks.[16] What these teaching techniques do (and often do well, of course) is to provide practice—or opportunities to practice—using various thinking skills or strategies. In effect, these techniques put students into situations in which they—the students—must execute one or more skills as best they can without instructive assistance in how to do so. Although such techniques are useful in learning how to think, the practice and testing they provide are only part—a small part—of what a student needs for becoming proficient in thinking.

One more effective way that we can teach thinking is to engage students in substantive tasks requiring the kinds of thinking we want them to develop and then to explicitly teach, as the occasion and need arise, the specific cognitive operations they need to complete these tasks successfully. To accomplish this, teachers can do three things: they can make thinking the subject of instruction, focus on the key attributes of the cognitive operations that constitute thinking, and provide continued explicit instruction and guided practice in how to execute these operations in a variety of contexts for a variety of purposes. Such instructions is often referred to as direct or explicit instruction.[17] When this instruction precedes using the methods described above to stimulate practice or independent use of thinking, teachers can sharply enhance student proficiency in thinking and maintain that proficiency for an extended period of time.[18]

Many teachers assume that students learn how to think while processing information that they are trying to learn. However, lessons that keep the focus on subject matter—history, science, the content of a short story, a particular kind of math problem—so obscure the nature of the thinking processes involved in manipulating the information that most students fail to understand or learn these processes.[19] A more effective approach is to make thinking itself the major substance of learning, especially in the introductory and early stages of learning thinking.[20] Thus, the various operations and rules that constitute thinking become the subject matter to be learned. Deliberate, conscious student attention should be focused on the cognitive operations being taught rather than on the academic or other content serving as a vehicle of such instruction or on the insights or knowledge developed by use of such content.[21] The most effective teaching of thinking concentrates for some time on the key thinking strategies and skills constituting various kinds of thinking; it keeps student attention consciously on these operations and the attitudes and knowledge supporting them.

In addition, effective teaching of thinking attends in detail to making as explicit as possible the major attributes of the cognitive skills and strategies selected for instruction. As each of these operations is introduced and becomes the object of repeated practice, student attention is directed at the specific steps through which one goes in executing the operation and any rules or principles that guide how the operation is carried out. Learning a thinking skill or strategy requires knowledge of what it is and how it works as well as practice in executing it.[22]

To provide such instruction, techniques commonly associated with direct instruction prove most useful. Such instruction in its initial stages keeps the focus of a lesson as much as possible on the attributes of each skill to be learned and provides repeated lessons in those attributes. It provides demonstrations and explanation of how to execute the skill as well as "systematic guidance through a series of practices to mastery."[23] It also provides explicit instruction in how and why a thinking operation may function in different ways in different subject matter or with different kinds of data or media.[24] Only after such direct instruction is provided can students be expected to benefit from opportunities or encouragement or "prodding" to practice on their own the thinking operations they are attempting to learn.

The direct teaching of thinking, it should be noted, does not consist of pouring into students' heads a single way to execute any given thinking skill or strategy or mindless training in executing an operation in a given way. Rather, it helps students articulate how, why and when particular operations can be effectively executed and offers "expert" models of how they can be so performed. Such models become targets or guidelines to be employed for developing student proficiency in employing these operations; they serve as take-off points, to be adapted or modified by students as they develop their own understanding of and proficiency in these operations. When the instructional techniques of direct instruction are applied to the teaching of specific thinking operations, their attributes and supporting attitudes, improved student thinking can become a reality.

WHERE CAN THINKING BE MOST EFFECTIVELY TAUGHT?

The teaching of thinking can and should be carried on throughout each school's curriculum, across all grade levels and in all subjects.[25] Regardless of which particular thinking operations are selected for schoolwide instruction, explicit attention to these operations should be a continuing feature from the point of introduction thereafter. While some of these operations may be introduced in nonacademic subject-matter units or contexts, all of these thinking skills and strategies must be taught, reinforced, elaborated and practiced in a variety of subject-matter areas as well as in content drawn from everyday, out-of-school life experiences of students. The teaching of thinking, to be most effective, should in fact permeate all curricula and be an object of continuing, conscious concern and attention throughout every educating institution.

Why should the teaching of thinking be carried on across all grade levels and in subject-matter courses? There are at least two kinds of reasons. One has to do with the nature of thinking. The other is related to the mutual interrelationships of thinking and subject matter. Both kinds of reasons are important.

The various cognitive skills and strategies constituting thinking are not learned once and for all at a particular grade level or time. Thinking operations grow and develop over time as an individual becomes more experienced in their use in a variety of increasingly complex contexts for a variety of purposes. To be successful, the teaching of thinking must provide continuing attention to these skills and strategies once they have been introduced.[26] One or two lessons in a particular thinking operation are simply not sufficient to teach or learn any cognitive operation to any degree of proficiency at all.

Moreover, thinking operations and the subject matter and types of data and media with which they are used affect one another in many ways. Thinking skills and strategies are shaped by the subject matter or media contexts in which they are introduced or first encountered.[27] These operations, it seems, do not automatically transfer to other contexts, nor do students seem inclined to make such transfer. Teachers must make deliberate efforts to help students learn how to execute in new subjects, or with new media or types of data, the thinking skills and strategies introduced and learned initially in other subjects, media, or data.[28]

Teaching thinking in subject-matter courses has value beyond improving proficiency in thinking. Teaching various thinking skills and strategies in subject-matter courses where they must be used to learn subject matter gives such operations practical value readily recognized by most students. Moreover, providing instruction at a point in such courses where students have a recognized need to know how to execute these skills or strategies produces better student motivation to learn them.[29]

Not surprisingly, instruction in these skills in subject-matter courses, as noted above, also produces better learning of subject matter.[30] Teaching thinking operations in subject-matter courses not only enhances learning to these operations but also contributes to increased achievement in subject-matter learning.

WHAT CAN TEACHERS DO TO MAKE THE TEACHING OF THINKING A REALITY IN THEIR CLASSROOMS?

The major goal of the teaching of thinking is—or ought to be—for students to become proficient enough in thinking so that they can learn and act responsibly and effectively on their own. Such proficiency, however, involves more than simply being able to *execute skillfully* the various mental operations that constitute thinking. Proficiency in thinking also includes *knowing when* it is appropriate to use these operations and *being willing* to employ them when it is appropriate to do so. Effective thinking consists of much more than technical performance.

Developing such thinking requires attention to affect as well as to technique, to knowledge as well as to application, to managing as well as to executing. It calls for deliberate, sustained, conscious effort on the part of teacher and student in a variety of contexts for a variety of purposes, in most instances, over considerable time! And such teaching begins with three assumptions. First, all students think. Second, all students can think better than they are inclined to do on their own. And, third, the teaching of thinking is for *all* students rather than for just a few. By intervening directly with appropriate instruction, teachers can help all students in our schools improve and refine their thinking. The chapters that follow present and illustrate practical approaches to accomplishing this goal.

These chapters address three of the questions with which any teacher must deal for successful teaching of thinking. *What* do I teach? *How* can I best teach it? *How* will I know if I have been successful? Dealing with the first of these questions, Chapters 1 and 2 present a functional model of thinking and describe various thinking operations that teachers could elect to teach.* Chapters 3 through 7 focus on how to teach these operations directly in any subject at virtually any grade level. After describing, in Chapter 3, classroom contexts and an instructional framework most suitable for organizing such instruction, subsequent chapters detail speci-

---

*For detailed descriptions of specific thinking skills and strategies and sequential skill models, see Barry K. Beyer, *Developing a Thinking Skills Program* (Boston: Allyn and Bacon, to be published).

fic teaching strategies and techniques for introducing, providing guided practice in, and transferring or elaborating thinking skills and strategies. Chapter 8 then addresses how teachers can help students develop meta-cognitive abilities of planning and directing their thinking and the dispositions that support such control. Finally, Chapter 9 suggests ways of assessing student proficiency in thinking—and, indirectly, teacher proficiency in teaching thinking. This chapter focuses especially on what teachers can do in their own classrooms and on their own tests to assess student learning as well as their own teaching.

A brief Epilogue calls attention to some of the more significant implications of the strategies and ideas presented herein. Those interested in pursuing this topic further will then find a list of selected references related to teaching thinking.

The systematic use of the instructional strategies and principles presented in these pages can sharply enhance proficiency in the skills and strategies constituting thinking in all areas at all grade levels, for all individuals.

NOTES

1. As quoted by Walter B. Kolesnik, *Mental Discipline in Modern Education* (Madison: University of Wisconsin Press, 1958), referred to in Bryce B. Hudgins, *Learning and Thinking* (Itasca, Ill.: F. E. Peacock Publishers, 1977), p. 146.

2. John Dewey, *How We Think* (Boston: D. C. Heath, 1910); Kolesnik, *Mental Discipline*, pp. 11–12.

3. *The Information Society: Are High School Students Ready?* (Denver: Education Commission of the States, 1982), p. 12.

4. These include, for example: The National Commission on Excellence in Education, *A Nation at Risk* (Washington: U.S. Government Printing Office, 1983); Task Force on Education for Economic Growth, *Action for Excellence* (Denver: Education Commission of the States, 1983); National Science Board Commission on Pre-College Education in Mathematics, Science and Technology, *Educating Americans for the 21st Century* (Washington: National Science Foundation, 1983).

5. Nelson Quimby/Robert J. Sternberg, "On Testing and Teaching Intelligence: A Conversation with Robert Sternberg," *Educational Leadership* 43:2 (October 1985), p. 53.

6. Hilda Taba, "Teaching of Thinking," *Elementary English* 42:15 (May 1965), p. 534; John E. McPeck, *Critical Thinking and Education* (New York: St. Martin's Press, 1981), p. 104; Edward M. Glaser, *An Experiment in the Development of Critical Thinking* (New York: Bureau of Publications, Teachers College, Columbia University, 1941), p. 69.

7. David N. Perkins, "Thinking Frames: An Integrative Perspective on Teaching Cognitive Skills" (paper delivered at ASCD Conference on Approaches to Teaching Thinking, Alexandria, Va., August 6, 1985), p. 1.

8. Reuven Feuerstein, *Instrumental Enrichment* (Baltimore: University Park

Press, 1980); Robert J. Sternberg, "How Can We Teach Intelligence?" *Educational Leadership* 42:1 (September 1984), pp. 38–50.

9. Thomas H. Estes, "Reading in the Social Studies—A Review of Research Since 1950," in James Laffery, ed., *Reading in the Content Areas* (Newark, Del.: International Reading Association, 1972), pp. 178–183.

10. William W. Purkey, *Self-Concept and School Achievement* (Englewood Cliffs, N.J.: Prentice-Hall, 1970).

11. Vermont Department of Education, *Basic Competencies: Reasoning* (Montpelier: State Department of Education, 1979).

12. *Assessment of the Critical Thinking Skills in History-Social Science* (Sacramento: California State Department of Education, 1985); Thomas Toch, "That Noble and Most Sovereign Reason . . .," *Education Week* June 9, 1982, pp. 7 and 16; Robert J. Sternberg and Joan B. Baron, "A Statewide Approach to Measuring Critical Thinking Skills," *Educational Leadership* 43:2 (October 1985), pp. 40–43.

13. Alvin Toffler, *Future Shock* (New York: Random House, 1970); John Naisbitt, *Megatrends* (New York: Warner Books, 1982/1984).

14. K. Patricia Cross, "The Rising Tide of School Reform Reports," *Phi Delta Kappan* 66:3 (November 1984), p. 172.

15. Quimby/Sternberg, "On Testing and Teaching Intelligence," p. 53.

16. Walter Doyle, "Academic Work," *Review of Educational Research* 53:2 (Summer 1983), p. 180; Catherine Cornbleth and Willard Korth, "In Search of Academic Instruction," *Educational Researcher* 9:5 (May 1980), pp. 1–9; Barry K. Beyer, "Improving Thinking Skills—Defining the Problem," *Phi Dela Kappan* 65:7 (March 1984), pp. 486–490; Ina V. S. Mullins, "What Do NAEP Results Tell Us About Students' Higher Order Thinking Abilities?" (Paper delivered at ASCD Wingspread Conference on Teaching Thinking, Racine, May 17–19, 1984).

17. Barak V. Rosenshine, "Teaching Functions in Instructional Progams," *Elementary School Journal* 83:4 (March 1983), pp. 335–352.

18. Doyle, "Academic Work," pp. 159–199; Barak V. Rosenshine, "Synthesis of Research on Explicit Teaching," *Educational Leadership* 43:7 (April 1986), pp. 60–96.

19. Taba, "Teaching of Thinking"; Howard Anderson, ed., *Teaching Critical Thinking in Social Studies, 13th Yearbook.* (Washington: National Council for the Social Studies, 1942), pp. v–vii.

20. Michael I. Posner and Steven W. Keele, "Skill Learning," in Robert M. W. Travers, ed., *Second Handbook of Research on Teaching* (Chicago: Rand McNally College Publishing Company, 1973), pp. 805–831.

21. Ann L. Brown, Joseph C. Campione, and Jeanne D. Day, "Learning to Learn: On Training Students to Learn from Texts," *Educational Researcher* 10:2 (February 1981), pp. 16–18; Sternberg, "How Can We . . .,"

22. Benjamin Bloom, "Mastery Learning," in James H. Block, ed., *Mastery Learning: Theory and Practice* (New York: Holt, Rinehart and Winston, 1971), p. 52; Sternberg, "How Can We . . .," pp. 38–50.

23. Psychologist R. E. Snow, as quoted in Norman Frederiksen, "Implications of Cognitive Theory for Instruction in Problem Solving," *Review of Educational Research* 54:3 (Fall 1984), p. 382; Posner and Keele, "Skill Learning."

24. Posner and Keele, "Skill Learning"; Hudgins, *Learning and Thinking*, pp. 142–172.

25. McPeck, *Critical Thinking*, pp. 132–150; Raymond S. Nickerson, "Kinds of Thinking Taught in Current Programs," *Educational Leadership* 42:1 (September 1984), p. 27.

26. Posner and Keele, "Skill Learning."

27. Nickerson, "Kinds of Thinking"; McPeck, *Critical Thinking*.

28. Posner and Keele, "Skill Learning"; Hudgins, *Learning and Thinking*, pp. 142–172.

29. Carl Bereiter, "Elementary School: Necessity or Convenience?" *Elementary School Journal* 73:8 (May 1973), pp. 435–446.

30. Estes, "Reading in the Social Studies."

1

Thinking and Thinking Skills

The nature of thinking seems at first to be rather obvious. After all, we do it all the time. Yet, when pressed, most of us find it difficult to describe thinking in very precise or detailed terms. But describe it, in detail, we must if we are to be successful at teaching it. For in the teaching of thinking, the subject—or content—to be taught and learned is thinking. Success in teaching any subject requires one to know that subject in considerable depth. Those who provide or supervise instruction in thinking or who prepare materials for use in such teaching or who design instruments for assessing both the teaching and learning of thinking must know what it is about thinking that is to be taught and learned.

Understanding the nature of thinking and those components of it serving as goals of instruction are a *sine qua non* for the effective teaching and learning of thinking. Such an understanding can emerge from three things: an understanding of the general nature of thinking; familiarity with a model of thinking that relates the major functions of thinking to each other; and knowledge of some of the specific operations that constitute thinking. This chapter briefly examines each of these three aspects of thinking.

THINK !

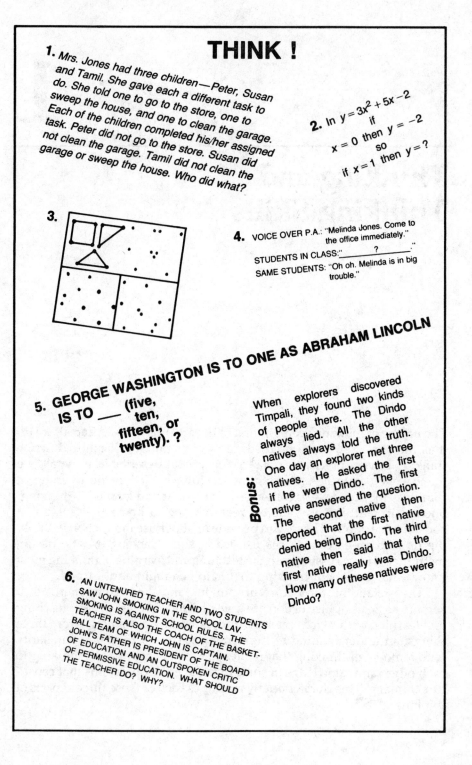

1. Mrs. Jones had three children—Peter, Susan and Tamil. She gave each a different task to do. She told one to go to the store, one to sweep the house, and one to clean the garage. Each of the children completed his/her assigned task. Peter did not go to the store. Susan did not clean the garage. Tamil did not clean the garage or sweep the house. Who did what?

2. In $y = 3x^2 + 5x - 2$
if
$x = 0$ then $y = -2$
so
if $x = 1$ then $y = ?$

3.

4. VOICE OVER P.A.: "Melinda Jones. Come to the office immediately."

STUDENTS IN CLASS:"_____?_____"

SAME STUDENTS: "Oh oh. Melinda is in big trouble."

5. GEORGE WASHINGTON IS TO ONE AS ABRAHAM LINCOLN IS TO ___ (five, ten, fifteen, or twenty). ?

Bonus: When explorers discovered Timpali, they found two kinds of people there. The Dindo always lied. All the other natives always told the truth. One day an explorer met three natives. He asked the first if he were Dindo. The first native answered the question. The second native then reported that the first native denied being Dindo. The third native then said that the first native really was Dindo. How many of these natives were Dindo?

6. AN UNTENURED TEACHER AND TWO STUDENTS SAW JOHN SMOKING IN THE SCHOOL LAV. SMOKING IS AGAINST SCHOOL RULES. THE TEACHER IS ALSO THE COACH OF THE BASKET-BALL TEAM OF WHICH JOHN IS CAPTAIN. JOHN'S FATHER IS PRESIDENT OF THE BOARD OF EDUCATION AND AN OUTSPOKEN CRITIC OF PERMISSIVE EDUCATION. WHAT SHOULD THE TEACHER DO? WHY?

THINK, AGAIN !

TASK	ANSWER?	WHAT DID YOU DO IN YOUR HEAD TO GET THIS ANSWER?	HOW DID YOU FEEL WHILE DOING THIS TASK?

THE NATURE OF THINKING

Thinking, in its broadest sense, is the search for meaning. It consists either of finding meaning assumed to exist already or of making meaning out of something that has no readily apparent meaning. It is, as John Dewey wrote years ago, "that operation in which present facts suggest other facts (or truths) in such a way as to induce belief in the latter upon the ground or warrant of the former."[1] Thinking, in short, is the mental process by which individuals make sense out of experience.

As informative as such general definitions of thinking may be, however, they are not precise enough to provide much guidance for teaching thinking effectively. This requires a much more explicit and detailed understanding of thinking than such broad definitions communicate. One way to develop this understanding is to engage in, and then examine, thinking as it is used to accomplish a variety of purposes to which it is commonly put. The preceding two pages—THINK and THINK AGAIN—offer such an opportunity.

As their titles indicate, these preceding pages invite you to think and then to reflect on your thinking. They present a number of tasks, each of which requires different types of thinking to complete. Try completing some of these tasks.[2] Write your answers in the appropriate column; then reflect on how you completed each task. What did you do in your head to produce each answer? Why? How did you feel as you executed each? Write your responses in the spaces provided in the next two columns. Completing thinking tasks like these and articulating how you did each can clarify the nature of thinking, what it is and how it works. What is thinking?

Thinking involves many things and serves many ends, as illustrated by the tasks just executed. Task 1, for example, is essentially a problem-solving task, as is task 2. To complete either successfully requires you to identify and clarify the specific problem, to pick an appropriate solution strategy and, after executing it, to check the results as well as the strategy itself. To replicate the figures in each of the blocks in task 3, however, requires other kinds of thinking, including distinguishing the relevant from the irrelevant, identifying relationships, and discriminating. Task 4 requires identifying an unstated assumption, while task 5 involves making an analogy. The rest of the tasks require additional kinds of thinking, including decision making (task 6), and reasoning (Bonus task). In at least two of these tasks, you even have to infer the nature of the task itself! Thinking, as exercised by these tasks, engages a multitude of mental operations, from recalling to processing to evaluating. In reflecting on how you executed these tasks, you can begin to articulate more precisely the nature of this complex process. Such reflection gives added insight into thinking as the mental process by which individuals manipulate sensory input and recalled perceptions to formulate thoughts, to reason about, and/or to judge.

But executing the preceding thinking tasks requires use of more than mental operations. It also requires a certain amount of knowledge, including knowledge of various mathematical rules (as in squaring x before multiplying x in task 2). Knowledge of American history and of American currency certainly prove useful in completing task 5. Furthermore, the Bonus task clearly requires more than knowledge or even skill in conditional logic. Completing this particular task successfully probably also requires a certain amount of persistence, a disposition to take the time required to figure out that only one of these natives was Dindo. And satisfactory resolution of task 6 certainly requires a willingness—indeed, a desire—to examine a variety of alternatives before settling on one as the best choice.

Thinking, as completion of these tasks suggests, is neither a vague process nor a one-dimensional endeavor. It is a complex phenomenon consisting of at least three key components. Any act of thinking involves one or more cognitive operations, certain kinds of knowledge, and certain attitudes or dispositions. Figure 1.1 presents a concept of thinking that identifies these key components and their major attributes. A brief explanation can provide the kind of detailed understanding of thinking required for effective teaching of thinking in any classroom.

If there is anything that experts agree on about thinking, it is that thinking consists of some type of mental activity. This activity can be described, in part, in terms of the operations that the mind seems to perform when thinking. These operations are of two general types: cognitive and metacognitive. The former consists of those operations used to generate or find meaning. These operations include a variety of complex strategies, such as decision making, problem solving, or conceptualizing, as well as more discrete, less complex skills such as the processing skills of analyzing and synthesizing, reasoning skills, and more complicated critical thinking skills such as distinguishing what is relevant from what is irrelevant.

The second type of operation, metacognition, consists of those operations by which we direct and control these meaning-making strategies and skills. Metacognition has often been described as thinking about thinking.[3] It consists, in part, of those operations involved in directing one's efforts to find or make meaning, especially the major operations of planning, monitoring, and assessing one's thinking. Any act of thinking combines operations designed to produce meaning (cognitive operations) with those that direct how that meaning is produced (metacognitive operations).

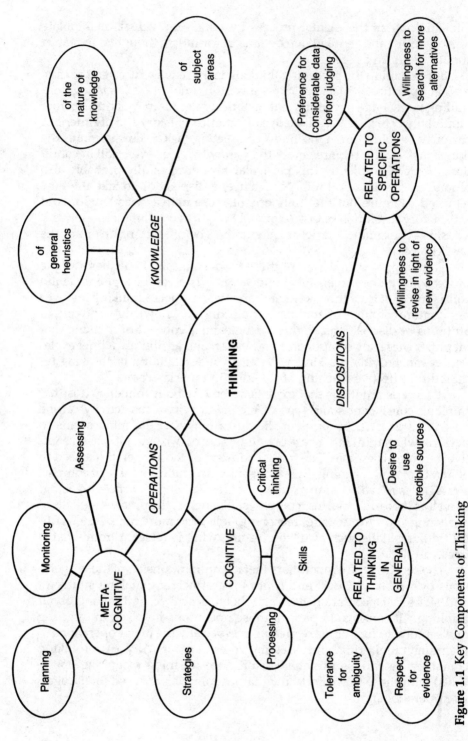

Figure 1.1 Key Components of Thinking

Thinking consists of more than doing, of course; it has as well an important knowledge component. This component consists, first, of general heuristics—rules of thumb—on how to execute various thinking operations. Heuristics are principles based on experience that usually, but not always, lead to the desired results. In learning to be a good teacher, for example, one heuristic that has proven important is that during the first year in a classroom, one "should not smile till Thanksgiving nor laugh till Christmas." In terms of thinking, a valuable heuristic is "look before you leap," meaning to consider all factors before drawing conclusions. Knowledge of such heuristics—often the result of accumulated experience—shapes how one goes about thinking almost as much as does skill in executing the operations that constitute thinking.

A second dimension of the knowledge component of thinking is knowing something about the nature of knowledge itself. This includes, for example, knowing that what we believe in as knowledge is highly selective, fragmentary, interpretive, ever-changing and, thus, most tentative.[4] Awareness of these aspects of knowledge grounds how we go about thinking as well as how we treat the products of our—and others'— thinking.

Knowledge of the subject area about which one is thinking—usually referred to as domain-specific knowledge—is also an important part of this knowledge component. This includes knowing various reliable sources of data in a particular field of knowledge, any special heuristics for handling this domain-specific data, and specific analytical concepts useful for generating, organizing, and making sense of information in specific fields.[5] It should come as no surprise to realize that those who are most successful at thinking in a given field or subject are those who know the most about that field or subject.[6] The assertion that "discovery favors the well-prepared mind" underscores precisely this relationship between thinking and knowledge.[7] Certainly, the ways we go about thinking are very much shaped and informed by our knowledge or lack of knowledge of subject matter. Yet, it should be noted, knowledge of subject matter is itself no substitute for knowledge of, and proficiency in, the operations employed in thinking. Both knowledge of subject matter and proficiency in thinking are essential for skillful, productive thinking.

Thinking also consists of a variety of attitudes, or what educator Robert Ennis calls dispositions, that support as well as drive it.[8] These dispositions are of two types—those that relate to thinking in general and those that relate to specific cognitive operations. Among the former are a tolerance for ambiguity as well as a willingness to suspend judgment, a respect for evidence and for the use of reason, a willingness to alter a judgment when reason and evidence make it appropriate to do so, a healthy skepticism and curiosity, and an objective respect for "the truth." Among the latter are a willingness—indeed a desire—to consider an issue from points of view other than one's own, a desire to secure as much information as possible before making a judgment, and a willingness to identify additional alternatives after an apparently acceptable alternative has been proposed. Effective thinking also requires, as David Krathwohl and his colleagues note, a powerful inclination to make judgments on the basis of the total situation, the issues involved, a clearly defined purpose, and explicitly considered consequences rather than on the bases of fixed, dogmatic precepts or emotional or wistful thinking.[9] An effective thinker is as much characterized by dispositions such as these as he or she is knowledgeable about thinking and skilled at executing the various operations of which thinking consists.*

These three components of thinking—operations, knowledge, and dispositions—are closely interrelated. Each builds out of, and contributes to, the others. The more knowledgeable one is about a subject and about various heuristics related to it, the better able one is to use general thinking operations to their maximum effect. What one understands about the nature of knowledge informs and supports attitudes of caution and care in processing information, generating thinking, and accepting as solid or reliable the products of thinking. In any thinking act these three components are so intertwined they are often impossible to separate one from the other.

But there is more to thinking than these key components. Thinking does not occur in a vacuum. And, because it does not, there is a contextual dimension to thinking. Any act of thinking involves not only the components of thinking just described but also factors external to the mind. For example, thinking is influenced considerably by the degree of expertise an individual brings to the various operations employed in any thinking act. Someone highly skilled at analysis will be more effective at thinking than will be one who has little proficiency in this important cognitive operation. Someone who is disposed to gather as much information as possible before making a judgment will be more likely to develop realistic conclusions than will someone who jumps to conclusions on the basis of very limited information. Proficiency in employing the operations of which thinking consists, as well as one's dispositions and knowledge related to thinking, shape thinking.

The environment in which thinking occurs also shapes thinking. This environment has a number of important dimensions. One of these is *time*. Any thinking act occurs over time, whether a short or long period. It is affected by this duration, or amount of time devoted to it, as much as by the data processed and the incidents occurring in the environment as

---

*A more detailed description of these dispositions and attitudes may be found in Chapter 8.

thinking occurs. Moreover, the tempo or degree of intensity of thinking varies. While at times thinking may be intense and very active, at others it may be more reflective, almost dormant, as thoughts and data mingle in seemingly unconscious ways.

The *arena* in which thinking occurs is a second part of any thinking environment. Thinking that occurs in the course of a dialogue requires use of knowledge, cognitive operations, and attitudes that in some instances differ considerably from those that occur in solitary, reflective settings. Participating in an argument whose purpose is to persuade others that a given position is the "best" position employs somewhat different cognitive operations, attitudes, and knowledge than does participating in an argument or discussion whose final goal is uncovering the "truth."

A third part of any thinking environment is the *subject* or topic being thought about and the data or subject matter being used.[10] This substantive content of thinking informs and shapes how one thinks about it. Thinking in history, for example, is shaped by the discipline of history, the kinds of causal questions typically asked by historians, and the kinds of connections or relationships typical of that discipline. Specific thinking operations employed in history may differ somewhat in construct from these same operations when performed with linguistic or mathematical data or in a literary environment. Environments shape thinking. As environments change, so to some extent does how we think.

Thinking is further distinguished by other important characteristics. It is, generally, purposeful. People think for a purpose, usually to resolve a discordant situation—to close a perceived gap between what is and what should or is desired to be. Moreover, thinking is developmental. The structures and contexts of any thinking operation and of thinking as a whole become more sophisticated and complex as individuals grow and develop physically and as they accumulate experience.[11] Futhermore, thinking occurs in different modalities: individuals think in figurative, symbolic, verbal, quantitative, and spatial modalities, and, as educator Barbara Presseisen notes, thinking is to some extent carried out differently in each modality.[12]

Thinking, in sum, consists of certain dispositions, knowledge, and operations. Giving it both character and substance, these elements are, in effect, the gears of thinking; as they mesh, thinking occurs. The proficiency of the individual doing the thinking, the environment(s) in which thinking occurs, the purposes for which it is engaged, and the modalities in which it is employed all shape how this process is executed. Yet, there is more to thinking than can be described by listing its components, those factors that shape it and its distinguishing features. Thinking is an action. It occurs at different levels and serves a multitude of functions. Examining the major kinds of thinking individuals engage in can help clarify even further exactly what constitutes thinking.

A MODEL OF FUNCTIONAL THINKING

While much more remains to be learned about thinking and how it occurs, specialists now agree that the mind is not a muscle but a complicated, processing mechanism, that thinking is not a muscular action but consists of many different cognitive operations often going on simultaneously or in combination with each other. Although the mind seems to operate in a holistic fashion, for purposes of teaching we can identify these major operations in terms of the functions they serve. By identifying these functional operations and addressing them directly, educators can improve the quality of thinking through direct efforts to improve one's abilities to employ those operations. In other words, we can improve the quality of thinking by improving, through instruction, specific strategies and skills that are employed in thinking.

As noted above, thinking involves two kinds of operations, cognitive and metacognitive. These two types of operations differ in the levels at which they are performed, the objects on which they act, and the thinking procedures of which they consist. This two-level conception of thinking functions can be illustrated by focusing on the major operations that constitute each of these levels of thinking. Imagine these operations as a series of concentric circles or rings as in Figure 1.2. The cognitive or meaning-making operations that constitute thinking make up the central core. The metacognitive, or thought-directing functions, make up the outer ring that wraps around and is superordinate to the inner core of operations used to produce meaning. A further explanation of this image will clarify the interrelationships of the types of operations and functions that constitute thinking.

Cognitive Functions and Operations

The goal of cognition is meaning-making. Any individual thinks for the purpose of producing a specific meaning—a solution to a problem, a new truth, a clearer understanding, a judgment, and so on. To produce such meanings, thinking employs both complex general strategies such as problem solving, decision making, and conceptualizing and more specific, subordinate thinking skills of which these strategies consist.[13]

For example, in making a decision or engaging in any other major thinking strategies, an individual takes in and processes all kinds of information, perceptions, and impressions. He or she records input gathered by the senses of sight, smell, touch, and so on, and recalls from memory related data, impressions, and previously constructed thoughts. As this input becomes available, it is manipulated and processed in a number of ways. Individuals reason with and about it, inductively and deductively, analogically, and sometimes even metaphorically. They take

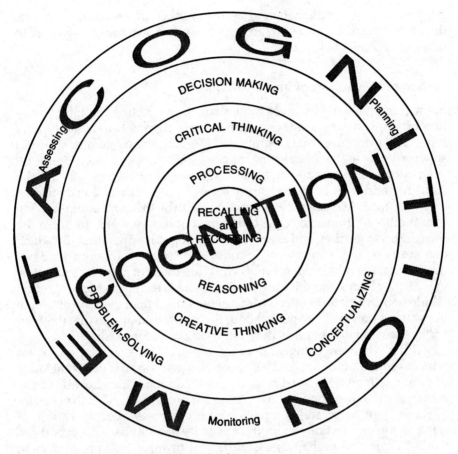

Figure 1.2 A Model of Functional Thinking

it apart by analyzing it. They manipulate it creatively to discover or make connections, patterns, and relationships within and among the input and emerging thoughts about it. And they examine it critically to judge the accuracy, worth, and reliability of the input as well as of the patterns, meanings, and connections perceived or invented. Any purposeful act of thinking—such as to resolve a problem, to make a choice, or to invent or elaborate a concept—involves all of these kinds of operations.

One might thus liken the operations that constitute cognition to a sort of gyroscope. The major thinking strategies or processes constitute a stationary outer rim, keyed to the prescribed strategic goal to be accomplished. The operations on the inner rings of the model—recording and recalling, reasoning and processing, and critical and creative thinking—engage in a variety of combinations (just as the various planes of a gyroscope spin simultaneously) as the thinker proceeds in a specific direction toward the thinking goal. The result is some meaning or truth that did not exist before.

Metacognitive Functions and Operations

But making meaning involves more than simply setting thinking in motion by applying the strategies and skills of cognition to some type of input. It also involves metacognition.[14] Metacognition operates at a level superordinate to that of meaning making, hence its position in Figure 1.2 as an outer ring of operations. Metacognitive operations are applied to the strategies and skills used to produce meaning rather than directly to data or experience. Metacognition seeks to control these meaning-making operations—to guide, to correct, to adjust and, in a word, to direct the selecting, sequencing, and executing of the cognitive operations by which one seeks to make meaning. It consists of several different kinds of operations, the most important of which are those of planning, monitoring, and assessing the thinking in which one is engaged. Metacognition requires individuals, in effect, to stand outside of their own heads and to be aware of how they are going about their own thinking so that they can better accomplish what it is they are trying to accomplish.

Thus, when engaging in decision making, for example, an expert remains conscious of the goal being sought, plans in advance what kinds of thinking operations must be undertaken, and monitors how he or she is carrying out these operations as thinking progresses. Alert to obstacles in the way of successful completion of the process—perhaps a lack of information or questions about the reliability of a source—this expert can "shift" gears and perhaps seek additional or more credible sources to overcome these obstacles or can redirect his or her thinking to otherwise overcome them. And, as the process unfolds, the expert continuously assesses the extent to which he or she is approaching the goal so that appropriate operations can be brought into play even if they were omitted from the initial plan. Thinking about one's thinking is a difficult kind of thinking in which to engage, but employing it is one characteristic of individuals who are rated as superior in thinking.

Thinking to make or find meaning differs considerably from metacognition, thinking about how one is engaged in that meaning making. The former seeks to produce a product, the latter to direct the cognitive operations being employed to produce that product. The former acts directly on data, experience, thoughts, and perceptions; the latter acts on the cognitive operations that generate and manipulate these phenomena. Mastery of the former is what educators customarily focus on in teaching thinking; mastery of both kinds of thinking, however, is what distinguishes effective and efficient thinkers from novices. The teaching of thinking, to be of greatest benefit to learners, should therefore focus on both the metacognitive and the cognitive.

Dealing with cognitive and metacognitive operations simultaneously, however, can be cumbersome and confusing, especially for novice learners. Thus, the teaching of thinking might best focus initially on developing those strategies and skills that constitute the meaning-making or cognitive functions of thinking. Teachers can then focus more explicitly on metacognitive operations when students have become somewhat proficient in the skills and strategies used to make meaning. The following pages thus describe first, in some detail, these cognitive operations. Subsequent chapters present ways to teach these operations. A detailed description of metacognitive operations and dispositions is presented in Chapter 8. While teachers of thinking should attend to both cognitive and metacognitive operations, concentrating on one set of functions at a time makes it easier to understand how this can be done.

THINKING STRATEGIES AND SKILLS

The labels used to describe the thinking operations discussed above do not by any means adequately describe what goes on in one's head when trying to make meaning. Each of the major thinking operations noted in the inner circles of Figure 1.2, for example, consists of sometimes many subordinate and interrelated operations. And each of these operations consists of a procedure driven by some rule(s) or principle(s) and informed by specific criteria or knowledge. The operations that constitute thinking consist of much more than can be described by simple, one-word labels or single-sentence definitions.

It is thus important, at the start, to distinguish clearly between and among these thinking operations and the terms used to describe them, particularly the terms of *skill*, *strategy*, and *operation*. In the realm of teaching thinking, the word *skill* has several different connotations. In one sense it means the ability to execute or perform in an expert, rapid, accurate way. (A skilled performance is one that is done rapidly, accurately, and in expert fashion.) In another sense, the word *skill* is often synonymous with a cognitive or thinking operation, such as recalling, analyzing, detecting logical fallacies, and so on. Such operations, if simple, are often called skills; if complex, such as decision making, they are often called strategies. In the pages that follow, the word *skill* refers to discrete, thinking operations such as clarifying, detecting bias, synthesizing, and operations of this order. The word *strategy* describes much more complex, sequential operations such as problem solving and decision making. The term *thinking operations* includes both skills and strategies. The teaching of thinking consists essentially of helping individuals learn how to execute a variety of thinking operations in a rapid, efficient, accurate, and reliable fashion.

What are some of the key thinking operations—skills and strategies—on which teachers might focus to improve the quality of students' thinking?

Cognitive psychologists, educators, and others have over the years identified literally scores of cognitive skills and strategies that can or should be taught or strengthened by some type of formal instruction. Figure 1.3 outlines those thinking operations that seem to cut across a wide variety of subject areas and disciplines and that are often included in inventories of thinking operations for teaching. These operations are arranged in three levels, based on their complexity, inclusivity, and functional interrelationships; they are related directly to the model of functional thinking presented in Figure 1.2. These operations are, in fact, the mental operations most frequently used by individuals when they think.

Thinking Strategies

The operations designated as Level 1 operations are extremely complex thinking processes or strategies. Three of these strategies—problem solving, decision making, and conceptualizing—are listed here and described briefly in terms of their constituent operations. Other operations, such as comprehension, may also appropriately be considered as strategies.

Four features distinguish thinking strategies from other kinds of thinking operations. These strategies are, first of all, major functions of purposeful thinking, as noted in the discussion of Figure 1.2. Moreover, each strategy consists of a number of subordinate operations, and each of these subordinate operations itself consists of even more refined and precise subordinate operations. Third, individuals proceed through these strategies generally in the sequence represented by the steps listed here, but not always. In some instances the various operations are repeated— the process is recursive—until one arrives at a final product. Finally, each of these strategies and its subordinate operations utilizes in varying combinations the other thinking skills listed in Figure 1.3. The strategies of problem solving, decision making, and conceptualizing all serve, in effect, as functional structures or frameworks in which individuals apply other, more precise skills in order to produce a meaningful product— such as a solution, a decision, a concept, or an understanding.

Many different descriptions of *problem solving* exist.[15] The strategy outlined here represents a model often used in mathematics or engineering, while somewhat different models are used in the social sciences and other disciplines. In engaging in problem solving, as described here, one first becomes aware of a problem. This step (as is each of the other steps in

I. THINKING STRATEGIES

Problem Solving

1. Recognize a problem
2. Represent the problem
3. Devise/choose solution plan
4. Execute the plan
5. Evaluate the solution

Decision Making

1. Define the goal
2. Identify alternatives
3. Analyze alternatives
4. Rank alternatives
5. Judge highest-ranked alternatives
6. Choose "best" alternatives

Conceptualizing

1. Identify examples
2. Identify common attributes
3. Classify attributes
4. Interrelate categories of attributes
5. Identify additional examples/nonexamples
6. Modify concept attributes/ structure

II. CRITICAL THINKING SKILLS

1. Distinguishing between verifiable facts and value claims
2. Distinguishing relevant from irrelevant information, claims, or reasons
3. Determining the factual accuracy of a statement
4. Determining the credibility of a source
5. Identifying ambiguous claims or arguments
6. Identifying unstated assumptions
7. Detecting bias
8. Identifying logical fallacies
9. Recognizing logical inconsistencies in a line of reasoning
10. Determining the strength of an argument or claim

III. MICRO-THINKING SKILLS

1. Recall
2. Translation
3. Interpretation
4. Extrapolation
5. Application
6. Analysis (compare, contrast, classify, seriate, etc.)
7. Synthesis
8. Evaluation

Reasoning

inductive
deductive
analogical

Figure 1.3 Major Cognitive Operations

this or any other thinking strategy) is much more complex than its label suggests. Recognizing a problem involves more than simply looking for key words or clues as to what needs to be accomplished. In nonacademic settings it involves sensing a discordant situation, a gap that needs to be bridged, or a contradiction that begs for resolution. At this point one must define the problem clearly enough to deal with it, and this sometimes requires breaking the overall problem as perceived into subproblems. Going even beyond these steps, expert problem solvers identify and verify the problem's causes or reasons for its existence.

Sometimes representing a problem assists one in identifying as precisely as possible the nature of that problem. Such an operation requires clear specification of the goal, the present situation, the factors that might change the condition from the present state to the desired goal, and those things that restrict these factors. Representing a problem clearly is fundamental to resolving it. This is a second major step in a general strategy of problem solving.

After a problem has been clearly defined or represented, one must select a plan for solving it—for closing the gap between the existing state and the desired goal. Many different plans exist. Some may be formulas. Some may be processes, like that of hypothesis making and testing. If uncertain of which solution plan to try, the problem solver may need to follow a general trial-and-error procedure or to work backward from the possible solutions that can be imagined. To do this requires two things: knowledge of a number of solution plans and proficiency in applying these plans to actually resolve problems. Once an appropriate solution plan has been recalled, or devised and implemented, the solution has to be evaluated or checked, not only to see if it is accurate but also to determine its reasonableness. Finally, what has been learned about the solution plan and how to execute it has to be stored and integrated into one's repertoire of problem-solving plans.

This brief explanation of problem solving is only one way to describe this complex thinking stragtegy. Regardless of how problem solving is conceptualized, however, most specialists seem to agree that effective problem solving employs a general strategy like that presented in Figure 1.3. Most experts also agree that keys to all problem-solving strategies are representing the problem and selecting appropriate solution strategies. But knowing how to execute a variety of specific solution plans is also crucial to effective problem solving. Most important here, however, is awareness of the complexity of the strategy and the extent to which problem solving consists of many subordinate operations, each made up of many more rather precise operations and skills.

Decision making, another major thinking strategy, is often considered to be identical to problem solving. Indeed, some experts combine the two into one extended procedure and treat all problems as essentially situations requiring decisions about solutions.[16] Other experts see decision making as a process that differs considerably from problem solving. In their view, decision making, unlike problem solving, involves (1) choosing from a number of acceptable alternatives when there is no single, objectively correct alternative, (2) simultaneous evaluation of such alternatives rather than serial testing of potential solutions, (3) use of qualitative as well as quantitative criteria in analyzing various alternatives, and (4) repeated reference to values in applying these criteria.[17] Whereas to some, decision making may seem very much like problem solving, to others it is a distinct type of thinking process. Here it is treated as a distinct strategy in its own right.

Like other major thinking strategies, decision making is extremely complex, consisting of a number of operations each of which consists of additional subordinate operations. The description of decision making listed in Figure 1.3 clearly distinguishes this strategy from a problem-solving strategy.

Each of the major steps in this strategy of decision making is important to the successful application of the strategy. Clear specification of the goal(s) to be achieved by a pending decision is perhaps one of the most important of all these steps because the desired goal becomes one of the criteria used in judging the appropriateness of the alternatives available. Part of this step is to identify the gap between the desired and present conditions as well as the possible reasons for such a gap. Alternatives that have been generated must be analyzed in terms of relevant criteria, criteria such as cost (perhaps in terms of time as well as money), resources required, and goals sought as well as consequences anticipated, both long-range and short-range. These criteria for analyzing alternatives usually vary according to the types of decisions to be made and the arenas in which they are to be applied. These criteria are also likely to increase in number and degree of sophistication as one gains experience in employing this strategy.

Alternatives that have been analyzed in terms of the specified criteria can now be ranked as to how well they meet these criteria. It then proves most useful to reevaluate the highest-ranked two or three options in terms of the risks involved in selecting each option and in terms of the risks involved in selecting each option and in terms of possible consequences not originally anticipated. Finally, a choice can be made from among these top-ranked options.

This is but one model of decision making. The strategy, as Joe B. Hurst and his colleagues point out, has been conceptualized in other ways, too.[18] The point to remember here is that in its most refined form decision making can be extremely complex, involving a host of rather precise cognitive operations at each step of the way.

Conceptualizing is a third major thinking strategy. Individuals engage in conceptualizing when they seek to generalize from specifics or to invent concepts or models. Like problem solving and decision making, conceptualizing is a lengthy and complex process, consisting of many operations and subordinate operations. The breakdown of key steps in conceptualizing in Figure 1.3 enumerates some of the most important of these operations.

Essentially, conceptualizing involves two major operations. First, one identifies the key attributes of several members of a class or category of phenomenon. Then, by continued application of these attributes to additional examples of the phenomenon, one builds a generalized mental image of that phenomenon.[19] Individuals build a concept of "pet" from examples of domesticated birds, cats, dogs, horses, and so on. They build a concept of analytical thinking from examining repeated examples of how it seems to operate.

In conceptualizing as outlined in Figure 1.3, one starts with several examples of whatever is to be conceptualized and, by comparing and contrasting these examples, identifies attributes common to all of them. In relating these attributes to one another in some type of pattern or patterns, a tentative model or image of the general concept emerges. By repeatedly applying this tentative image to additional examples of the phenomenon as well as to nonexamples, one refines the conceptual image in terms of key attributes and their interrelationships as well as in terms of variations of the phenomenon that it designates. Through this or similar processes, individuals build mental models that enable them to organize and to make sense out of the increasingly voluminous and disparate experiences and data that constitute life.[20]

Micro-Thinking Skills

These Level III thinking skills are of two types—basic information-processing operations and reasoning operations. The information-processing operations are derived from Benjamin Bloom and his colleagues' analysis of cognitive educational objectives.[21] The reasoning operations are those traditionally taught in logic and philosophy.[22] Bloom and his colleagues, it may be recalled, identified only six key operations, combining translation, interpretation, and extrapolation as comprehension. However, for purposes of clarity and efficient teaching these three operations are recognized here as important enough to stand individually. Bloom and his colleagues conceptualized all these operations as a taxonomy in which each operation included all those antecedent to it; thus, analyzing data engages one in recall, translation, interpretation, extrapolation, and application as well as in those specific procedures that constitute analysis.

Reasoning is the lubricant by which the various processing operations of interpreting, analysis, synthesis and evaluation are operationalized and executed. By reasoning inductively from many specifics, one can infer broad meanings such as generalizations, principles, and the like. By reasoning deductively, one can move from general principles to specifics. Most syllogisms, for example, involve deductive reasoning, as for instance:

- Only students in trouble get called to the office.
- Ronnie, a student, was just called to the office.
- Ronnie is in trouble!

The process involved in such reasoning is used in many critical thinking operations including, for example, identifying unstated assumptions, bias, and author's frame of reference or point of view. Not only are these (and related reasoning skills) basic processing operations, they are also used in many other higher-level skills to move us from accepted truths to new ones.

The micro-thinking operations in Figure 1.3 are, in fact, the building blocks constituting those operations described as Level I strategies. None of the micro-thinking skills is as complex as the major strategies; each micro-thinking operation consists of only a limited number of steps, procedures, and rules. These skills are relatively simple and straightforward, as are the others at this level of thinking.

This skill of analysis, for example, comes in many forms, including comparing, contrasting, classifying, and identifying all kinds of relationships and patterns. In general, putting this skill into operation involves:

- determining the purpose of the analysis
- recalling or identifying the clues or criteria needed to achieve the purpose
- searching data piece-by-piece to find evidence of these clues or criteria
- determining the pattern among this evidence or these clues
- stating the results of the analysis

The skill of evaluation seems a bit more complicated than analysis because it incorporates analysis as well as other lower-level skills. Evaluation consists essentially of these steps:

- determining the trait to be evaluated
- identifying the criteria to be applied (by recalling criteria, inventing one's own, or using given criteria)
- defining these criteria in terms of exemplars
- examining the data to find evidence or exemplars
- judging the extent to which evidence matches the criteria
- stating a judgment

Each micro-thinking skill is used repeatedly in the course of any purposeful thinking whether to resolve a problem, to make a decision, or to conceptualize. The skill of analysis, for example, is used in virtually each major step of decision making. It is employed to identify obstacles to a desired goal and to identify the probable cause(s) of these obstacles. Determining the value of a particular alternative in terms of the various criteria of cost, consequences, and so on requires a detailed analysis of each alternative. Choosing the "best" alternative occurs only after selected alternatives are submitted again to further analysis. This specific skill is employed continuously in a variety of thinking strategies, as are the other processing and reasoning operations listed here.

Critical Thinking

The term *critical thinking* is one of the most abused terms in our thinking skills vocabulary.* Generally it means whatever its users stipulate it to mean. In some circles the term *critical thinking* is used to mean all thinking operations, from decision making to analysis of part–whole relationships to interpreting. In other circles it means the skills drawn from Bloom's taxonomy. Yet critical thinking is *not* to be considered as encompassing all, or identical to any, of these operations. Critical thinking, for example, is obviously not the same as recall. Neither is critical thinking synony-

---

*As commonly interpreted by the general public, the term "critical" has negative connotations. These connotations are reflected by a National Association of Elementary School Principals' wall plaque (often found in many school buildings), displaying a statement entitled *Children Learn What They Live* that starts:
> If a child lives with criticism,
> He learns to condemn. . . .

When the word "critical" is attached to the term "thinking," as in "critical thinking", this negative connotation is transfered to the entire concept of critical thinking. For many people, such thinking is assumed to consist of harsh criticism, fault-finding, carping negativism. Use of this term to describe important skills of analytical/evaluative thinking thus frequently evokes suspicion and, at times, even open hostility. Such hostility often finds expression in open opposition to efforts to teach these skills in schools. To eliminate or minimize the chances of this happening in the future, the term "critical thinking" probably ought to be replaced by a more precise and less inflammatory term, such as, perhaps, "evaluative thinking."

However, to avoid adding to an already confusing labyrinth of ill-defined terminology and concepts regarding thinking skills, the technical term of *critical thinking* will be used throughout these pages to describe what experts today generally mean by this label. Until some agreement is reached on exactly what ought to be included under this rubric, it seems unproductive to add to the existing uncertainty or lack of consensus by introducing a new term into the thinking skills lexicon.

mous with decision making or problem solving. Researchers R. R. Allen and Robert K. Rott describe this latter distinction as follows:

> Critical thinking begins with a previous claim, conclusion or product and considers the question, "Of what truth or worth is it?" Problem solving, on the other hand, begins with a perceived problem and asks, "How might this difficulty be resolved?"[23]

Experts in the study of critical thinking have for years been rather specific about what they mean by the term. Critical thinking, according to them and as used here, means judging the authenticity, worth, or accuracy of something.[24] That something may be a piece of information, a claim or assertion, or a source of data. Contrary to assumptions that critical thinking is of necessity negative or carping, this type of thinking, properly employed, is objective and value-free, frequently resulting in judgments that are positive, affirmative, and even laudatory. Essentially evaluative in nature, critical thinking analyzes persistently, and objectively any claim, source, or belief to judge its accuracy, validity, or worth. Critical thinking also involves dispositions and ways of thinking that support such analysis and evaluation.[25]

Unlike problem solving, decision making, or other Level I operations described above, critical thinking is not a strategy. It does not consist of a sequence of operations and subordinate procedures that one follows in generally sequential fashion. Critical thinking, instead, is a collection of specific operations that may be used singly or in any combination or in any order.[26] Figure 1.3 lists ten of these critical thinking operations. An individual may engage in one or more of these—in any order—and have engaged in critical thinking. For instance, one can search for bias, distinguish statements of fact from value judgments, and identify logical fallacies without engaging in any other of the operations listed in Figure 1.3 and can have engaged in critical thinking.

Each critical-thinking operation contains both analysis and evaluation. That is, each operation involves, first, taking data apart to find evidence related to certain criteria and, then, judging the extent to which what has been found meets the criteria implied by the skill. In trying to determine if a paragraph is relevant to a given claim, for example, one first takes the paragraph apart sentence-by-sentence and judges how closely each sentence and then the overall paragraph pertain to the claim. Consequently, critical-thinking operations are more complex than the micro-thinking skills listed as Level III skills but less complex than the Level I thinking strategies.

Like the Level III micro-thinking skills, however, the operations constituting critical thinking are used at various points in each of the major thinking strategies listed in Level I. Thus, for example, the skill of distinguishing relevant from irrelevant is performed in the course of defining a problem as well as in testing hypotheses, in evaluating alternatives, and in identifying essential attributes of concept examples. In trying to determine the acceptability of an alternative or hypothesis, one must distinguish statements of fact from value judgments, detect bias and unstated assumptions, and determine the credibility of sources. Critical-thinking operations are thus somewhere between major strategies and micro-thinking skills in complexity, function, and inclusivity.

Many thinking operations may properly be described as critical-thinking operations. The critical thinking operations in Figure 1.3 are those most often referred to in the literature of science, language arts, and social studies teaching. They appear here not as a taxonomy of critical thinking, but in an order that distinguishes simpler operations—such as distinguishing verifiable facts from value claims; distinguishing relevant from irrelevant; identifying components of a statement, claim, or argument—from more complex critical-thinking operations such as determining the strength of a claim or argument. The list of critical-thinking operations in Figure 1.3 enumerates these operations more in a teachable sequence than in any other sequence.

Probably the most all-inclusive act of critical thinking is that of argumentation—argument making and argument analyzing. An argument, in critical thinking terms, is an assertion or claim accompanied by evidence, a line of reasoning and general principles supporting this claim and denying any alternative claims. Most of the critical-thinking skills listed in Figure 1.3 are used in producing and examining such arguments.[27] Either of these processes constitutes a useful framework for teaching and practicing the other skills of critical thinking.

It should be noted that not all operations commonly assumed to be useful in critical thinking are, in fact, useful. While some specialists include separating facts from opinions as such a skill, many do not. In this particular instance, some specialists such as social studies educator Jean Fair claim that this operation is often performed unsuccessfully because of ambiguities in the meanings of *fact* and *opinion*.[28] Fair suggests, instead, that it is more useful to distinguish between verifiable facts and value claims or between hypotheses and generalizations, or between verified and unverified statements of fact. There will probably always be some disagreement about which operations are important critical-thinking operations. However, the single most important criterion for delineating a thinking operation as a critical-thinking skill must remain the criterion that, as educator Isidor Starr once wrote, the skill seeks to "differentiate truth from falsehood, fact from fiction."[29] The operations presented in Figure 1.3 as components of critical thinking fit this criterion exactly.

Unlike micro-skills, critical thinking is distinguished also by a large and unique number of dispositions that inform and drive it. As educators Dorothy McClure Fraser and Edith West note, individuals adept at critical thinking exhibit (1) an *alertness* to the need to evaluate information, assertions, and sources, (2) a *willingness* to test opinions, and (3) a *desire* to consider all viewpoints.[30] Critical thinking, as Henry Giroux notes, seeks to identify the "set of filters through which [authors] view information, select facts . . . (and) define problems."[31] A critical thinker approaches information, assertions, and experience with a healthy skepticism about what is *really* true or accurate or real as well as with a desire to search through all kinds of evidence and engage in considerable analysis to determine that "truth." As philosopher John McPeck writes, critical thinking involves not only knowing "when to question something and what sorts of questions to ask" but an inclination to do so.[32] Critical thinking in its most refined state is a frame of mind and set of attitudes and dispositions as well as a number of cognitive operations.

Creative Thinking

Although Figure 1.3 contains no skills specifically labeled as creative thinking, a word about creative thinking should be added here. Figure 1.2 suggests that creative thinking is related to critical thinking. Clearly, however, they are not the same. Whereas creative thinking is divergent, critical thinking is convergent; whereas creative thinking seeks to generate something new, critical thinking seeks to assess worth or validity in something that exists; whereas creative thinking is carried on often by violating accepted principles, critical thinking is carried on by applying accepted principles. Although creative and critical thinking may very well be different sides of the same coin, they are not identical.

On the other hand, creative thinking, like critical thinking, is distinguished by a number of very unique dispositions. In fact, as Alan J. McCormack and David Perkins note, creative thinking is largely a state of mind.[33] It seems to be primarily thinking guided—indeed driven—by a desire to seek the original. It values mobility; it revels in exploration; it requires flexibility; and it honors diversity. As Perkins notes, creative thinking attends to purpose as much or more than to results, works at the edge of one's competence rather than within the comfortable core of such competence, and is driven by an intrinsic motivation to be original.[34] Creative thinking may well be more the application of these dispositions and motives to thinking operations like problem solving than it is any particular set of unique thinking skills.

Many experts, in fact, consider creative thinking and problem solving to be quite similar. For them, creative thinking is problem solving applied to creative ends.[35] Cognitive psychologist John R. Hayes, for example, asserts:

> A creative solution is a problem solving act, and, in particular, it is the solution of an ill-defined problem.[36]

Hayes points out that the key cognitive operations in creative thinking—problem finding, idea generating, and planning—are in effect all part of problem solving. The more specific operations constituting these key operations furthermore appear to be largely what Benjamin Bloom and his colleagues labeled *synthesis*. One may invent a rather creative hypothesis out of an in-depth analysis of a problem; one may develop an original solution to a problem; one may invent a unique argument by combining reasoning and evidence in a new way. All of these are, in effect, the products of synthesis making. As such, creative thinking clearly involves *analysis* of the parts of any phenomenon in an effort to form new and original relationships or patterns resulting in a new synthesis; it involves *application* of data in varying unique combinations and, indeed, the collection of unusual data or data not commonly used, to produce these syntheses; it requires *comprehension* and *recall* of considerable experience and data. These operations sometimes appear to function in a way often described as preparation, incubation, illumination, and verification or one of incubation, representation, construction, and revision or polishing.[37] These procedures are said to be as recursive as often as they are linear. But none are skills or cognitive operations in the sense of those terms as used here.

Whatever the exact relationship is between creative and other forms of thinking, it seems quite clear that creative and critical thinking are closely related. Perhaps philosopher Michael Scriven has described this relationship most accurately in noting:

> Critical skills go hand in hand with creative ones; creativity is not just a matter of being different from other people, it's a matter of having a different idea that works as well or better than previous ideas. . . .(O)riginality . . . means novelty and validity.[38]

Loren D. Crane expressed this mutual relationship another way:

> When reason fails, imagination saves you!
> When intuition fails, reason saves you![39]

Like critical thinking, creative thinking is employed at various points in the broad thinking strategies of problem solving, decision making, and conceptualizing. Thinking up alternatives, as Scriven points out, is a creative aspect of decision making.[40] And these alternatives, as are other products of creative synthesis making, are themselves repeatedly subjected to critical appraisal, as one judges the extent to which they may be original or be leading toward an effective, pleasing product.

Perkins has described heuristics for fostering or harnessing creative thinking. His "design" procedure asks questions regarding purpose, structure, model cases, and arguments for and against whatever is under consideration.[41] Other techniques such as brainstorming, elaboration, synectics, and so on also are employed to stimulate, trigger, or facilitate creativity.[42] But these are not cognitive operations as much as they are heuristics or techniques applied for creative purposes. The thinking operations constituting creative thinking are, in fact, the various operations listed in Figure 1.3, not the least of which are reasoning and the other basic micro-thinking operations.

In thinking for virtually any purpose—to resolve a problem or make a decision or conceptualize—one engages in creative as well as critical thinking over and over again. One invents new combinations and critically evaluates them. One also employs reasoning and processing skills. And all these operations are performed in executing problem solving and other major cognitive strategies. The intermixing of these various kinds of thinking in any specific thinking act merely attests to the complexity of thinking. Yet these thinking operations can be identified as discrete operations. It is thus possible to attend to them individually, to intervene and to provide instruction in each of them; this will enable the entire process of thinking to work better whenever it engages.

THINKING AND THE TEACHING OF THINKING

Thinking operations can be conceptualized in a number of ways. Figure 1.2 presented one such conceptualization, a model of functional thinking. Beyond its major functions, thinking consists of many discrete operations and strategies, some quite complex, others less so. Some of these operations are so general as to cut across and undergird various types of thinking; others are very precise and primarily related to specific cognitive tasks. Figure 1.3 identified some of the more important of these strategies and skills. Most of these operations are used in different combinations with one another in order to achieve different purposes.

Thinking and thinking skills, it should be remembered, are not synonymous. Just as we need to distinguish clearly between thinking and thinking skills, we need to distinguish between teaching thinking and teaching thinking skills. Thinking is a holistic process by which we mentally manipulate sensory input and recalled data to formulate thoughts, reason about, or judge. It involves perception, prior experience, conscious manipulation, incubation, and intuition. Through this complex and only partially understood phenomenon, we give meaning to experience. Thinking skills, on the other hand, are very specific operations we deliberately perform on, or with, data to accomplish our thinking goals—operations like identifying a problem, finding unstated assumptions, or assessing the strength of an argument. In a way, thinking is like playing tennis or any other skilled performance. Combining many procedures, it is still greater in sum than all these procedures combined. Just as tennis consists of many specific skills—serving, making drop shots, lobbing, and volleying, thinking too consists of specific skills, the mastery of each of which contributes to effectiveness in the entire process. Just as playing tennis requires the integration of specific skills with an overall strategy in a given context for a purpose, so too does thinking require the integration of specific skills with an overall strategy in a given context for a purpose. Thinking, like tennis or any other skilled performance, is more than a bag of individual skills.

In this same vein, teaching thinking is not the same as the teaching of specific thinking skills. The former generally consists of providing opportunities for youngsters to engage in thinking (if they choose to do so)—of stimulating and encouraging their thinking, indeed often of actually prodding them to "Think!" and "Think again!" The latter—the teaching of thinking skills—consists of deliberate instruction in *how* and *why to execute* the very specific operations used in thinking, operations such as shown in Figure 1.3.

Thinking, like all similar skilled performances, is a general process that certainly does require encouragement and opportunities to exercise. But simple exercise or practice is *not* enough. One does not become proficient at thinking without explicit instruction also in how to execute the very precise skills or operations of which it consists. The teaching of thinking, as described in the following chapters, consists of providing such instruction in thinking skills and strategies and their related dispositions and knowledge.

NOTES

1. John Dewey, *How We Think* (Boston: D. C. Heath, 1910), pp. 8–9.

2. Analogy from Robert J. Sternberg, "How Can We Teach Intelligence?" *Educational Leadership* 42:1 (September 1984), p. 40; diagram from Reuven Feuerstein's, *Instrumental Enrichment* program. Used by permission of Frances R. Link, Curriculum Development Associates, Inc.

3. Ann L .Brown, Joseph C. Campione, and Jeanne D. Day, "Learning to Learn: On Training Students to Learn from Texts," *Educational Researcher* 10:2 (February 1981), pp. 14–21; Arthur L. Costa, "Mediating the Metacognitive," *Educational Leadership* 42:3 (November 1984), pp. 57–62.

4. Barry K. Beyer, *Teaching Thinking in Social Studies*, rev. ed. (Columbus: Charles E. Merrill Publishing Company, 1979), pp. 22–26.

5. Walter Doyle, "Academic Work," *Review of Educational Research* 53:2 (Summer 1983), especially pp. 163–173.

6. John McPeck, *Critical Thinking and Education* (New York: St. Martin's Press, 1981); Raymond S. Nickerson, "Kinds of Thinking Taught in Current Programs," *Educational Leadership* 42:1 (September 1984), pp. 35–36.

7. Jerome Bruner, *The Process of Education* (Cambridge: Harvard University Press, 1960), pp. 181–185.

8. Robert Ennis, "A Logical Basis for Measuring Critical Thinking Skills," *Educational Leadership* 43:2 (October 1985), p. 46, and "Rational Thinking and Educational Practice," in Jonas F. Soltis, ed., *Philosophy and Education: 80th Yearbook of the National Society for the Study of Education, Part I* (Chicago: National Society for the Study of Education, 1981).

9. David R. Krathwohl et al., *Taxonomy of Educational Objectives—Handbook II: Affective Domain* (New York: David McKay, 1964), pp. 181–185.

10. Doyle, "Academic Work," pp. 159–199.

11. Irving E. Sigel, "A Constructivist Perspective for Teaching Thinking," *Educational Leadership* 42:3 (November 1984), pp. 18–21; Irving Sigel and R. R. Cocking, *Cognitive Development from Childhood to Adolescence* (New York: Holt, Rinehart & Winston, 1977).

12. Barbara Z. Presseisen, *Thinking Skills Throughout the Curriculum: A Conceptual Design* (Philadelphia: Research for Better Schools, 1985).

13. See, for example, Robert J. Sternberg, *Beyond I.Q.: A Triarchic Theory of Human Intelligence* (New York: Cambridge University Press, 1985); John Anderson, *The Architecture of Cognition* (Cambridge: Harvard University Press, 1983); Richard W. Burns and Gary D. Brooks, "Processes, Problem Solving and Curriculum Reform," *Educational Technology* 10 (May 1970), pp. 10–13.

14. J. H. Flavell, "Metacognitive Aspects of Problem Solving," in Lauren B. Resnick, ed., *The Nature of Intelligence* (Hillsdale, N.J.: Lawrence Erlbaum Associates, 1976); Brown, Campione, and Day, "Learning to Learn," pp. 14–21.

15. Norman Frederiksen, "Implications of Cognitive Theory for Instruction in Problem Solving," *Review of Educational Research* 54:3 (Fall 1984), pp. 363–407.

16. Charles E. Wales and Anne Nardi, *Successful Decision-Making* (Morgantown: West Virginia University Center for Guided Design, 1984).

17. Charles H. Kepner and Benjamin B. Trego, *The New Rational Manager* (Princeton: Princeton Research Press, 1981).

18. Joe B. Hurst et al., "The Decision Making Process," *Theory and Research in Social Education* 11:3 (Fall 1983), pp. 17–43.

19. Peter H. Martorella, *Concept Learning: Designs for Instruction* (Scranton, Pa.: Intext Educational Publishers, 1982); David Merrill and Robert D. Tennyson, *Teaching Concepts: An Instructional Design Guide* (Englewood Cliffs, N.J.: Education Technology Publications, 1977).

20. Beyer, "Teaching Thinking," pp. 184–190.

21. Benjamin Bloom et al., *Taxonomy of Educational Objectives—Handbook I: The Cognitive Domain* (New York: David McKay, 1956).

22. See, for example, Michael Scriven, *Reasoning* (New York: McGraw-Hill, 1976); W. H. Werkmeister, *An Introduction to Critical Thinking—A Beginner's Text in Logic* (Lincoln, Nebr.: Johnsen Publishing Company, 1957).

23. As summarized by John P. Madison, "Critical Thinking in the English Classroom," *English Journal* 60:8 (November 1971), p. 1136.

24. Robert Ennis, "A Concept of Critical Thinking," *Harvard Educational Review* 32:1 (Winter 1962), pp. 81—111; McPeck, *Critical Thinking*.

25. Soltis, ed., *Philosophy and Education*.

26. For an elaboration of this point, see Barry K. Beyer, "Critical Thinking: What Is It?" *Social Education* 49:4 (April 1985), pp. 270—276.

27. Steven Toulmin, Richard Rieke, and Allan Janik, *An Introduction to Reasoning*, 2d ed. (New York: Macmillan, 1984).

28. Jean Fair, "Skills in Thinking," in Dana Kurfman, ed., *Developing Decision-Making Skills: 47th Yearbook* (Washington: National Council for the Social Studies, 1977), pp. 38—39.

29. Isidor Starr, "The Nature of Critical Thinking and Its Application in Social Studies," in Helen McCracken Carpenter, ed., *Skill Development in Social Studies: 33rd Yearbook* (Washington: National Council for the Social Studies, 1963), p. 36.

30. Dorothy McClure Fraser and Edith West, *Social Studies in Secondary Schools* (New York: Ronald Press, 1961), p. 222.

31. Henry Giroux, "Writing and Critical Thinking in the Social Studies," *Curriculum Inquiry* 8:4 (Winter 1978), p. 298.

32. McPeck, *Critical Thinking*, pp. 7, 9, 152.

33. Alan J. McCormack, "Teaching Inventiveness," *Childhood Education* (March/April 1984), pp. 249—255; David Perkins, "Learning by Design," *Educational Leadership* 42:1 (September 1984), pp. 18—25.

34. Perkins, "Learning by Design."

35. See, for example, Sidney Parnes, *Creative Problem Solving* (Buffalo: D.O.K. Publishers, 1978); A. F. Osborn, *Applied Imagination* (New York: Scribner's, 1963).

36. John R. Hayes, *The Complete Problem Solver* (Philadelphia: Franklin Institute Press, 1981), p. 125.

37. Bryce B. Hudgins, *Learning and Thinking* (Itasca, Ill.: F. E. Peacock Publishers, 1977), pp. 256—294; Robert Marzano and C. L. Hutchins, *Thinking Skills* (Aurora, CO: Mid-continent Regional Educational Laboratory, 1985).

38. Scriven, *Reasoning*, p. 37.

39. Loren D. Crane, "Unlocking the Brain's Two Powerful Learning Systems," *Human Intelligence Newsletter* 4:4 (Winter 1983), p. 7.

40. Scriven, *Reasoning*.

41. Perkins, "Learning by Design."

42. Hudgins, *Learning and Thinking*.

Selecting and Defining Thinking Skills and Strategies for Teaching

Literally dozens of thinking skills and strategies could be taught in classrooms. Because instructional time is short, however, and teaching any thinking operation to a reasonable degree of proficiency requires continued instruction over an extended period of time, it is not possible to teach directly all the thinking operations that we might wish to teach. Instead, teachers will find it most productive to select only a limited number of thinking operations for instruction. And, because many thinking operations are so ill-defined, it is also necessary to clarify their attributes in enough detail so they can be taught explicitly. This chapter suggests principles and procedures teachers can use to select and define thinking operations for teaching to their students.

SELECTING THINKING SKILLS AND STRATEGIES TO TEACH

Teachers can turn to a number of sources for assistance in selecting thinking operations to teach. They might, for example, consult a district's curriculum documents in their subject areas or for their grade levels. Using as guides the examples and definitions of thinking operations from the preceding chapter, they can examine these curriculum documents to find similar thinking operations. As an alternative, teachers could survey the textbooks(s) used at a particular grade level or in a particular course to identify any thinking operations that these materials claim to teach or at least provide opportunities for students to practice. Similar surveys can be made of standardized tests administered to students or of commercially developed thinking skills programs available for use in a classroom or district. Teacher self-reports about which thinking operations they already teach or believe should be taught also serve this same purpose well. Consulting any or all of these sources allows one to determine which thinking operations are already presumably considered worth teaching; it eliminates the task of deciding from scratch which could—and then should—be taught.

Teachers can also consult the recommendations of experts. Such recommendations abound. Virtually every specialist in the teaching of thinking has developed a list of thinking operations that he or she feels is the most appropriate array of such operations to teach. Examination of these recommendations will reveal four kinds of thinking operations most often recommended for instruction. One type is best described as generic thinking operations, or general thinking skills and strategies that underlie all other thinking tasks or subject-specific operations. Albert Upton identified six such operations: thing-making (conceptualizing), qualification (identifying attributes), classification, structure analysis (identifying the parts of something), operations analysis (identifying the steps in a process), and analogy.[1] Psychologist Reuven Feuerstein, on the other hand, emphasizes such operations as identifying spatial relationships and patterns, analytic perception, and syllogistic reasoning, among others.[2] On the basis of Guilford's work, psychologists Mary and Robert Meeker recommend teaching such operations as spatial conservation, inferential reasoning, making notational transformations, and evaluating symbol relations.[3] Similar kinds of general thinking operations could readily be added to this list. Operations such as these are generally considered to undergird all thinking and thus are not usually associated with any particular subject area or academic discipline.

Experts offer three other kinds of thinking operations for instruction, as well. Some recommend heuristics or rules of thumb rather than specific cognitive operations. Edward de Bono's CoRT (Cognitive Research Trust) thinking program, for example, teaches such heuristics as PMI (Plus, Minus, Interesting) as a technique for thinking around a topic or issue, CAF (Consider All Factors) as a rule for dealing with alternatives in a decision-making situation, and similar rules of thumb.[4] Such heuristics are not themselves cognitive operations as much as they are rules that call into play such operations, but, by so doing, they prove useful in thinking.

Other experts recommend a range of very specific information-processing skills and strategies for instruction. Researcher Robert Marzano, for example, suggests teaching content thinking skills such as concept attainment, pattern recognition, and synthesizing; storage and retrieval skills; matching skills such as deductive and analogical reasoning and extrapolation; and restructuring skills such as problem solving.[5] Many others recommend teaching the skills constituting the educational objectives described by Benjamin Bloom and his colleagues, especially the skills of application, analysis, synthesis, and evaluation.[6] Philosophers often recommend teaching such operations as syllogistic reasoning, detecting logical fallacies, identifying contradictions in reasoning, inferring, predicting and distinguishing between premises, conclusions, assumptions, and inferences.[7] Operations like these are most frequently included in most recommended thinking skills curricula.

Still other experts, however, suggest teachers teach for certain kinds of selected behaviors that seem to demonstrate effective thinking.[8] These behaviors include clearly defining all problems to be resolved, persisting in any thinking task, looking at issues from a variety of points of view, continuing to seek alternatives after hearing a reasonably attractive one, seeking and giving evidence and reasoning in support of a claim, and so on. Focusing on behaviors like these, they assert, stimulates and encourages the development of thinking in general.

Dealing with the myriad of cognitive operations recommended by others for instruction or found in existing instructional programs, materials, and curricula can be most confusing. Careful analysis of all these sources, however, can help identify a number of thinking operations that seem to be widely recommended as basic to purposeful thinking. The thinking strategies and skills listed in Figure 2.1 represent one compilation of such thinking operations. This is the same list of operations presented in Figure 1.3 (in the preceding chapter) as the essential ingredients of the cognitive operations component of thinking.

The operations in Figure 2.1 constitute an inventory of operations from which curriculum developers or teachers may select to build a thinking skills program. In fact, these operations might well constitute the core thinking operations to be taught in any K–12 curriculum, across a variety of subject areas. Or, teachers charged with the teaching of thinking in their own individual classes might select from this list those most useful for teaching to their own students in the context of their subjects or grade levels. These operations are limited in number, are of recognized practical value, are readily identified with a number of subject areas, are closely interrelated, and are meaningful and functional for both students and teachers, out-of-school as well as in academic settings.

Given all the thinking operations one could teach or even the list in Figure 2.1, selecting exactly which operations to teach in any curriculum or single course or grade level is still extremely challenging. For assistance

I. THINKING STRATEGIES

Problem Solving

1. Recognize a problem
2. Represent the problem
3. Devise/choose solution
   plan
4. Execute the plan
5. Evaluate the solution

Decision Making

1. Define the goal
2. Identify alternatives
3. Analyze alternatives
4. Rank alternatives
5. Judge highest-ranked
   alternatives
6. Choose "best" alternative

Conceptualizing

1. Identify examples
2. Identify common attributes
3. Classify attributes
4. Interrelate categories of
   attributes
5. Identify additional
   examples/nonexamples
6. Modify concept attributes/
   structure

II. CRITICAL THINKING SKILLS

1. Distinguishing between verifiable facts and value claims
2. Distinguishing relevant from irrelevant information, claims, or reasons
3. Determining the factual accuracy of a statement
4. Determining the credibility of a source
5. Identifying ambiguous claims or arguments
6. Identifying unstated assumptions
7. Detecting bias
8. Identifying logical fallacies
9. Recognizing logical inconsistencies in a line of reasoning
10. Determining the strength of an argument or claim

III. MICRO-THINKING SKILLS

1. Recall
2. Translation
3. Interpretation
4. Extrapolation
5. Application
6. Analysis (compare, contrast,
   classify, seriate, etc.)
7. Synthesis
8. Evaluation

Reasoning
inductive
deductive
analogical

Figure 2.1 Major Cognitive Operations

44

in making such selections, teachers can use the criteria embodied in the following questions:

1. Does the skill or strategy have frequent, practical application in the student's everyday, out-of-school life?
2. Does the skill or strategy have frequent, practical application in a number of subject areas?
3. Does the skill or strategy build on previously taught thinking operations or lead to the development of other, more complex operations?
4. Does the subject matter in which the operation is to be taught lend itself to teaching the operation?
5. Can an understandable form of the skill or strategy be mastered relatively easily by the students, given their degrees of readiness and experience?

Thinking skills and strategies that receive the most positive responses to each of the above questions will be those most appropriate for teaching across a K−12 curriculum or in any particular class or course. The final number selected, of course, will have to be limited; thus, priorities will have to be established for deciding which are *most* worth teaching. Because of the limited time available for teaching and because of already crowded curricula, teachers should limit to two to four a year the number of thinking operations introduced each year in each grade or in a single subject or pair of subjects. Even by introducing only three new operations a year, a teacher would still have to reinforce and elaborate all the thinking operations introduced in preceding years, a number that could become unwieldy for secondary teachers unless care is taken. Teachers can work in conjunction with other subject-matter teachers at the same grade level and with teachers of preceding and following grade levels to coordinate the selection of thinking operations to teach and then spread the number of operations selected across a number of subjects and grade levels. This procedure reduces the number of operations to be introduced by any single teacher or in any one subject or grade, and it makes such instruction more manageable for learners as well as for teachers.

DEFINING THINKING OPERATIONS FOR TEACHING

Teaching thinking, to be most effective, requires a rather detailed understanding on the part of teachers of the specific thinking skills and strategies being taught. Unfortunately, however, thinking skills and strategies are not adequately described for this purpose by a single word, or short phrase or even a sentence or two. These operations are much more complex than such limited definitions can communicate. Indeed, strategies such as problem solving are even much more complex than is suggested by the outline of steps under "Problem Solving" in Figure 2.1 or the brief description of it in the preceding chapter. For teaching purposes it is much more valuable to know and work from a model of a problem-solving strategy like that in Figure 2.2 than it is to work from a simple dictionary definition of the term or from a sketchy outline. The same can

1. *Identifying a problem*

   Picking out problem statement or finding a problematic condition in given data or a situation

   Identifying the elements of the desired state (goal), the present state, and any obstacles between the two

   Identifying controversy or obstacle-producing elements

   Identifying primary and secondary problems

2. *Representing (clarifying) the problem*

   Defining key terms and conditions

   Identifying key elements: goals, operations, knowns, unknowns

   Putting elements of problem into own words or symbols (via pictures, diagrams, numbers, and so on)

3. *Choosing a solution plan*

   Restating the problem to be resolved

   Selecting a plan appropriate to the type of problem perceived, from such plans as:
   trial and error
   multi-dimensional matrices
   hypothesis making and testing
   specific formulas
   turning the problem into auxiliary or subordinate problems
   working backward from imagined solutions
   working analogous problems

   Anticipating and planning for obstacles

4. *Carrying out the solution plan*

   Monitoring the process

   Removing obstacles

   Adapting procedures

5. *Concluding*

   Stating the findings

   Providing supporting evidence and reasoning

6. *Evaluating (checking)*

   Validating the findings in terms of goals and procedures

   Validating the procedures and overall process in terms of efficiency and effectiveness

Figure 2.2 A Problem-Solving Strategy[9]

1. *Define the goal/purpose to be achieved*

   Identify the goal(s) or purpose(s)
   Define the goal(s) in operational terms
   Identify the attributes of the current condition or state
   Identify the nature of the gap between the goal and current state
   Identify the obstacles to closing the gap and their causes

2. *Identify alternatives (options)*

   Brainstorm options
   Elaborate on options
   Recall analogous cases and options

3. *Analyze alternatives in terms of:*

   Goals sought
   Consequences, both long-range and short-range
   Costs, including real costs and opportunity costs
   Resources required

4. *Rank alternatives in terms of the above criteria*

5. *Judge the two or three highest-ranked alternatives, in terms of:*

   Risks involved
   Unanticipated consequences
   Constraints

6. *Choose the "best"alternative*

Figure 2.3 A Decision-Making Strategy[10]

be said of decision making, a detailed model of which is presented in Figure 2.3.

The descriptions of problem-solving and decision-making strategies presented in Figures 2.2 and 2.3 elaborate the brief outlines of these strategies presented in Figure 2.1. Each assumes some prior familiarity with basic major steps in the respective strategy and, as a result, seems particularly appropriate for instruction in the middle school grades. Understanding the essential features of any thinking operation as outlined in models or descriptions such as these is invaluable to effective teaching and learning of these operations and of thinking as a whole.

To understand a thinking operation sufficiently well to teach it to novices, a teacher must know the major principles or rules or criteria guiding its use as well as the major steps or procedures by which these principles or criteria are applied. In most instances teachers find it useful to study or generate rather detailed descriptions of these aspects of the thinking operations they seek to teach *before* teaching them. Such descriptions assist them in planning effective lessons, in selecting appropriate examples of the operation in action, in selecting useful instructional materials, and in preparing assessments of student learning as well as of their own teaching. Interestingly enough, developing such descriptions makes one better at executing these thinking operations as well!

Most thinking operations, whether discrete skills or complex strategies, can be conceptualized as having a label or name, a definition, a number of unique, interrelated attributes, and some type of relationship to other skills. Proficiency in a thinking operation consists as much of knowing the operation's components as it does of being able to execute the operation in a rapid, efficient manner.

Knowledge of an operation's attributes seem most useful in defining the operation for purposes of teaching and learning. Figure 2.4 diagrams the kinds of attributes typical of most thinking operations. The *procedure* that typifies a thinking skill or strategy consists essentially of the steps through which one goes in executing the operation—these steps generally occur in some sequence and sometimes consist of a number of subordinate steps or procedures. Thinking skills and strategies also incorporate certain *principles* or *rules* that guide one through an operation's procedure. The more important rules concern when to use the operation, how to initiate it, what to do when obstacles arise to effective execution of its procedures, and what other thinking operations are often used with this operation.

Finally, each thinking skill or strategy is distinguished by certain kinds of *knowledge* informing the use of the operation. Some thinking operations, especially critical thinking skills, apply specific criteria in their operations; that is, when distinguishing statements of fact from value judgments, one uses specific criteria for determining whether a statement is a fact or a value judgment. These criteria are part of one's knowledge related to this particular thinking skill. Other skills, such as analyzing for certain purposes, use analytical concepts as search cues. Still other kinds of thinking operations, such as analyzing to identify value claims, employ certain kinds of informational clues or principles to look for. Virtually all thinking operations have a knowledge component that shapes how these skills are executed.

To clarify this conception of any thinking skill or strategy, consider how one engages in the skill of using a textbook's index. Try finding, or imagining how to find, the page number in a science text where Boyle's Law is explained. As you do this, try to remain aware of what you do and why you do it.

Individuals actually executing this skill indicate that in so doing they usually go through the following procedure:

1. First, they decide to use the index (rather than to thumb through the book or to use the table of contents).

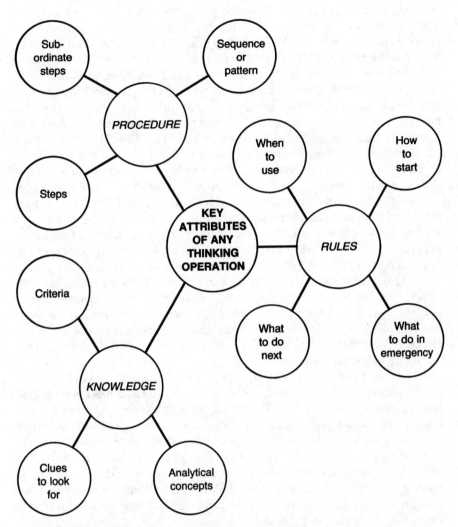

Figure 2.4 Key Attributes of Any Thinking Skill or Strategy

2. Then they decide to look under *B* for Boyle's Law.
3. Next they open the text and flip to the back to locate the index.
4. Upon finding the index, they go straight to the *B*'s and then to *Bo* where they skim to find the entry: *Boyle's Law*.
5. Finding the entry, *Boyle's Law*, they search under this term to find the specific topic—in this example, its explanation—and then identify the page number(s) following this topic entry.

Individuals possess certain knowledge that enables them to engage in this procedure effectively and efficiently. They know, for example, what an index is and what it looks like. They know that an index is customarily found at the back of a book and that certain items such as people's names are listed surname first, whereas events or other items are listed first word first. They know that under each heading they can find related, subordinate headings—sometimes in chronological order, sometimes in alphabetical order, and sometimes in the order presented in the text. And they know the meaning of symbols, such as 114–117; 114, 117; and 114ff.

Those expert at using an index also follow certain rules or guidelines in executing the skill procedure. For example, these individuals use this skill when they wish to find text information quickly. They initiate the task by deciding what particular search word they will hunt for. If they can't find that particular term or word, they identify synonyms or associated terms—in the case of this example, perhaps Combined Gas Laws, pressure, or so on—and search for them. They use the same "emergency" approach in searching for specific aspects of any subtopic, if they can't find them under the main term they are using. If they cannot find the index, they flip to the Table of Contents to see if there is one and where it begins. And they know what to do after they have identified the page numbers they seek. Individuals successful at using a textbook index, in effect, follow these guidelines as if they were rules to guide the way they go about using an index.

The conceptualization of a thinking operation presented in Figure 2.4 can be applied to any thinking skill or strategy, just as it has been applied here to make sense of the skill of using an index. Teachers who use this conceptual model to organize what they know about the thinking operations they seek to teach will be able to teach them better than will those who possess only a fuzzy notion or one-sentence definition of the same operation. Students who work toward describing a thinking skill or strategy in terms of its procedure, rules, and knowledge attributes will come to understand it better than if they treat it simply as a definition or even a sequence of steps alone.

It should be noted here that any conceptual model of a thinking operation provides simply a glimpse of that operation at a given point in time. One's understanding of the operation grows and evolves in complexity and degree of sophistication as the operation is used over and over in a variety of contexts for a variety of purposes. Such a model can help make sense out of information about a thinking operation, but what it reveals ought not be considered the last word or the only legitimate description of any particular operation. A model of any thinking operation should be considered as a device for organizing knowledge of the operations for purposes of instruction or as a general target of instruction.

The exact conceptualization, however, will vary with the data in which it is developed and the degree of expertise of the developer.

Presently, the states of cognitive science and skill teaching are such that descriptions of most skills tend to concentrate almost exclusively on their procedures. While explications of this attribute are certainly crucial for those charged with teaching a given thinking skill or strategy, the absence of descriptive information relative to the other types of attributes—rules and knowledge—makes for an incomplete understanding of the total skill or strategy. Yet, descriptions of thinking operations in terms of their procedures alone are better than no descriptions at all. Moreover, focusing attention on the procedures by which a thinking skill or strategy is put into operation proves to be the easiest way to generate awareness and eventually some knowledge of the other major attributes of that skill or strategy. Teachers can use such limited descriptions to create lessons in which students, through application of the given procedure, gradually articulate key rules and knowledge associated with the procedure and, in time, generate for themselves and for teachers a more complete conceptualization of the skill. Both teacher and student knowledge of thinking skills or strategies thus continues to develop while such skills are actually being taught.

IDENTIFYING THE ATTRIBUTES OF THINKING SKILLS

Asserting the importance of detailed descriptions—or even the procedural attributes of each thinking operation selected for instruction—is one thing; finding such descriptions is quite another. There is at present no single complete source of such descriptions. But there are at least three kinds of sources to which teachers can turn in order to find or develop partial descriptions of these attributes. These include (1) the work of theoreticians and researchers reported in the professional literature, (2) teachers' own attempts to carry out a skill, and (3) student efforts to execute a skill. Each of these kinds of sources can provide skill descriptions of differing degrees of completeness, utility, and precision. All should be consulted in building descriptions of thinking operations for use in teaching and testing.

Professional Literature

Over the past several years researchers and experts have produced a number of rather precise descriptions of how selected thinking operations are, or can be, effectively executed. Some of these descriptions have been constructed from analyses of records of expert thinkers in action.[11] Other descriptions have been produced by the experts themselves to describe what they believe to be the ideal way to carry out a given thinking operation.

For example, analogy making is a widely tested and sometimes taught thinking skill. This skill is used in making such relationships as:

$$A \quad : \quad B \quad = \quad C \quad : \quad D$$

George Washington is to one   as   Abraham Lincoln is to _____ .

(five, ten, fifteen, twenty)?

Psychologist Robert Sternberg reports that protocols—written transcripts—of how experts execute operations such as this one indicate that the key steps in making analogies are to:

1. Identify/translate the key terms or elements in the first part of the analogy (A and B).
2. Recall knowledge associated with each of these key terms or elements (A and B).
3. Infer the appropriate relationship between the key elements in the first pair (A and B).
4. Superimpose the inferred relationship onto the key elements of the second part of the analogy (C and D).
5. Apply the relationship inferred in the first part to find the missing element(s) of the second part (D) in order to complete the analogy.[12]

Similar descriptions of other thinking operations can be found scattered through the literature on teaching, critical thinking, cognitive learning, and skill teaching.

Figure 2.5 lists a number of sources that present descriptions of various thinking operations. Although they are of uneven quality, these sources are among the best and most readily available. Teachers seeking workable and reasonably detailed, if sometimes only partial, "starter" descriptions of various thinking operations may find these most helpful.

Teacher Execution of a Skill

Teachers can also identify some of the key attributes of any thinking skill or strategy by analyzing what they themselves actually do as they engage in a task requiring execution of that skill or strategy. Such a task analysis can be done with the aid of a colleague (or some other individual recog-

1. Bloom, Benjamin, et al. *Taxonomy of Educational Objectives—Handbook I: Cognitive Domain.* New York: David McKay, 1956.
   This volume describes the nature of different types of educational objectives presented in the form of a taxonomy of cognitive behaviors moving from recall to comprehension, application, analysis, synthesis, and evaluation.

2. Damer, T. Edward. *Attacking Faulty Reasoning.* Belmont, Calif.: Wadsworth Publishing Company, 1980.
   In this small, college-level book, philosopher Damer describes fifty-eight common logical fallacies, providing for each a definition, several examples, and the way to attack it.

3. Ennis, Robert H. "A Concept of Critical Thinking." *Harvard Educational Review* 32:1 (Winter 1962), pp 81–111.
   This classic analysis of critical thinking includes the identification of key critical thinking skills and a general description of various attributes of these operations.

4. Frederiksen, Norman. "Implications of Cognitive Theory for Instruction in Problem Solving." *Review of Educational Research* 54:3 (Fall 1984), pp 363–407.
   In this summary of research studies into the nature of problem solving, Educational Testing Service psychologist Frederiksen analyzes various models of the process and how it is used with ill-defined as well as with clearly defined problems. He also explains a number of key implications for teaching problem solving.

5. Friedman, Michael and Steven Rowls. *Teaching Reading and Thinking Skills.* New York: Longman, 1980.
   On pages 169–211 the authors describe some of the characteristics of different thinking skills including categorizing, fact/opinion, relevant/irrelevant, deductive reasoning, inductive reasoning, predicting, and conceptualizing.

6. Hayes, John R. *The Complete Problem Solver.* Philadelphia: Franklin Institute Press, 1981.
   This text in general problem solving for college students includes sections on problem representation, memory and ways to use it, learning strategies, decision making, and creativity and invention. This is best read after Polya's work (below).

7. Hurst, Joe B., et al. "The Decision-Making Process." *Theory and Research In Social Education* 11:3 (Fall 1983), pp. 17–43.
   Although less complete than Frederiksen's analysis of research on problem solving, Hurst's survey of studies and articles on decision making provides a useful insight into various models and components of this major thinking process.

8. Kepner, Charles H., and Benjamin B. Tregoe. *The New Rational Manager.* Princeton, N.J.: Princeton Research Press, 1981.
   One of the clearest and most detailed explications of a decision making process available, this large work presents a step-by-step description of decision making from problem analysis to decision analysis. It can provide a basis for teaching this process throughout a curriculum.

9. Nickerson, Raymond S. *Reflections on Reasoning.* Hillsdale, N.J.: Lawrence Erlbaum Associates, Publishers, 1986.
   This exploration of reasoning explains in detail the nature of beliefs, assertions, arguments, and stratagems and then briefly describes twenty-one common reasoning fallacies. It concludes with ten basic rules for rational thinking.

Figure 2.5 Sources of Thinking Skill Descriptions

10. Polya, Gyorgy. *How to Solve It*, 2d ed. Princeton: Princeton University Press, 1957, 1973.
    This classic explication of problem solving presents basic principles and procedures for problem solving with examples illustrating each major step.

11. Raths, Louis, et al. *Teaching for Thinking: Theories, Strategies, and Activities,* 2d ed. New York: Teachers' College Press, 1986.
    This is a new edition of a classic title. Chapter 1 provides general descriptions of such skills as summarizing, observing, classifying, interpretating, criticizing, looking for assumptions, imagining, hypothesizing, applying, decision making, and designing. Following that are chapters on ways for students to practice each in elementary and secondary grades.

12. Scriven, Michael. *Reasoning.* New York: McGraw-Hill, 1976.
    One of many good college texts on reasoning, Scriven's book describes and explains briefly the nature of reasoning and explains in detail key steps in analyzing an argument.

13. Toulmin, Steven, Richard Rieke, and Allan Janik. *An Introduction to Reasoning,* 2d ed. New York: Macmillan, 1984.
    An extremely clear introduction to argumentation, this text explains the structure of arguments and then how to determine the soundness and strength of arguments and how to identify common fallacies in argumentation. The authors then discuss applications of argumentation in different fields including science, the arts, and ethics. Examples, applications, and visual diagrams enhance understanding of the principles explained.

14. Wales, Charles E., and Ann Nardi. *Successful Decision Making.* Morgantown: West Virginia University Center for Guided Design, 1984.
    In this manual for college students Wales and Nardi outline twelve key steps in a useful process that combines problem solving and decision making as well as a four-part model of the essential components of problem solving.

15. Weddle, Perry. *Argument—A Guide to Critical Thinking.* New York: McGraw-Hill, 1978.
    In this guide, the author explains the nature of argument, selected fallacies, and the use of language in argumentation. He then examines the role of authority, generality, comparison, and cause. Numerous examples and applications are provided.

16. Whimbey, Arthur, and Jack Lochhead. *Problem Solving and Comprehension,* 3d ed. Philadelphia: Franklin Institute Press, 1982.
    This small book illustrates errors in reasoning and then provides instruction in problem solving, verbal reasoning, analogy making, analyzing of trends and patterns, and solving word problems; it is replete with examples, explanations, and opportunities for application.

Figure 2.5 (*continued*)

nized as having some degree of proficiency at executing this operation) or by the teacher alone. Either procedure requires a number of cases or tries, however. One cannot come to understand any thinking operation on the basis of a single try or example. However, analysis of how someone—

even one's self—actually executes a thinking task can contribute significantly to one's awareness and introductory understanding of the major attributes of important thinking operations.*

In using this approach to identifying the attributes of any thinking operation, teachers can engage in an adaptation of what is often called retrospective analysis.[13] Working with a partner or two, teachers audio or video tape themselves as they engage in the skill. Upon completion of the task, together they analyze the tape to help them clarify what they did as they executed the skill. In the absence of recording devices or of an observer-recorder, individuals can, as an alternative, simply execute the skill and then attempt to recall from memory exactly how they went about doing it. In the analysis of such efforts, the following questions prove useful in focusing on the key steps in the skill procedure, important principles or rules followed in executing the procedure, and knowledge that proved useful in the process:

- What did (I, we, you) do to get the result? What did (I, we, you) do first, next, next, and so on?
- Why were these things done?
- What do (I, we, you) know that allowed or led (me, us, you) to do each step?
- How did (I, we, you) know what to do next?
- How did (I, we, you) know (I, we, you) was/were achieving or getting closer to achieving the goal?

By answering these or similar questions, teachers can reconstruct—even if tentatively—what went on in their own or other's minds as they executed the thinking skill. They can then use this information to prepare a tentative description of the operation; this description can then be the basis for planning a series of lessons in that thinking operation.

An example of how an individual or several individuals can do this on their own may clarify this approach. Suppose a teacher wishes to identify the major attributes of the skill of distinguishing relevant from irrelevant information. First, the teacher can look up several dictionary definitions of the terms *relevant/relevance* and *irrelevant/irrelevance* and then find some common synonyms for these terms. Upon so doing, the teacher may note that *relevance* commonly means "related or pertaining to the topic at hand," while *irrelevance* usually means "having no application to or effect on" the topic at hand. Then a number of statements can be examined to see what in them is relevant to a stipulated topic. Upon completing this

---

*For detailed explanations of specific procedures for conducting such analysis, see Barry K. Beyer, *Developing a Thinking Skills Program* (Boston: Allyn and Bacon, to be published).

task those involved can reflect on how they executed the task, why they did what they did, and what they knew that enabled them to proceed as they did.

Suppose the following statement—written about the European discovery of a large city in the sixteenth century—were used to show how one goes about distinguishing relevant from irrelevant information. The task could be to determine the extent this statement is relevant to this claim:

The city described here would be easy to conquer.

Statement:

1	Then Montezuma. . .told (us) to look at his great city and all the other
2	cities standing in the water. . . .So we stood there looking, because that
3	huge accursed (temple) stood so high that it dominated everything. We
4	saw the three causeways that led into Mexico. . . .We saw the fresh water
5	which came. . .(by viaduct) to supply the city, and the bridges. . .at
6	intervals on the causeways so that the water could flow in and out from one
7	part of the lake to another. We saw a great number of canoes, some
8	coming with provisions and others returning with cargoes and merchandise;
9	and we saw too that one could not pass from one house to another. . .except
10	over wooden drawbridges or by canoe. We saw (temples) and shrines. . .
11	that looked like gleaming white towers and castles: a marvelous sight.
12	. . .(W)e turned back to the great market and the swarm of people buying
13	and selling. . . .Some of our soldiers who had been in many parts of the
14	world, in Constaninople, in Rome. . , said they had never seen a market
15	so well laid out, so large, so orderly, and so full of people.[14]

In reading this statement one may have identified sentences beginning on lines 1, 3, 4, and 7 as relevant to the given claim. Sentences beginning on lines 2, 10, 12, and 13 may have been considered, initially at least, to be irrelevant to this claim. Analysis of why these choices were made can help articulate some of the key components of the skill of distinguishing the relevant from the irrelevant.

What is it one did to execute this skill—to determine what information is relevant or irrelevant to a given claim? In retrospect it seems on first thought as if one:

1. Restated the goal of the task—to distinguish what in the statement was relevant to the given claim from what is not relevant.
2. Read the statement sentence-by-sentence, even phrase-by-phrase, to identify what was relevant.
3. Judged the overall degree to which the statement as a whole was relevant to the given claim.

Why were certain sentences judged to be relevant? Sentences beginning on lines 1 and 3 seemed relevant because they explained or gave examples of how the island city related to the mainland and they implied that cutting the bridges would isolate the city. These sentences, in effect, seem to be evidence supporting the claim. Sentences beginning on lines 4 and 7 seem to be of the same type. They explain and give examples of how the city is linked to the outside world. Thus, those items judged to be relevant seem to be so judged because they give examples or explanations or details directly related to the given claim. It appears, then, that examples, explanations, and details may be three criteria of relevancy.

Discussion with others of how relevancy is determined can help further articulate and clarify some additional steps, principles, or rules to follow, and useful things to know in executing this skill. Repeating this task with several other claims and appropriately related information may add to one's insights into how this skill can be executed effectively. Such repeated efforts to use the skill and then to analyze retrospectively how it was executed might suggest eventually that someone accomplished in this skill might well carry out this operation by:

1. Stating the nature of the topic or matter at hand. By so doing, one sets up a criterion to keep on task.
2. Recalling or identifying various criteria to use in determining relevancy—criteria such as whether statements give details, examples, explanations, contradictions, or evidence directly related to (but *not* necessarily supportive of) the given claim.
3. Searching the statement piece-by-piece to find evidence of such criteria.
4. Matching each piece—each sentence—to the above criteria or other criteria that pop into mind.
5. Judging the degree to which the statement as a whole pertains or connects to the matter at hand.

Like other procedures for identifying the major attributes of a thinking skill or strategy, this, too, has its limitations. There is obviously more to the skill of determining relevance than one or two tries at it may reveal. Initial analyses may not produce any recognizable rules or principles being followed, for example. Much depends on the media being used, the type of data involved, the informational and experiential background of the person executing the skill, and the purpose to which the skill is being put. However, reflective analysis such as this can produce at least tentative insights into some of the attributes and workings of any thinking skill or strategy. As one becomes experienced in using the skill and consciously reflecting on the process involved, understanding of it deepens. What this preliminary investigation can do in most cases is to enable a teacher to prepare at least a tentative description of a thinking operation as in Figure 2.6. Using this description as a guide and perhaps as an

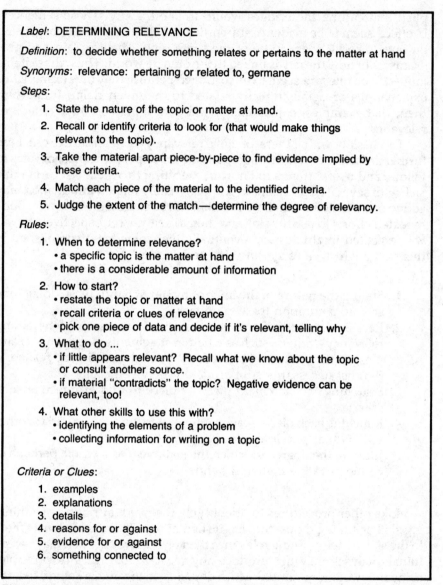

Label: DETERMINING RELEVANCE

Definition: to decide whether something relates or pertains to the matter at hand

Synonyms: relevance: pertaining or related to, germane

Steps:

1. State the nature of the topic or matter at hand.
2. Recall or identify criteria to look for (that would make things relevant to the topic).
3. Take the material apart piece-by-piece to find evidence implied by these criteria.
4. Match each piece of the material to the identified criteria.
5. Judge the extent of the match—determine the degree of relevancy.

Rules:

1. When to determine relevance?
   • a specific topic is the matter at hand
   • there is a considerable amount of information
2. How to start?
   • restate the topic or matter at hand
   • recall criteria or clues of relevance
   • pick one piece of data and decide if it's relevant, telling why
3. What to do ...
   • if little appears relevant? Recall what we know about the topic or consult another source.
   • if material "contradicts" the topic? Negative evidence can be relevant, too!
4. What other skills to use this with?
   • identifying the elements of a problem
   • collecting information for writing on a topic

Criteria or Clues:

1. examples
2. explanations
3. details
4. reasons for or against
5. evidence for or against
6. something connected to

Figure 2.6 A Tentative Description of a Thinking Skill

initial target, the teacher can then introduce this operation to students in a direct, explicit fashion.

Written descriptions of individuals engaged in thinking can also provide insights into the major attributes of a thinking skill. The thinking illustrated in Chapter 8's story of the scholar exemplifies such a description. Thoughtful analysis and discussion of exactly what this scholar does in his mind—and why he does it—can reveal a useful description of a strategy of problem solving. Such descriptions abound in literature. Teachers can use them to identify the key attributes of thinking operations they wish to introduce and as instructional materials in lessons designed for helping students develop their own understanding of thinking.

Student Execution of a Skill

Analysis of student efforts to engage in a thinking operation can also provide insights into the key attributes of a thinking skill or strategy. In fact, teachers can use the efforts of students in their classes to carry out a skill or strategy to identify some of the major elements of the procedure, some rules or principles, and any useful knowledge that may constitute any thinking operation. Continued use of this procedure and sharing of what is discovered with other teachers engaged in similar teaching can lead to at least a tentative, introductory acquaintance with the operation. Armed with this information about a thinking skill or strategy, a teacher can then introduce and teach this operation to students in a very direct way.

One way to employ this procedure is to engage students in executing the skill and then have them, as best they can, describe how they went about doing it. The following procedure proves useful for this purpose with entire classes as well as with much smaller groups of students. It works best with secondary level students.

1. Introduce the thinking operation in question by giving its name and a simple definition of it.
2. Have the students execute the operation as best they can, using material provided for them.
3. Then have the students recall how they carried out the operation, the steps in the procedure they used, and any rules, principles, or knowledge they knew or used to guide them through the task. Even though not all students will have done the same things in the same ways, a tentative outline of several procedures, some rules, and some associated knowledge may emerge.
4. Next, have the students execute the operation again, keeping in mind the discussion about how they executed it previously.
5. Finally, have them report how they did the operation the second time, seeking the same kinds of information as above about the operation and revising the tentative outline of its attributes to accommodate new information.

Using this strategy with average to above-average students can help teachers develop a tentative, though sketchy, outline of the major attributes of many thinking operations. Repeatedly using this strategy on the same operation in different classes can help clarify and elaborate its attributes. As teacher and students continue to apply the operation and to reflect on how they do it, the teacher's knowledge of it will grow, as will student expertise in using it. This procedure, in fact, can enable teachers to begin actually to introduce a skill while at the same time learning more about what it is.*

The procedures described in this section have been used in varying combinations to develop descriptions of selected thinking skills and strategies. Applying these procedures—especially in consulting the recommendations of experts and in analyzing how individuals execute it—has provided some insight into the nature of certain critical thinking skills. Figure 2.7 describes the two major dimensions of four of these skills: determining relevancy, distinguishing factual statements from value judgments, detecting bias, and determining the credibility of a written source. This figure lists in the left-hand column the criteria that are used in executing each skill.[15] In the right-hand column it lists the steps through which one generally proceeds in executing any of these skills.

If, for example, one has decided to determine the credibility of a written source—a newspaper article, for instance—one then goes to his or her memory to recall the criteria of credibility. Figure 2.7 lists these in the box at the bottom of the left column. Next, one searches through the data—by going through the steps listed down the right-hand side of Figure 2.7—to find evidence related to these criteria. The next step is trying to identify any relationships among the evidence found—in this instance perhaps a search for evidence relating to criteria such as the source's having any conflict of interest or the extent to which the source knew that its reputation was at stake. Finally, the searcher would match the evidence found against all the criteria to judge the extent to which the source is credible. Proficiency in critical thinking skills such as these requires skill in executing these steps and knowledge of the criteria or clues that should be applied in executing these steps.

CAUTIONS ABOUT DEFINING SKILLS

Each of the sources of skill descriptions described here provides some insight into the nature of thinking and into thinking skills and strategies. Each, however, has its limitations as well. How expert is the expert selected to read or observe or interview? How does one reconcile different sets of attributes for the same thinking operation? How does one know

---

*This procedure is the basis of one of the strategies for introducing a thinking operation, presented in Chapter 4.

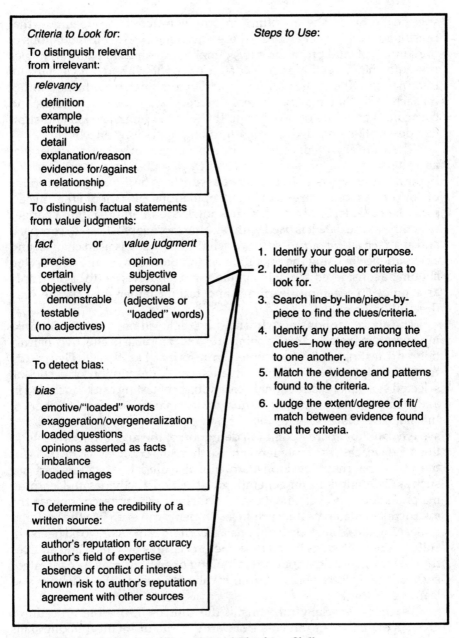

Figure 2.7 Components of Four Critical Thinking Skills

specifically he or she is getting information about the operation that presumably is being analyzed? These questions expose the limitations of the sources of, and procedures for, defining thinking skills and strategies presented here. Yet these procedures are productive and can yield useful information. When used judiciously and in combination with one another on each skill, they may be the only practical way open to teachers and curriculum builders for developing the detailed thinking skill and strategy descriptions needed to teach thinking operations effectively.

There are also other caveats. The most important is to remember that any thinking skill or strategy attributes described represent working hypotheses only. They should not be assumed to be the only descriptions of how one proceeds to execute these operations. Nor should they necessarily be considered accurate. Our knowledge of an operation changes over time as the data it is used with become more sophisticated, complex, and abstract; as the purposes for which the operation is used change; and as experience in using the operation accumulates. Thus, any description should be considered at best incomplete and tentative; it is to be used only as a guide in teaching, learning, and testing rather than as the only description or model.

The above cautions notwithstanding, detailed descriptions of thinking operations selected for teaching are indispensable to effective instruction and testing. When presented in a format like that in Figure 2.6, these descriptions have many advantages. A description of each skill selected as a major instructional goal or object of testing can be included in a curriculum guide, textbook manual, or test manual to inform teachers of the major attributes of skills they are supposed to teach. All teachers in a system can thus share a common definition of the major thinking operations they teach. Test designers can use these descriptions as the basis for the test items they develop. Instructional materials designers can use such skill descriptions for generating instructional activities and learning materials and may even find it useful to include similar descriptions in the instructional materials they produce. Students can even use the building or fleshing out of such descriptions as learning targets or worksheets. In spite of the limitations inherent in the procedures by which and sources from which many descriptions of thinking operations may be generated, such detailed descriptions can be invaluable aids to the teaching and learning of thinking.

Teachers especially can consult the sources or use the procedures given in this chapter to articulate or clarify the nature of the thinking skills and strategies they are charged with teaching *before* they introduce them in their classrooms. If these thinking operations are to be taught well, teachers cannot enjoy the luxury of waiting for some experts to prepare such descriptions before they attempt to start teaching them. Fortunately, in the process of helping students learn thinking skills and strategies, teachers can learn more about these operations, too.

NOTES

1. Albert Upton, *A Design for Thinking* (Palo Alto, Calif.: Pacific Books, 1961); John Glade and Howard Citron, "Strategic Reasoning," in Arthur L. Costa, ed. *Developing Minds: A Resource Book for Teaching Thinking* (Alexandria, Va.: Association for Supervision and Curriculum Development, 1985), pp. 196–202.

2. Reuven Feuérstein, *Instrumental Enrichment* (Baltimore: University Park Press, 1980).

3. J. P. Guilford, *Way Beyond the I.Q.* (Great Neck, N.Y.: Creative Synergetic Associates, 1977); Mary N. Meeker, "SOI," in Costa, ed., *Developing Minds*, pp. 187–192.

4. Edward de Bono, *CoRT Thinking* (New York: Pergamon Press, 1973/1983).

5. Robert Marzano and C. L. Hutchins, *Thinking Skills: A Conceptual Framework* (Aurora, Colo.: Mid-continent Regional Educational Laboratory, 1985).

6. Benjamin Bloom et al., *Taxonomy of Educational Objectives—Handbook I: Cognitive Domain* (New York: David McKay, 1956).

7. For example, Matthew Lipman et al., *Philosophy in the Classroom* (Montclair N.J.: Institute for the Advancement of Philosophy for Children, 1977).

8. Benjamin Bloom and Lois Broder, *Problem-solving Processes of College Students* (Chicago: University of Chicago Press, 1950); Arthur Whimbey and Linda Shaw Whimbey, *Intelligence Can Be Taught* (New York: E. P. Dutton, 1975); Arthur L. Costa, "Teaching for Intelligent Behavior," *Educational Leadership* 39:2 (October 1981), pp. 29–32.

9. John R. Hayes, *The Complete Problem Solver* (Philadelphia: Franklin Institute Press, 1981); Norman Frederiksen, "Implications of Cognitive Theory for Instruction in Problem Solving," *Review of Educational Research* 54:3 (Fall 1984), pp. 363–407; Gyorgy Polya, *How to Solve It*, 2d ed. (Princeton, N.J.: Princeton University Press, 1957/1973).

10. Charles H. Kepner and Benjamin B. Tregoe, *The New Rational Manager* (Princeton, N.J.: Princeton Research Press, 1981); Joe B. Hurst et al., "The Decision Making Process," *Theory and Research in Social Education* 11:3 (Fall 1983), pp. 17–43; Charles E. Wales and Ann Nardi, *Successful Decision-Making* (Morgantown: West Virginia University Center for Guided Design, 1984).

11. As, for example, in Linda S. Flower and John R. Hayes, "Problem Solving Strategies and the Writing Process," *College English* 39:4 (December 1977), pp. 449–461.

12. Robert J. Sternberg, "How Can We Teach Intelligence?" *Educational Leadership* 42:1 (September 1984), p. 40.

13. John Edwards and Perc Marland, "What Are Students Really Thinking?" *Educational Leadership* 42:3 (November 1984), pp. 63–67.

14. Reprinted with permission from *Bernal Díaz, The Discovery and Conquest of New Spain*, translated by J. M. Cohen (London: Penguin Books, Ltd., 1975), pp. 234–235.

15. Adapted from Robert H. Ennis, "A Logical Basis for Measuring Critical Thinking Skills," *Educational Leadership* 43:2 (October 1985), p. 46.

3

Organizing for the Teaching of Thinking

Experts in thinking consistently point out that thinking does not occur in a vacuum. Neither does the teaching of thinking. The contexts, or environments, in which thinking is taught and practiced very much shape the development of student proficiency in thinking. At least four different dimensions of the teaching-learning context are of major importance in this regard: the environment of the classroom and school, the subject matter used in teaching, the teaching process employed, and the framework used to provide actual instruction in thinking. By giving continuing attention to these four contexts, teachers can establish and maintain the kinds of settings or contexts best suited to developing effective and skillful student thinking.

CLASSROOM ENVIRONMENT AS A CONTEXT FOR THE TEACHING OF THINKING

The feelings about learning that pervade a school and the climate they reflect and shape affect what is learned as much as does the kind of instruction carried on in its classrooms. Schools in which the behaviors of students and teachers contradict what is being taught are at best rather sterile environments for achieving the objectives of instruction. To be effective, the teaching and learning of thinking, like any subject, requires environments that reinforce and support this teaching and learning.[1]

Classrooms can provide much of the richness for thinking that a student's out-of-school environment may lack but that are essential to improving student thinking. Some everyday environments in which students find themselves, for example, fail to offer stimulating opportunities to engage in the more complex kinds of thinking. Authoritarian environments, whether associated with teacher, peer group, parent or sibling, may tend to inhibit thinking rather than to promote it. Some of these environments may also lack the mediation of individuals who can challenge, probe, and encourage thinking and who can actually show how to do it more effectively. Teachers and schools can counter such limiting environments by providing classrooms that support thinking and that provide the kinds of mediation useful in helping students develop proficiency in their own thinking skills and abilities.

The most supportive classroom environment for the teaching and learning of thinking exists where student and teacher *thinking can occur* continuously, where *learning activities regularly require thinking*, and where students and teachers frequently *reflect on and discuss their thinking*. In such classrooms the active search for knowledge constitutes the focus of learning. Teachers can develop and maintain such an environment by attention to the physical arrangements of the classroom, to the kinds of instructional materials used, and to the kinds of interactions and activities that occur in these classrooms.

Classrooms conducive to the teaching of thinking continuously invite—almost beg—students to think. These environments are shaped (as well as typified) not only by the student and teacher behaviors that go on there but also by their physical attributes and arrangements. Lecterns and fixed, theater-style seating do not typify thinking classrooms; neither do furniture arrangements where the instructor's desk is the single, front-of-the-room focus of attention. Instead, seating arrangements that facilitate grouping and face-to-face interaction serve this goal better. So also does the classroom where a teacher's desk or work table is located to the side or at the rear of a room, where it is used as a work station rather than as a bastion or pulpit or command center.[2]

The kinds of instructional materials used in classrooms also shape the learning environment. Exclusive use, in most subject areas, of conventional workbooks or activity books often has as negative an impact on thinking as does having all students use the same textbook. In the former instance, such workbooks commonly provide drill and practice without the instruction necessary to produce productive practice. In the latter instance, reliance on single texts gives the distinct impression that learning consists essentially of finding and remembering already-given authoritative answers. When, however, activity books are combined with instruction in how to executive thinking, they are more useful in developing thinking. Distributing a variety of texts to a class—ten copies of each of three texts among a class of thirty students, for example—greatly enhances opportunities for processing different kinds of information as well as for using more complex thinking skills and strategies.

In classrooms that support and reinforce thinking, students feel free to, and regularly do, take the initiative to risk, challenge, question, guess, invent, and test.[3] These classrooms are typified by considerable student-to-student and student-to-subject matter interactions. By providing continuing opportunity and encouragement for students to engage in thinking, teachers create more receptivity to, and motivation for, learning specific thinking skills and strategies. And such classroom environments also nurture student attitudes and behaviors supportive of thinking.

Information processing, rather than only information telling or receiving, typifies classrooms that honor student thinking. In these classrooms students compare, analyze, and judge the quality of arguments, the accuracy of hypotheses, the adequacy and accuracy of evidence, and the quality of the reasoning given in support of claims or conclusions. They invent or discover relationships among data; they infer; and they test inferences. Students go beyond simply reciting subject matter. They dissect, reflect on, and add to what they read, hear, see, or feel to give it new meaning.

In these classrooms students do not interrupt one another; instead, they do consider the ideas, contributions, and arguments of their peers. Students in these environments focus on the substance of the notions put forward as well as one the quality of reasoning and evidence offered in support rather than on the personal characteristics of those who offer these notions or arguments. Here students deliberately seek more information, other points of view, and a variety of alternatives. A willingness to suspend judgment and a desire to be as accurate as possible typify their study and discussion.

Teachers create such classroom climates by providing thought-provoking learning tasks and time for students to engage in these tasks.[4] These teachers exhibit a willingness to deal with questions to which neither they nor texts nor other authorities have ready answers. And they remain open to and honor the products of student thinking. Rather than always asking questions or telling, these teachers help youngsters articulate and critically analyze their own ideas, hunches, and hypotheses. They frequently respond to student statements with silence, with requests for elaboration or supportive evidence and reasoning, with questions designed to extend student guesses and thoughts, and with alternatives that invite further exploration. They build tasks on previous tasks. They model and share with students how to execute appropriate thinking skills and strategies, and they focus student attention on how hypotheses are tested and on how conclusions are reached. Importantly, both teachers and students submit textbooks and other sources, as well as their own views, to careful examination. And teachers assist students in generating and then answering their own questions rather than dealing always with text or teacher-given questions.[5]

The behaviors and activities of a classroom that values thinking reflect certain assumptions about students, thinking, and the teaching of thinking. Educators who maintain classroom environments such as these assume that all students are capable of thinking and of thinking better than they are wont to do on their own. They assume further that learning how to think better is worth doing in all classes for all students. These teachers realize that the time spent in productive thinking and in the teaching of thinking is time well spent. They know that while the payoff from such teaching may not be fully realized in their own classes, it will come eventually in the form of greater student learning and achievement in later coursework as well as in student proficiency in thinking in general.

The teaching of thinking will be most productive in classrooms that employ physical arrangements, utilize instructional materials and activities, and exhibit teacher and student behaviors like those just described. Such classrooms virtually call out, "Its okay to think! It's useful to think! Come on, let's think to learn!" Such environments make students more receptive to, and most likely to profit from, instruction in those skills, strategies, and dispositions that constitute effective, skillful, informed thinking.

SUBJECT MATTER AS A CONTEXT FOR THE TEACHING OF THINKING

Subject matter is a second important dimension of the context in which thinking and the teaching of thinking are carried on. It is commonly accepted that subject matter and what we know by using it are very much influenced by the kinds and quality of thinking we apply to it. Less obvious may be the converse of this observation: thinking and the operations of which it consists are very much influenced by the subject matter to which they are applied.[6] Our thinking is both limited and enhanced by the nature and amount of subject matter in which it is used. For not only does thinking seek to do something to or with subject matter, but also subject matter and knowledge shape considerably how one goes about thinking in general and executing various thinking skills in particular.

Knowledge of subject matter usually serves as a goal of classroom or other learning. That is, a major purpose of thinking is to understand better or learn more about particular subject matter, whether it be to learn a concept, develop a generalization, build an explanatory theory, solve a problem, and so on. Doing something with subject matter gives both purpose and direction to thinking. Achieving a subject-matter goal drives thinking. Interestingly, research suggests that motivation to learn or improve a skill is enhanced when instruction in that skill is provided at a time that the skill is needed to achieve a subject-matter goal.[7] Subject-matter using or learning gives purpose to thinking.

Subject matter also serves as a vehicle for thinking. Individuals exercise thinking skills and strategies by processing or manipulating some kind of subject matter or body of information. Three kinds of subject matter are customarily used in classroom settings as vehicles for thinking: (1) academic subject matter, such as literature, history, geometry, French, music, chemistry, and so on; (2) community or school-life experience shared by the students; and (3) personal, out-of-school life experiences common to all students. Information in each of these areas can be used to hone student thinking.

Subject matter, furthermore, of whatever kind, serves as an arena in which thinking can occur. And, like any arena, this subject matter sets parameters on thinking as well as facilitates it. Proficiency in any thinking skill or strategy is as much enhanced by knowledge of the subject matter being thought about—and by interest in that subject matter—as it is by proficiency in the thinking operation being employed.[8] Success in thinking can be limited or restricted as much by ignorance or misunderstanding of the subject matter being used as by less-than-adequate proficiency in a specific thinking operation. The kinds and quality of inferences one can draw from classifying chemical formulas, for example, are affected as much by what one knows about chemistry as they are by one's proficiency in the skill of classifying. Knowledge of a subject, or lack of it, very much shapes how one thinks about it besides affecting the results of such thinking.

What are the implications for the teaching of thinking of these interrelationships between subject matter and thinking?

First, research suggests that for best results in learning thinking skills, a teacher should introduce and provide instruction in any skill when students perceive that they need this skill to achieve a subject-matter related objective.[9] Students who are asked to make sense out of disorganized data have a felt need to somehow organize that data. Instruction in a skill useful in accomplishing this task is thus clearly appropriate. Teaching thinking skills on a "need-to-know basis" in dealing with subject matter capitalizes on a natural relationship between subject-matter learning and thinking.

Second, the subject matter used should be meaningful to the student—understood by them and be perceived as worth learning or using.[10] Subject matter used simply to exercise a thinking skill may produce so little motivation to execute a thinking skill or strategy that the result may well be mindless attention to the task.

Third, the kinds of subject matter used in the teaching of thinking should be appropriate to the thinking skill learning task. In the initial stages of learning a thinking operation, for example, the subject matter must be already understood by or familiar to the learners in order to attend fully to understanding the new skill.[11] A teacher cannot introduce an unfamiliar thinking operation with unfamiliar subject matter and expect students to attend to the operation; in such instances, students attend primarily to the subject matter, since past experience tells them that they will be held accountable on tests for that rather than for any skill or strategy. Moreover, some understanding of the subject matter is required to execute the operation even in its simplist form.

If the subject to be used in introducing a new thinking operation turns out to be unfamiliar to students, a teacher has two options. Students can first give attention to understanding—defining, explaining, and studying—the subject matter to comprehend it, and after that use it to learn about the operation. Or, the class can put the regular subject matter aside temporarily and use subject matter more familiar to the students, perhaps data from a school setting or from shared out-of-school student experience. Taking this latter approach, however, seems inadvisable because it implies that we cannot use thinking skills or strategies in regularly assigned subject matter; this is not only untrue but is also contrary to the role of subject matter in schools. Clearly, the first alternative is preferable.

Fourth, any thinking skill or strategy should be used with a variety of academic and other subject matter over a period of years. Thinking operations are often tied closely to the subject matter in which they are originally introduced, whether academic or experiential, not only by the association of the two in the minds of the learners but also because the cues to use of these operations are likely to be unique to that subject matter.[12] Cues for using the same skill with different subject matters often differ. Attributes useful in classifying words according to grammatical form differ considerably from those useful in classifying the same words to identify lifestyles. The greater the variety of subject matter in which a thinking skill or strategy is taught, the more likely the students will be able to generalize the skill or strategy so as later to transfer it to any new subject area on their own initiative.[13] Learning a skill or strategy in a variety of academic subject areas also introduces students to the different points of view inherent in different subjects, a knowledge of which allows more options in thinking when unfamiliar subject matter appears. And learning a skill to this degree of independent usage is an important goal of the teaching of thinking.

Finally, the subject matter used should be appropriate to the thinking skill that is to be taught. If the skill of detecting bias is to be introduced, the subject matter to be used must contain clear examples of bias. Teachers should not have to step out of the regularly used subject matter to find repeated examples or data for a particular skill being taught. Such practice merely reinforces a student's impression that the particular skill is not of much value in the subject under study. Where thinking skills are carefully keyed to appropriate subject matter, better learning of *both* occurs. [14]

In sum, the subject matter used in teaching skills constitutes an important context in which skill teaching and learning occur. This subject matter affects the quality of skill learning as much as the degree of proficiency in the skills used. Efforts to ensure that thinking skills and subject matter reinforce each other in the classroom contribute significantly to the success of the teaching of thinking throughout the entire curriculum.

TEACHING PROCESSES AS A CONTEXT FOR THE TEACHING OF THINKING

Teachers use a variety of teaching processes to guide or direct student learning. Some, such as the read-recite-test-process are essentially expository in nature. Others are much more inductive, such as those employing problem-solving or discussion processes. Besides providing useful contexts or structures for the teaching and learning of thinking skills and strategies, these teaching processes directly shape the quality of the skill learning that occurs as a result.

Teaching processes used in classrooms shape the teaching and learning of thinking in at least three ways. First, these processes provide numerous "teachable moments"—opportunities to provide students direct instruction in how to execute a particular thinking operation needed at that point in the process. Second, by seizing these "teachable moments," by temporarily interrupting the overall teaching process to provide direct instruction in thinking operations, teachers can capitalize on students' felt needs to know how to executive these operations, thus providing instruction when motivation to learn is at its highest.[15] And, finally, providing instruction in a thinking skill or strategy at a point in a learning process where it is needed and useful embues the thinking operation with meaning both in terms of its function in learning as well as its relationship to other thinking operations with which it is normally used.

One commonly used teaching process involves essentially reading (or listening or viewing)-reciting-reviewing-and testing. Designed to help students learn subject matter or authoritative statements about subject matter, this process also provides numerous opportunities for direct instruction in various thinking operations—operations such as information storage and retrieval skills, comprehension skills, and skills of analysis and synthesis as well as selected critical thinking skills. At various points in the read-recite-review-test process the teacher may interrupt to show or help students learn how to use a specific thinking operation to understand or remember better the subject matter under discussion.

Suppose, for example, that in a biology class recitation about the parts of the human body, the teacher realizes that students see the various components of the body as unrelated, disparate items. To help them make better sense of these parts, perhaps so that they can remember them, a teacher may wish to introduce students to the skill of classifying. Students can then use this skill to organize these data in a meaningful way. So, in the middle of the general class recitation the teacher can interrupt the planned lesson, provide instruction in how to execute the skill of classifying, and then resume the lesson by having students apply this skill to the subject matter at hand to learn it better. In subsequent lessons the teacher can seize appropriate opportunities to have students practice this skill—with guidance—to process other kinds of subject matter.

Or, to give another example, suppose a teacher, in directing a recitation of a reading assignment, becomes aware that students are unable to get the main idea of the assignment. Interrupting the read-recite-review-test process, the teacher could introduce the skill of generalizing (a form of what Bloom calls synthesis making), showing students how to pull together a general statement about the reading from all the paragraphs they have read. Such instruction in this skill could be followed by additional practice in executing the skill as opportunities arise in later lessons.

Structuring learning tasks around problem solving, decision making, or conceptualizing provides even greater opportunities for showing students how to execute a thinking skill that is useful in carrying out a particular part of such a strategy. For example, in dealing with a particular math problem, students may be unable to recall a solution plan appropriate to the math problem. Such a situation presents an opportunity to stop the problem-solving process for a time to provide direct instruction in a skill needed in that situation—such as, perhaps, working backward from a possible answer. After the introduction and some practice, the class can resume the general problem-solving task at hand. Any teaching built around problem-solving strategies or similar thinking strategies offers opportunities at each step for instruction in the numerous thinking skills useful in carrying out that strategy.

Philosopher Richard Paul describes another teaching process he calls dialogical.[16] In this process students investigate ethical issues or issues of general human concern or controversial topics to develop their abilities of rational thinking as well as to understand themselves better. In this process students articulate claims, provide evidence, and reason in support of these claims, then do the same from other points of view. In so doing, students identify and respond to challenges to the different points of view articulated; identify and examine the assumptions underlying the reasoning behind these positions, challenges and responses; and examine the consistency of their standards and reasoning. Although generally student-centered, this teaching process, too, offers numerous opportunities for teachers to interrupt the process for instruction in how to execute any of a number of important thinking skills in which students demonstrate less-than-the-desired or required proficiency. If in the course of such a process, for example, students have difficulty in detecting unstated assumptions, the teacher can temporarily interrupt the dialogical process for instruction in how to execute this important operation. This dialogical process provides yet another useful context for the direct teaching of virtually all the thinking operations presented in the preceding chapters.

Regardless of which specific teaching process is employed, all present some opportunities for direct teaching of thinking skills and strategies. Of course, expository processes such as that of read-recite-review-test may offer fewer opportunities than other, more inductive teaching processes and may, in fact, provide opportunities for instruction in only the most elemental thinking operations. Indeed, if one were to provide instruction in some critical thinking operations in the context of expository teaching, the operations taught might actually prove dysfunctional to successful completion of that teaching process itself. Teaching critical thinking skills in the context of reading and reciting to prepare for a test on the subject matter under study might well undermine the teaching process as students begin to use the skills being taught to challenge or deconstruct the subject matter, thus rendering it useless to remember! However, other teaching-learning processes, including discovery and student-centered processes, present wider opportunities for instruction in virtually any of the thinking operations that teachers might select for teaching.

Besides providing more opportunities for the teaching of specific thinking operations, the teaching processes described here also provide motivation for learning these operations. Research suggests that student motivation to learn a new skill or strategy is sharply enhanced when instruction in how to execute that skill or strategy is provided at a time it is needed to accomplish another assigned task.[17] If the task assigned involves decision making, instruction in how to generate alternatives is most appropriate when it is time to identify such alternatives. Using teaching processes that create points where students need to know how to execute particular thinking operations enables teachers to capitalize on natural student desires to have these needs met. Teaching thinking operations as students feel they are needed takes advantage of the heightened motivation to learn inherent in such situations.

Providing instruction in specific thinking operations in the context of problem-solving, dialogical, or other teaching processes also gives meaning to the thinking operations being taught. Teaching thinking skills or strategies as discrete operations often fragments such learning and produces a grab-bag effect. It tends to develop thinking operations as technical "tricks of the trade" without providing any meaningful context in which to employ them. On the other hand, teaching a specific thinking operation when it is needed by the students gives the operation added meaning by associating it with how it functions in learning. Thinking operations learned in a context where they have demonstrated utility are more likely to become a permanent part of one's thinking repertoire than are those learned simply as a collection of techniques.[18]

The overall teaching processes teachers use to facilitate student learning influence considerably the teaching—and learning—of thinking. These processes not only provide opportunities for teaching specific thinking skills and strategies, but by seizing on these opportunities, teachers can capitalize on enhanced student motivation to learn the skills and strategies taught. And by providing such instruction at these points teachers can help give thinking skills and strategies added meaning and thus greater utility. The teaching process context in which the teaching of thinking is carried on certainly shapes the teaching and learning of thinking as much as does the subject matter used and the classroom climate in which such learning and teaching occur.

AN INSTRUCTIONAL FRAMEWORK FOR THE TEACHING OF THINKING

Effective learning of the skills, strategies, knowledge, and dispositions that constitute thinking requires more than the use of appropriate classroom climates and subject matter and teaching processes that provide encouragement, opportunity, and exercise. These are necessary components of the teaching of thinking, of course. But they are simply not sufficient, by themselves, to develop the proficiency in student thinking that schools can and should develop. As educators Benjamin Bloom[19], Bruce Joyce, Beverly Showers [20], and others have pointed out, developing some degree of proficiency in a skill also requires education and training. By combining such education and training with the encouragement and nurturance provided in classroom environments such as those described above and with use of appropriate subject matter and teaching processes, teachers can create instructional and learning contexts that sharply enhance the learning of thinking.

Research in skill learning and recommendations of experts in cognition and thinking suggest an instructional framework well suited for providing direct instruction in thinking skills and strategies. Such research and advice indicate that:

1. To be mastered, a skill should be overlearned initially. [21]
2. In the initial stages of learning a skill focus should be explicitly on the skill. Interference from subject matter and other skills should be minimized, if not eliminated altogether.[22]
3. Initial instruction in a skill should be followed by frequent, intermittent, guided practice in the skill.[23]
4. To facilitate transfer, skills should be applied in a variety of contexts and settings with appropriate instructional guidance.[24]
5. Generalizing a skill may best occur by executing a variety of non-cued tasks, each requiring use of different thinking operations.[25]

These findings and recommendations will be elaborated in later chapters. For the moment, their significance lies in the framework they suggest for structuring the teaching of thinking skills and strategies. This instructional framework consists of six stages:

1. Introduction
2. Guided practice
3. Independent application
4. Transfer and elaboration
5. Guided practice
6. Autonomous use

Any thinking skill or strategy can be learned to a high degree of proficiency when instruction in that skill or strategy proceeds in a series of lessons through all six stages of this teaching framework. Stages 1–3 constitute the first phase of teaching any thinking skill or strategy—introducing it and teaching it to independent use in a simplified form. Stages 4–6, the second phase, complete this instruction by helping students generalize the skill to a wide variety of applications and to internalize it in its more sophisticated, complex forms. A brief explanation of each of these stages will clarify the nature of this framework.

Describing the Framework

Introduction. Instruction in any thinking operation may be initiated whenever a teacher senses a need for students to be able to execute it better than they seem able to do. Such initial instruction can take the form of a single lesson, perhaps of 30 to 50 minutes. The actual length of such a lesson will depend on the abilities of the students, the complexity of the operation to be introduced, and the degree of student proficiency in prerequisite skills. The purpose of this lesson is to introduce students to the major attributes or components of the new operation, if only at a rudimentary, rather simplified level. Instruction here focuses directly on the thinking skill or strategy being introduced as students not only see the operation modeled but also have one or more opportunities to engage in it with appropriate teacher guidance.[26]

Introductory lessons in a thinking skill or strategy obviously do not, by themselves, teach a skill. As a result of such a brief introduction, students will not have developed any significantly increased proficiency in executing the operation being introduced. But they will have launched their study of it. This lesson is but one-sixth of the kinds of lessons needed to develop such proficiency. Subsequent lessons allow students to internalize their knowledge of the operation through repeated practice and, with the help of teacher and peers, in reflecting on and articulating how it seems to work.

Guided Practice.   Once a thinking skill or strategy has been formally introduced, students benefit from a number of lessons in which they practice executing it *with instructive guidance*. In these lessons students deliberately and explicitly practice executing and applying the major attributes of the thinking skill or strategy being learned, always using the same kind of subject matter and the same media or same type of data used in their introduction to the skill or strategy. Experience suggests that these lessons should require relatively brief amounts of time devoted to actually applying the operation, accompanying such application with considerable teacher or peer-provided guidance, assistance, or direction in how to do so. Such guidance may take the form of structured previews of how the operation to be used can be executed as well as follow-up reviews of how it actually worked out in practice. These guided practice lessons should be spaced out, intermittently, over several weeks. They can easily be incorporated into lessons that seek important subject-matter learning objectives as well.[27]

Unlike introductory lessons in which students must focus exclusively on the operation, guided practice lessons allow time and opportunity to deal with the subject matter used in the lesson and the substantive products of skill use. After discussing and analyzing how the thinking operation being practiced was employed, students can then use the knowledge generated by their application of it to carry forward the subject-matter learning in which they are engaged. Gradually, as students become more proficient with the new thinking operations, teachers can reduce the amount of explicit guidance to eventually little, if any, skill instruction.

The exact number of guided practice lessons in any thinking skill or strategy will vary according to the operation being practiced and the abilities of the students. Such lessons should be offered until students demonstrate an ability to execute the operation, on request without teacher guidance. Teachers may well have to conduct three, four, or even more guided practice lessons in a single thinking skill or strategy, once it has been introduced, before moving into the next stage of instruction.[28]

Independent Application.   As students demonstrate an ability to execute the thinking operation being practiced without assistance or guidance, they can then be provided repeated opportunities to use it on their own. These applications should continue to be in the same kind of data or subject matter or media in which the operation was originally introduced and practiced. When students independently apply the skill or strategy, as specifically required by the teacher or text, they integrate the various steps in the procedure by which it is made operational, and they begin to internalize the rules, principles, and other knowledge that inform it.[29] Such application is an important step en route to automatizing a thinking operation and to taking ownership of it.

Many techniques exist for such independent practice of a thinking operation. Teacher, text, or workbook questions may initiate such skill or strategy use. Class discussions, debates, and writing journals or paragraphs or short essays are ways for students to apply designated thinking operations. This is the point in the teaching of thinking at which students can legitimately and productively be put into situations requiring them to think. It is at this point that encouragement and nurturance can contribute most to skill learning as students apply on their own over and over again the thinking operations they have been learning. Such opportunities for independent application of a thinking skill being newly learned may be combined with subject-matter learning and use of other skills in order to advance learning of both the thinking skill or strategy and subject matter.

Again, there is no precise rule or guideline for determining how many opportunities for independent application of a specified thinking operation are required to achieve a high degree of proficiency in executing it. But however many opportunities are required, they should be spaced out intermittently over several months.[30] Reoccurring use of the operation as an integral part of the subject-matter learning process helps to maintain it as well as to give it purpose and utility. Such lessons complete the initial phase of teaching a thinking skill or strategy.

Lessons in each of the first three stages of the instructional framework outlined here—introduction, guided practice, and independent application—enable students to develop a degree of proficiency in a new thinking skill or strategy in the setting (or with the kind of data) in which it was first experienced. The entire sequence of lessons may number a half-dozen or more, depending on the complexity of the operation being introduced and the abilities of the students. Once students have demonstrated that they can do it on their own, the teacher can then offer additional instruction designed to help students apply the operation in a variety of settings to thus generalize it beyond the introductory setting.

Transfer and Elaboration.   Showing students how to apply a previously introduced skill or strategy in new, unfamiliar settings launches the second phase of teaching any thinking operation. No instruction in thinking would be complete without considerable attention to this task. For thinking skills or strategies are not learned, in their most complex forms, once and for all at a specific time, remaining unchanged thereafter. Learned initially in rather simplified forms and limited by the settings in which they are first encountered, understanding of specific thinking operations grows and develops in sophistication as students repeatedly experience executing them in a variety of settings for a variety of purposes. As students learn how to apply these operations in settings, data, or media other than those in which they were first encountered, they learn more about them. This learning continues beyond school, but helping students to begin this process is an important function of this phase of teaching thinking.

Transferring a thinking operation consists of helping students learn how to execute a newly learned skill or strategy in settings other than that in which it was introduced. This means helping them identify the cues in these settings that signal the appropriateness of using the operation. It also means helping them identify any subtle changes in how to engage in the operation required by these new settings.[31] Lessons that launch such transfer are, in effect, reintroductions of the thinking operation but in new subject matter or with new kinds of data or media. In these reintroductions students review what they already know about the operation being learned and then receive instruction in how to execute it in the new setting. As with the original introduction, focus remains on the thinking operation rather than on attaining any subject-matter goals. A transfer lesson may not require as much time as is required to introduce a completely new thinking operation—perhaps only thirty minutes or so. This however, depends on the complexity of the operation, the closeness of the new setting to that in which the operation was originally learned, the degree to which students mastered it in the original setting, and the extent to which students are familiar with the new setting. Every time it is appropriate to execute a previously introduced and practiced thinking skill or strategy with new data or in new subject matter, a lesson like this can initiate learning how to make the transfer.

Guided Practice.   Once a thinking skill or strategy has been initially transferred—with instruction—to a new context, it must be practiced, again with teacher guidance, in that new context a number of times until students demonstrate appropriate proficiency in using it in this context.[32] The same principles and procedures need to be followed in conducting these lessons as are followed in the guided practice lessons conducted after a skill or strategy has been initially introduced and for the same reasons. The crucial ingredient of such lessons remains, as before, instructive guidance in how to execute the operation, provided as needed by teacher, text, or peers. As students become proficient in applying it in the new context, guidance can be reduced. Lessons applying a thinking skill or strategy in the original context can also be interspersed with lessons where students apply it in the newer context, always with teacher guidance as necessary.

Research provides no specific guidance for how many guided practice lessons are required for any particular thinking operation at this point. The number varies. Of course, all students do not develop proficiency at the same rate with the same types of instruction, so some may need more instructional help than others. Some may move more quickly into autonomous use of a skill than will others. Much instruction in this stage of the teaching framework may be with individuals or small groups rather than with the class as a whole. But it readily becomes evident when students have become familiar enough with a new skill or strategy to be able to engage in it on their own—when on their own initiative they can do it without assistance or correction.

Autonomous Use.   Being able to use a thinking operation or strategy to generate knowledge on one's own and on one's own initiative is, of course, the major goal of the teaching of thinking. The sixth, and last stage of the instructional framework presented here thus provides repeated opportunities for precisely such behavior. Again, all the techniques useful for independent application in the first phase of learning a thinking operation are also useful in this stage of the framework. These include responding to questions, engaging in discussions and debates, writing, completing research or action projects, and so on. Teachers must provide enough opportunities for students to engage in a specific thinking operation in a new setting to allow students to become proficient at doing so on their own.

One feature of practice at this stage deserves special note. The kinds of tasks in which students are asked to engage here ought not to be directed solely or explicitly at the thinking operation being worked on. As Professor Carl Bereiter asserts, students at this stage of skill learning should be confronted with tasks that require use—on their own choice—of any of a variety of the thinking operations they have been learning.[33] Thus, students in the midst of learning how to classify information might work at tasks that require classification interspersed with tasks that require sequencing or other skills without receiving any cues from the teacher as to which skills should be used or when. Knowing when to use a thinking operation and being wiling to do so are very much parts of proficiency in thinking. Students need practice at this point in *selecting which* operations to use as well as in applying them accurately, efficiently, and effectively.

As important as autonomous use is in learning thinking skills and strategies, it should be clear that this also is only one-sixth of what is necessary to learn a thinking operation. Thus, providing opportunities for autonomous use is *no substitute* for the instruction required in the other stages of the framework outlined here. Students need instruction in *how* to execute a thinking skill or strategy as well as guided and unguided practice in doing it. To develop student competencies in thinking to the highest degree of proficiency and maintaining this proficiency for the longest time possible requires instruction through all six stages of the framework presented here.

Transferring or extending newly introduced thinking skills and strategies thus constitutes the second and final phase of this framework for the teaching of thinking. For unless students are assisted in learning how to execute a particular thinking operation in settings different from that in which it is introduced, they will remain limited in their ability to use the operation on their own. By showing students how to transfer or elaborate a thinking operation in a variety of settings, by providing guided practice in executing it in these settings, and by offering repeated opportunities to apply it in these settings autonomously, teachers can help students to generalize the operation to the point where they can use it appropriately in a variety of novel settings and on their own initiative. The ultimate goal of the teaching of thinking is for students to be self-directed and self-starting skillful thinkers. This phase of teaching moves them toward this point.

Applying the Framework

The framework described here may be used for organizing instruction and learning in any thinking skill or strategy. To teach any of these operations to a high degree of proficiency, teachers can:

1. Introduce the thinking operation in a single lesson that focuses explicitly on the skill or strategy being introduced.
2. Provide guided practice in executing this operation in the same kind of setting as in the introductory lesson as many times as necessary for students to exhibit some initial proficiency in it.
3. Provide repeated opportunities for students to apply the operation on their own in the same kind of setting or with the same kind of data as in the preceding lessons.

4. Show students in another single lesson how to execute the operation in a new context (or add a new attribute to it), again focusing directly on the operation (and doing this each time it is used in a new context).
5. Conduct additional lessons providing guided practice in executing the operation in each new context.
6. Provide additional lessons in which students can execute the operation on their own in all the contexts in which students have been receiving instruction.

Figure 3.1 illustrates this sequence of lessons. As shown in this figure, teaching any new thinking operation may well require a dozen or more lessons in that operation over a semester or longer as students move from introductory instruction through the remaining stages of the sequence.[34] Exactly how many lessons will be needed to achieve a desired level of student proficiency will vary depending on the extent to which students have mastered prerequisite operations, the complexity of the new operation, the abilities of the students, and the quality of instruction.

The number of lessons in a sequence using this framework will depend also on the number of new contexts into which the operation is extended or the number of new attributes to be added; each of these contexts or added attributes requires a transfer lesson followed by enough lessons for students to begin achieving proficiency in this "version" of the operation. Each transfer lesson then requires guided practice lessons in the new context or in using the newly added dimensions of the operation, as well as repeated opportunities for autonomous use of it in the new and previously practiced forms and applications.

For example, a biology teacher using this instructional framework could sequence lessons in the skill of classifying by providing an introductory lesson in the skill early in a course when students need to distinguish between living and nonliving things.[35] Such a lesson could present data in the form of lists. Guided practice lessons in this skill could then follow when students need to be able to distinguish between various kinds of living organisms such as vertebrates and invertebrates; land, air, and water organisms; and so on—data that could always be presented in list form. The skill could then be transferred, perhaps, to use with pictorially presented data in a lesson when students study various circulatory systems. Again, several lessons could follow in which students receive guided practice in classifying other data presented pictorially—the respiration and nervous systems, perhaps. Finally, lessons could require autonomous use of the skill of classifying as well as of other skills to develop generalizations about biological systems. Teaching the skill of classifying thus means conducting a number of lessons through each stage of this framework as students move toward proficiency in the skill over the

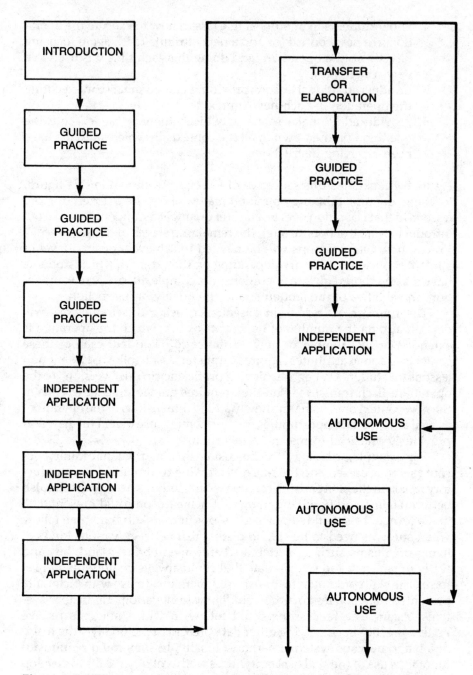

Figure 3.1 A Sequence of Lessons for Teaching a Thinking Skill or Strategy

duration of this course. Similar teaching sequences could be developed for any thinking skill or strategy selected for introduction in any subject-matter course.

Teachers, instructional materials developers, and curriculum builders can use this framework to sequence instruction in any thinking operation throughout any course or an entire curriculum. What is important to remember is that if students are to develop any degree of proficiency in a thinking skill or strategy, whatever lessons a teacher plans or conducts in it must include lessons in each of the six stages of this framework. When combined with purposeful study of appropriate subject matter, use of an appropriate teaching process, and a classroom environment supportive of thinking, this framework is a most useful and practical structure for organizing instruction in thinking.

THE TEACHING OF THINKING

Establishing and maintaining a structure that facilitates the teaching and learning of thinking is extremely important to improving student thinking. But this structure will be for naught unless teaching strategies appropriate to this structure are employed. Many such strategies already exist. Others can be devised. Like the instructional framework described above, these strategies are—and can be—derived from research in effective teaching and skill learning. Teachers seeking to improve student proficiencies in thinking can employ these strategies at various stages in the instructional framework and in the classroom and subject-matter contexts outlined above. The remaining chapters present, explain, and illustrate some of the most useful of these strategies.

NOTES

1. Larry Cuban, "Policy and Research Dilemmas in the Teaching of Reasoning: Unplanned Designs," *Review of Educational Research* 54: (Winter 1984), pp. 655–681; Henry A. Giroux, "Developing Educational Programs: Overcoming the Hidden Curriculum," *The Clearing House* 52:4 (December 1978), pp. 148–151.

2. Cuban, "Policy and Research," p. 657.

3. Arthur L. Costa, "Teaching for Intelligent Behavior," *Educational Leadership* 39:2 (October 1981), pp. 29–32.

4. Ibid.

5. Francis P. Hunkins, "Helping Students Ask Their Own Questions," *Social Education* 49:4 (April 1985), pp. 293–296.

6. John McPeck, *Critical Thinking and Education* (New York: St. Martin's Press, 1981); Michael I. Posner and Steven W. Keele, "Skill Learning," in Robert M. W. Travers, ed., *Second Handbook of Research on Teaching* (Chicago: Rand McNally College Publishing Company, 1973), pp. 805–831.

7. Janet Kierstead, "Direct Instruction and Experimental Approaches: Are They Really Mutually Exclusive?" *Educational Leadership* 42:8 (May 1985), p. 26; Carl Bereiter, "Elementary Schools: Necessity or Convenience?" *Elementary School Journal* 73:8 (May 1973), pp. 435–446.

8. Walter Doyle, "Academic Work," *Review of Educational Research* 53:2 (Summer 1983), p. 168; Raymond S. Nickerson, "Kinds of Thinking Taught in Current Programs," *Educational Leadership* 42:1 (September 1984), pp. 26–37; David S. Perkins, "Creativity by Design," *Educational Leadership* 42:1 (September 1984), p 12; Ann Brown, Joseph C. Campione, and Jeanne D. Day, "Learning to Learn: On Training Students to Learn from Texts," *Educational Researcher* 10:2 (February 1981), p. 18.

9. Bereiter, "Elementary Schools."

10. Posner and Keele, "Skill Learning."

11. Posner and Keele, "Skill Learning"; Bryce B. Hudgins, *Learning and Thinking* (Itasca Ill.: F. E. Peacock Publishers, 1977), p. 154.

12. Hudgins, *Learning and Thinking*, pp. 142–169.

13. Hudgins, *Learning and Thinking*; David N. Perkins, "Thinking Frames" (Paper delivered at ASCD Conference on Approaches to Teaching Thinking, Alexandria, Va., August 6, 1985).

14. Thomas H. Estes, "Reading in the Social Studies—A Review of Research Since 1950," in James L. Lafferty, ed., *Reading in the Content Areas* (Newark, Del.: International Reading Association, 1972), pp. 178–183.

15. Bereiter, "Elementary Schools."

16. Richard Paul, "Dialogical Thinking: Critical Thought Essential to the Acquisition of Rational Knowledge and Passions" in Joan Baron and Robert Sternberg, eds., *Teaching Thinking Skills: Theory and Practice.* (New York: W. H. Freeman, 1987).

17. Bereiter, "Elementary Schools"; Doyle, "Academic Work."

18. Jerome S. Bruner, *The Process of Education* (Cambridge: Harvard University Press, 1963), pp. 17–68.

19. Benjamin Bloom, *Developing Talent in Young People* (New York: Ballantine Books, 1985).

20. Bruce R. Joyce and Beverly Showers, *Power in Staff Development Through Research on Training* (Alexandria, Va.: Association for Supervision and Curriculum Development, 1983).

21. Barak V. Rosenshine, "Teaching Functions in Instructional Programs," *Elementary School Journal* 83:4 (March 1983), pp. 335–352; Hudgins, *Learning and Thinking*, p. 146; Posner and Keele, "Skill Learning."

22. Hudgins, *Learning and Thinking*; Posner and Keele, "Skill Learning"; Robert J. Sternberg, "How Can We Teach Intelligence?"; *Educational Leadership* 42:1 (September 1984), pp. 38–50; Edward de Bono, "The Direct Teaching of Thinking as a Skill," *Phi Delta Kappan* 64:10 (June 1983), pp. 703–708; Arthur Whimbey, "Teaching Sequential Thought: The Cognitive Skills Approach," *Phi Delta Kappan* 59:4 (December 1977), pp. 255–259.

23. Posner and Keele, "Skill Learning"; Hudgins, *Learning and Thinking*, pp. 92–99; Jane Stallings, "Effective Strategies for Teaching Basic Skills," in Daisy G. Wallace, ed., *Developing Basic Skills Programs in Secondary Schools* (Alexandria, Va.: Association for Supervision and Curriculum Development, 1983), pp. 1–19; Rosenshine, "Teaching Functions"; Doyle, "Academic Work."

24. Herbert J. Klausmeier and J. Kent Davis, "Transfer of Learning," *Encyclopedia of Educational Research* (New York: Macmillan, 1969), pp. 1483–1493; Hudgins, *Learning and Thinking*, pp. 142–169; Perkins, "Thinking Frames," pp.14–15; Doyle, "Academic Work"; Brown, Campione, and Day, "Learning to Learn."

25. Carl Bereiter, "How to Keep Thinking Skills from Going the Way of All Frills," *Educational Leadership* 42:1 (September 1984), pp. 75–78; Posner and Keele, "Skill Learning"; Hudgins, *Learning and Thinking*, pp. 92–99; Doyle, "Academic Work."

26. Rosenshine, "Teaching Functions"; Stallings, "Effective Strategies"; Posner and Keele, "Skill Learning"; Whimbey, "Teaching Sequential."

27. Barry K. Beyer, "Teaching Critical Thinking: A Direct Approach," *Social Education* 49:4 (April 1985), pp. 297–303; Rosenshine, "Teaching Functions"; Hudgins, *Learning and Thinking*, pp. 92–99.

28. Posner and Keele, "Skill Learning"; Joyce and Showers, *Power*; Rosenshine, "Teaching Functions."

29. Hubert Dreyfus, "Expert Systems Versus Intuitive Enterprise" (Paper delivered at George Mason University, Fairfax, Va., May 29, 1984); Doyle, "Academic Work"; Posner and Keele, "Skill Learning."

30. Posner and Keele, "Skill Learning"; Doyle, "Academic Work"; Hudgins, *Learning and Thinking*, pp. 92–99.

31. Hudgins, *Learning and Thinking*, pp. 142–169.

32. Hudgins, *Learning and Thinking*; Doyle, "Academic Work."

33. Bereiter, "How to Keep."

34. Joyce and Showers, *Power*.

35. Barry K. Beyer and Ronald E. Charlton, "Teaching Thinking Skills in Biology," *American Biology Teacher* 48:4 (April 1986), pp. 207–212.

4

Introducing a
Thinking Skill—I

Each of the stages in the framework for teaching a thinking skill or strategy serves an important function in helping students to develop proficiency in that operation. However, the introductory stage may well be the most important. For most students this is the first formal instructional encounter with a new thinking skill or strategy. What happens during this encounter goes a long way in helping students understand it. If this introduction is frustrating because a new skill seems impossibly abstract or complex or irrelevant, students may well avoid future opportunities to apply the skill which they take up only half-heartedly, or they may attempt to shortcut it in a way that negates its effective use. Consequently, teachers should give careful attention to how, where, and in what form they introduce new thinking skills and strategies in classrooms.

At times some teachers introduce a new skill simply by throwing the students into a task that requires its use as best they know how, providing a bit of exhortation or encouragement and concentrating thereafter upon the substantive insights—the answers—generated through use of the skill by those who can execute it. Unfortunately, little understanding of the skill itself results from such introductions, for at least two reasons. There is usually no effort to reflect on, or to provide, actual instruction in how to execute it. Moreover, the focus of such lessons remains almost completely, if not wholly, on subject matter.

A more effective way to introduce a new thinking skill or strategy in any course makes the thinking operation itself the subject and content of the lesson. Although the lesson may use subject matter regularly studied in the course as a vehicle in which to employ the skill, the teacher seeking to enhance student understanding of the skill should keep student attention continuously and consciously on the skill being introduced.

An introductory lesson in a thinking skill or strategy presents teachers with their first opportunity to employ what should be done (as indicated by research and thoughtful skill teaching experience) to help beginners understand a skill. The main purpose of such a lesson is to help students see the operation as a skill—by feeling what it is like to engage in a simplified version of it and by becoming aware of some of its key attributes. It is in such a lesson that modeling of the operation can most profitably occur, that the specific components or attributes of the operation can be articulated by the students, and that the operation can be performed in a risk-free, supportive environment. For many thinking operations such a lesson may well be sufficient to launch very effective and rapid learning of the newly introduced skill, via subsequent guided practice; for other operations, especially those that upon first encounter appear to be very complex, such a lesson may serve mainly to increase awareness of the value of the skill and to stimulate a felt need to become better at executing it.

Lessons introducing a new thinking or strategy usually require thirty to fifty minutes, depending on its complexity and the abilities and prior experience of the students. Any of a number of teaching strategies can be used to conduct such lessons. These strategies range from inductive, student-directed strategies on the one hand to rather didactic, teacher-directed strategies on the other. Some strategies combine elements of both. The inductive strategies allow students, in effect, to articulate for themselves the main attributes of the thinking operation being introduced and to elaborate and refine these attributes with subsequent guidance and practice. In the most directive strategies, teachers or other models present the key attributes of a new skill right at the start so that students can replicate them and elaborate them while practicing the skill in subsequent lessons. A strategy combining elements of both the inductive and directive strategies can be used to heighten motivation, to accommodate more complex skills or subject matter, or to respond directly to varying ability levels and learning styles of the students. Each of these types of strategies is useful in introducing new thinking skills and strategies.

AN INDUCTIVE STRATEGY

An inductive introduction to a thinking skill involves students almost immediately in executing the new operation in order to identify the main procedures, rules, or criteria that seem to be implicit in how it works. Such a strategy is most useful with average to above-average students, students with considerable background in the subject matter being used, and students who have already demonstrated some proficiency in thinking. It is also useful when the thinking operation itself is relatively uncomplicated. What emerges from this type of lesson is the students' initial view of the operation.[1] While there is some risk that a skill or strategy first developed in this way may confuse more than enlighten, properly conducted such an introductory lesson can, in effect, set up a hypothetical model of the operation for students to flesh out in subsequent practice by applying it with the guidance of teacher and peers.

In general, introducing a new thinking operation inductively consists of having students engage in the operation on their own, working perhaps in pairs or small groups to identify whatever procedures or rules they find themselves using. Once they have identified and discussed such attributes, the lesson continues with a second application of the operation and concludes with an explicit review of what has been discovered about it. Such a lesson need not be a special event, breaking the subject-matter sequence, nor need it be conducted in a "subject-matter free" context. It can—and indeed should—be presented when using the new operation is clearly necessary for understanding the subject matter or for accomplishing a subject-matter objective.

In conducting an inductive introductory lesson, a teacher can guide the class through five steps:

1. First, the teacher introduces the new thinking operation in the context of the subject matter being studied.
2. Then the students execute the operation as best they can to complete a short assigned task.
3. Next, students reflect on and share what they did in their minds as they executed the operation.
4. Another opportunity to execute the new operation follows in which students consciously try to use what they have discovered about it to complete a second task.
5. Students conclude by again reporting on what they believe they did in their heads to execute the new skill or strategy and what rules they seemed to follow in carrying it out.

By conducting lessons through these five steps of *introduce, execute, reflect, apply, review,* teachers can provide the kind of introduction to a thinking skill or strategy that lets students begin where they are in terms of what they know about it and that raises to a level of consciousness what they do in executing it. Follow-up lessons providing guided practice can build on what emerges to elaborate, flesh out, and even correct the attributes of the operation identified in this lesson.

Applying the Strategy

To demonstrate and clarify the details of this inductive strategy, an example of this strategy follows. Suppose an American history teacher is charged with the responsibility of teaching the skill of classifying information into self-invented categories.* This skill could be introduced early in the typical fifth or eighth grade American history course, perhaps at the point where students are supposed to learn the characteristics of life in England's American colonies just prior to the American Revolution. Students will be motivated to learn this skill when introduced in this context because being able to classify information will obviously help them achieve the given subject-matter objective. To introduce this skill at this point, then, a teacher could use the inductive strategy as follows.

After introducing the topic of the lesson—"life in the thirteen colonies around 1750"—and relating this topic to the students' previous study of the period, the teacher can set the substantive purpose for studying the skill by posing a question requiring student use of the skill. Such a question might be, "What was life like in the thirteen English North American colonies around 1750?"

To launch study of the skill itself, the teacher should then *introduce the skill* and provide a rationale for studying it. This can be accomplished by presenting the class with some data to classify. In this case the words in Figure 4.1 serve the purpose well. Pointing out that these words, presented as a handout or via an overhead transparency, were commonly spoken by the inhabitants of the New England colonies about 1750, the teacher can then ask the students to use these words to identify what life

---

*Because it is important to use familiar, uncomplicated subject matter in introducing a new skill, we can use the skill of classifying as the subject for illustrating the introductory strategies presented here. This skill is quite straightforward for adults. The objective of the example lessons that follow is not to learn how to classify data but to understand how to execute the key steps in the particular skill-introducing strategy being illustrated. Rather than attending exclusively to the skill of classifying itself, the reader should focus on the teaching strategy being employed, for it is *teaching* skills that constitutes the focus of this and the next few chapters.

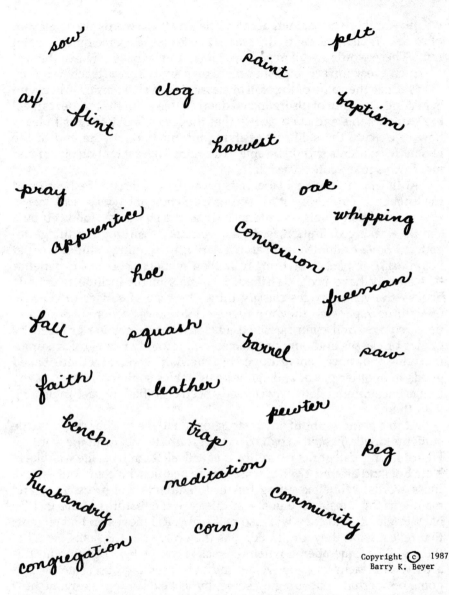

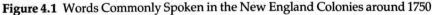

Figure 4.1 Words Commonly Spoken in the New England Colonies around 1750

was like for these people at that time. The way these words are displayed, of course, is challenging to the students because, as some quickly point out, "These words are all mixed up. How can we make sense of them?"

Such a reaction accomplishes more than anything the teacher can say to introduce the value of the skill of classifying, a skill particularly useful in making sense out of disorganized data. At this point the teacher can tell the students this and state clearly that the lesson's objective is to learn how to execute the skill of classifying information. By the end of the lesson the students should be able to describe, at least tentatively, one or more ways to execute this skill.

At this point, the skill label *classify* can be written on the board and the teacher can underline it for emphasis. Synonyms (*group, sort, categorize*) can be then given—by the teacher or the students—followed by a simple working definition, such as, perhaps, "putting like things together." Since examples are useful in clarifying meanings, students could volunteer examples of anything from their school or personal experience that already have been classified. Examples might include telephone books—the yellow pages classify things by type of service or product offered; newspapers—they are divided into news sections, sports sections, comics, and even classified ads; students—they are grouped by grades or classes and, among themselves, into other categories; supermarkets—they have items grouped by type: dairy here, meat there, baked goods in another place, and canned vegetables somewhere else. Many things encountered daily have already been classified for ease in dealing with them.

At this point, without any instruction at all, the teacher can have the students *execute the skill*. In pairs or small groups they can put the words in Figure 4.1 into categories or groups that will tell them what life was like in New England around 1750, at least for the people who commonly spoke those words. While executing this task, students will probably attend mainly to the substantive goal—in this case the features of life in 1750 New England—but they will also make physical moves and statements that reveal what they are thinking as they carry out the tasks. Some of these will be remembered when the task is completed. Throughout this activity the teacher may move around the classroom observing what is going on, perhaps encouraging some, but *not* explaining to anyone how to execute the task. This task is one students are to do on their own.

Having grouped most of the words on the handout, students then should *reflect* aloud on what they have been doing and how they have been doing it. The ensuing discussion should focus on the skill of classifying itself rather than on what the students found out about life in colonial New England. Yet to give substantive value to the activity, the teacher might initiate the discussion by having students report for a minute or two on several categories they invented, on the words they placed in each, and on what they infer from each category about life at this time. However, detailed discussion and analysis of these responses should wait until the next class period. At this point, attention should focus as much as possible on what the students did, in as much step-by-step detail as possible, to put these words into groups.

Talking about what went on in their minds while executing a thinking operation is a difficult task for most students, especially initially, because it requires them to stand outside of their heads and be alert to what is going on in them, something to which most students are not accustomed. Some students above the sixth grade level, though, will be able to report some things they do or did, such as, "First, I read—skimmed—the words. Then I found two that were the same—*hoe* and *ax*—and then there were more tools, like *trap* . . . so. . . . Then I started on another group—*baptism*, *faith*, and others. . . .But then later I broke the tools down into farming things, hunting things, and building things." Other students might indicate that first they skimmed the list of words and that, as they did so, categories of words seemed to jump out at them, such as religious words, farming words, and so on. So they then went back to find and list all the words related to each of these labels. Still other students may indicate that after hearing what their goal was and skimming the data, they looked at each word, recalled its meaning and a category to which it belonged, and marked it with some symbol or number to indicate its category. Then they went back to connect or list all those in the same category together and even, once or twice, to combine two categories (farm tools and farm crops, for example) to make a single category (such as farming).

As students report, elaborate on, and rework what they did or heard being done, the teacher can list their remarks on the chalkboard under *steps*, *rules*, and *knowledge used* columns as appropriate. In this way the teacher and students can gradually build a list of key attributes or components of this skill, as articulated by the students. What emerges is a tentative, first impression of some of the key procedures in which one engages in classifying data, some rules that may guide the execution of this skill, and some things students know about the skill or data to which it was applied that make it possible to execute the skill. A variety of procedures will be described, partially at best, as may be two or three rules—like putting data they didn't understand (such as the word *clog*) or data that they couldn't handle (perhaps *whipping*) into a category they called miscellaneous to work with later. At this point the goal is to get several different ways to execute this skill on the board for all to see, and to encourage students to articulate as many attributes of the skill as they can.

Students can now *apply the skill* again. Using the procedures, rules, and other items just discussed and on the board, they can, in pairs or alone this time, execute the skill a second time, using words like those in Figure 4.2, that were commonly spoken by colonists living in the Middle Atlantic colonies around 1750. Unlike the items on the initial list, these words appear to be organized, but, as students are quick to point out, not in a useful fashion. Besides, they complain, there are too many words. Classifying data thus proves to be a useful operation when one has so many data that it seems impossible to learn or use them all; these data can be made meaningful, however, if they are grouped into fewer, more easily processed and remembered "chunks" or categories. Thus, students can proceed to classify these words into categories to determine what life was like in the Middle Atlantic colonies just before the American Revolution. Again, the teacher can move about the room offering assistance, encouraging, and this time suggesting how students can proceed to execute this skill.

To conclude this lesson, students should *review* what they have found out about the skill. They may initiate this final step in the strategy by reporting several categories they made out of these words and what each category implied about life in 1750 for the people using these words frequently. But again, as in the reflection step, focus should be constantly on the skill and its identified attributes. Students may report that they followed one or more of the sequences of procedures already listed on the board or that they did so but added or modified some steps or rules. For

alien	apprentice	compact
faith	banish	wheelbarrow
exile	loft	clapboard
saw	musket	flint
ball	cold	community
net	shingles	freeman
heresy	conversion	writ
chimney	trap	pelt
cannon	discipline	shovel
thatch	covenant	bean
kettle	powder	maple
live	court	bedstead
sabbath	stranger	meeting
corn	bench	squash
will	pray	clay
barrel	ax	saint
keg	cloak	muskrat
wind	sandy	oak
harvest	fall	berry

Figure 4.2 Words Commonly Spoken in the Middle Atlantic Colonies around 1750

example, they may indicate that after finding just two words that seemed similar, they wrote the similarity as the label for the group and *then* wrote under it all the other words on the list fitting this label; they probably repeated this process until they had made several categories of words. Others might indicate that after just glancing at these words they decided to use their previous categories because, since this task and data were similar to the initial task, they thought the earlier categories would work here, too. And they did, to a point.

After volunteering any additional procedures used, rules followed, or knowledge used, and after raising any questions about the skill, students can refine the working definition given at the beginning of the lesson. They can describe some places in the course to date where the data they used had already been classified (in the chapter on explorers, for instance) and report some instances in their out-of-school activities where this skill may be most useful (perhaps in categorizing the advantages and the disadvantages of choosing any particular activity when deciding on what to do on Saturday). Some key procedures and rules can be entered into their notebooks or put on butcher paper or on the bulletin board to display for later reference.

A follow-up assignment could then be to classify a list of words commonly spoken in Maryland, Virginia, Georgia and the Carolinas about 1750 in order to identify the key features of life there at that time. In the next class session, students and teacher can review how these words were classified. Then they can focus on the subject matter they have been studying by using the substantive products of all three classifying activities to probe in detail the nature of life in the thirteen colonies on the eve of the American Revolution. The class can continue subject-matter learning and go back to practicing the newly introduced skill of classifying in a day or two when the data to be used in class make it appropriate to do so.

Analyzing the Strategy

Figure 4.3 outlines in some detail what should be done at each of the five major steps in this inductive introductory strategy to carry it out effectively. This outline can serve as a guide in writing a teaching plan for any lesson in any subject where a teacher wishes to introduce a thinking skill using this inductive strategy. The following explanation of the more important features of this strategy will clarify what ought to occur in each step and the importance of each.

In using this inductive strategy, a teacher first sets the substantive context of the lesson and then introduces the thinking skill or strategy which the lesson is to introduce. First, the teacher places the lesson in the context of the subject matter under study and gives, or has students invent, a subject-matter task—in this case, "What was life like for these

STEP 1 *INTRODUCE THE SKILL*

State that "learning" the skill is today's objective.
Give the skill label/name.
Give synonyms.
State a tentative/working definition.
State ways the skill can be or has been used:
   • in students' personal experiences,
   • in school activities,
   • in this course.
Explain how the skill is useful and why it's worth learning.

STEP 2 *EXECUTE THE SKILL*

Use the skill (as best one can) to accomplish a task.
Work in pairs, triads, or groups.
Use subject matter familiar to students and appropriate to course (or if necessary, from students' experience).

STEP 3 *REFLECT ON WHAT WAS DONE*

Students report what went on in their heads as they engaged in the skill.
Identify the key steps/rules used and sequence of each.
Clarify the procedure and any criteria used.
Focus on the skill and its attributes.

STEP 4 *APPLY SKILL TO NEW DATA*

Use what has been discussed about the skill to complete a second task.
Work in pairs, triads, or groups.
Use subject matter appropriate to the course but in the same structure and media as in Step 2.

STEP 5 *REVIEW THE SKILL*

Report on what students did in their heads as they applied the skill.
Review the steps/procedure that seem to constitute the skill.
Review the rules that direct use of the skill as well as when it is to be used.
State the relationship of this skill to other skills.
Review or revise the skill definition.
State where the skill can be used in personal or out-of-school situations.

Figure 4.3 An Inductive Strategy for Introducing a Thinking Skill or Strategy

people in 1750?"—that makes it useful for them to learn a particular skill. Then the teacher shifts the focus of the lesson to the skill itself. Such an introduction serves two purposes: it places the lesson in the subject-matter context of the course and gives purpose to learning about the skill to be introduced.

Giving a few minutes of concentrated attention at this point to the skill is important for both pedagogical as well as psychological reasons. Pedagogically, by writing the skill label—"classify"—on the board, adding synonyms and a tentative definition, and discussing some examples briefly, the teacher reinforces the stated goal of the lesson—to "learn" at an introductory level a specific thinking skill, in this case classifying.

Psychologically, the four or five minutes required to complete this introduction to the new skill or strategy helps students develop the mental set necessary for what they are about to do—execute the operation. Whenever individuals decide to do something, psychologists report, the mind searches long-term memory to bring into short-term memory for immediate use anything it knows related to the task to be undertaken.[2] It uses various cues in making this search. If all a teacher does to aid students to search their memories is to use a single skill label, the students' search may be limited to that one cue, the skill label. Adding synonyms, a definition, and examples in effect provides additional potential cues for those who may have something stored away in the past experience associated with *any* of these cues. The time devoted to this "cueing" allows time for the search and for students to develop the set or readiness to engage in the skill. Too many times teachers fail to help students develop the set needed to execute a skill. This attention to the skill in introducing it counters such an omission. In teaching a new thinking operation, especially in the early lessons, teachers should launch their instruction by introducing the skill as described here so that students can develop the set they need to have some success at executing the skill.

In conducting this part of an introductory lesson, the teacher may wish to involve students as much as possible. Students can volunteer synonyms for the skill label or simple definitions of the skill and even examples of its use. But the teacher should not strain to get these out of the class. In the case of complex or unfamiliar skills, this often proves impossible, so the teacher should be prepared to supply them directly. The point of the introduction is not to play guessing games with these skill descriptors but to get as many up on the chalkboard as possible in a brief time as cues for students trying to recall whatever they may know about the skill so that they can better understand or use it.

It is most useful for students to execute a newly introduced skill (Step 2) in pairs, triads, or small groups. This minimizes any risk involved. Those unable to do the skill can ride the coattails of those who can. This "teaming" also allows for some peer teaching, as those more familiar with the skill usually step right in and do it, occasionally even explaining to their partners why they are doing what they do.

Once students have some experience in lessons of this type, one or two of them can be assigned as observers to record what other students do or seem to do as they execute the new skills, but this is not absolutely necessary. Such a procedure does serve to alert students to the kinds of thinking operations that may be going on as others in the groups or triads actually execute the skill. It also provides a number of resource people somewhat more prepared than other students to discuss, after this part of the lesson has been completed, how the skill was carried out. But when such an activity is first used (as in the above example with the skill of classifying), it is just as useful to have all students engage in doing the skill and later all take part in reconstructing what they did.

Students' reflecting on and verbalizing (Step 3) what they did in their minds as they executed this skill is a key step in this, as in any, introductory strategy. This activity requires students to engage in metacognition, to look inside their heads to report what went on there in the course of—in this example—forming categories of data.[3] More will be said about metacognition in Chapter 8, but for now it is sufficient to know that at this point students must attempt to explore how they executed the skill and to articulate any rules they seem to have followed or special knowledge about the skill they used.

The teacher can initiate this step by discussing briefly—without writing anything on the board—ideas about life in 1750 New England generated by the groupings made by the students. But most of the class discussion at this point must focus on the skill. It is the skill that is to be "learned" in this lesson, not information about the subject; that information can be the focus of the next day's lesson. For the moment, it is crucial for students to hear how others did the skill and to share with them how they did it, for there is no "right" way to execute a skill, though some procedures are more efficient and productive than are others. Talking about the skill and hearing others talk about it are among the most effective devices in the initial stages of learning any thinking operation.

In the final two steps of this teaching strategy, students use what they have done, heard, and articulated to execute the skill again (Step 4), and then once again share with each other how they did it and what they have found out about the main attributes of the skill (Step 5). The skill definition offered at the beginning of the lesson can be revised here to reflect what has been learned, and perhaps additional synonyms will be volunteered. References can be made here, too, about where students can use this skill in other classes or out-of-school as well as where they have used it previously in the text or in their own course. The lesson concludes as it started, with emphasis on the skill, its attributes and uses. A follow-up assignment using the skill once more provides one more opportunity to begin to make it part of a student's intellectual repertoire.

Reviewing the Strategy

This inductive introductory strategy allows students and teacher to "discover" or at least become more conscious of the major steps, knowledge, and rules that constitute the skill being introduced, albeit perhaps only at a beginning and probably an incomplete level. Its use allows field-independent students to share their intuitive insights with their more field-dependent peers who rely more often on explicit directives to complete such tasks. It also requires field-independent students to become more conscious of how they think, thus giving them even more control over their own minds than they might otherwise develop. And, most important of all, this strategy allows teachers to introduce a thinking skill even when they themselves are not clear about its operations, rules, or special knowledge. In effect, this strategy allows students to "teach" the teacher as well as one another how to execute the skill. Conducting several inductive introductory lessons in the same skill in the same day will contribute immensely to a teacher's knowledge of how to do and how to explain a skill, thus making it much easier to use another, more direct introductory strategy when introducing this same skill another time.

This inductive strategy appeals to many teachers for a variety of reasons. Chief among these is belief that whatever students figure out on their own, as they do in using this strategy, they learn better. Indeed, research indicates that self-invention or student induction of thinking skills and strategies may lead to better retention of whatever operations are "discovered." However, this same research indicates that such an approach to learning thinking skills and strategies can also easily result in the invention of dysfunctional skills and strategies and a commitment to these that inhibits learning more useful, effective ways to execute these operations.[4] Thus, this inductive introductory teaching strategy must be used judiciously. It is not for all students nor for all times nor for all skills. Selection of the right teaching strategy for introducing a thinking operation must take into account the abilities of the students, their previous experience in using the operation to be introduced, the complexity of the operation, and the type of subject matter being used to introduce it. In many instances, especially for slower students or novices or in the case of complex thinking operations, more direct expository strategies will be more effective and appropriate in introducing a new thinking skill or strategy.

A DIRECTIVE STRATEGY

In introducing a new thinking operation, sometimes it is more efficient or effective, in terms of student learning, for teachers to be much more direct in their instruction than if they used the inductive introduction strategy. Such occasions include those when the thinking skill or strategy to be introduced is very complex, when the students may be less able than average students, or when the students have had no previous experience with the operation at all—when they are truly beginners or novices. In instances such as these, teachers can use a rather didactic introductory strategy.[5] For want of a better label, this introductory strategy can be called a directive strategy.

Analyzing the Strategy

With the directive strategy, the teacher plays a much more expository role than with the inductive strategy described above. This directive strategy presents the key attributes of the new thinking operation directly to the students right at the start of the lesson.[6] Thereupon, the students use whatever data have been provided them to execute the operation themselves in an effort to replicate it as it has been introduced. In so doing, they in effect test out the procedure and rules already presented and may even discover or invent additional ones. But the teacher retains almost complete control of what is to be learned about the new operation, first by presenting its key attributes; second by controlling its application; third, by accepting or rejecting student ideas about how it works; and, finally, by providing a standard description of the operation to conclude the lesson. A directive introduction actually minimizes student input at this initial stage of learning a new thinking skill or strategy. It does so in order to provide a common base on which students can elaborate with later guidance, practice, and reflection. In effect, this strategy has students execute a new thinking operation as others more proficient in it than they do it, before they—the students—try to execute it on their own.

In introducing a thinking operation using a directive strategy, a teacher guides students through six steps:

1. First, the teacher introduces the operation in the context of the subject matter being studied, just as in the inductive strategy.
2. Next, the teacher explains in some detail the key steps, in sequence, that constitute the operation's procedure as well as important rules and other information relating to the operation.
3. Then, the teacher, with student assistance as available, shows the students in step-by-step fashion just how the operation is executed—how the procedures are employed in sequence, how major rules work, and how specific criteria or cues are used.
4. At this point students discuss the demonstration, reviewing how the attributes of the operation are illustrated by the demonstration.
5. Then the students, with teacher guidance as necessary, apply the operation following as closely as possible the way it was demonstrated and explained.
6. Finally, the students reflect on how they executed the operation, focusing on the key procedures, rules, and knowledge that constitute the newly introduced operation.

By moving through these six steps—*introduce, explain, demonstrate, review, apply, reflect*—teachers can initiate student understanding of a new, often complex, thinking skill or strategy. This directive strategy allows teachers to control the various features of an operation as they are introduced, presenting a simplified version of it before presenting its more complex or sophisticated nuances. This approach can minimize confusion and provide all students a common baseline of knowledge about a new thinking operation on which to build in subsequent lessons. It also satisfies a commonly expressed desire of beginners and less able students faced with a seemingly impossible task to "show me what you want me to do" before they are willing to risk doing it. Figure 4.4 identifies the key operations that constitute each of the major steps in this teaching strategy. Teachers can use this outline as a guide in planning or evaluating lessons to introduce any thinking operation employing this directive strategy.

Applying the Strategy

A teacher can use a directive strategy just as easily as an inductive strategy to introduce any thinking operation. For example, in introducing the skill of classifying information in the imaginary American history lesson described above, a teacher using the directive strategy could start exactly as with the lesson using the inductive strategy. The teacher should *introduce* this skill at precisely the same point in the course and for the same purposes as in that example (Step 1). The four- to five-minute introduction of the skill should focus on the skill label—*classify*, provide synonyms, generate a tentative definition, and point out some examples from the everyday experiences of the students in the class. But after this initial introduction, the lesson should differ considerably from a lesson using the inductive approach.

Instead of having the students apply the skill immediately after its brief introduction, in this directive strategy the teacher should *explain* carefully the key attributes of the skill (Step 2). In this instance, for example, the teacher might project an overhead transparency showing some of the key rules and/or steps constituting the skill as executed by "experts." The teacher could thus point out that to classify data some experts:

1. State their goals—what they hope to find out by classifying the data.
2. Skim the data to see what's there.
3. Recall the meaning of the data.
4. Select one piece of the data—or let these data "jump up" and select them.

STEP 1 *INTRODUCE THE SKILL*

State that "learning" the skill is today's objective.
Give the skill label/name.
Give synonyms.
State a tentative/working definition.
State ways the skill can be or has been used:
  • in students' personal experience,
  • in school activities,
  • in this course.
Explain how the skill is useful and why it's worth learning.

STEP 2 *EXPLAIN THE SKILL*

State the procedure constituting the skill in step-by-step sequence, explaining
  what one does and why for each step.
State key rules and "things to know" about the skill.

STEP 3 *DEMONSTRATE THE SKILL*

Lead the class step-by-step through the skill:
  • state the goal,
  • refer to each step in the procedure,
  • give reasons for doing each step.
Show how rules are carried out.
Use course subject matter familiar to the students (or, if necessary,
  from their experience).

STEP 4 *REVIEW WHAT WAS DONE*

Review the procedures and rules.
Review the reasons for each (as illustrated in the demonstration).

STEP 5 *APPLY THE SKILL*

Execute the skill with teacher guidance.
Work in pairs, triads, or groups.
Complete material used in demonstration or use new but same kind of
  data/media as used in Step 3.

STEP 6 *REFLECT ON THE SKILL*

Review the steps comprising the skill and the rules guiding its use.
Reflect on ways in which the skill is used and when it is appropriate to use.
State the relationship of this skill to other skills.
Review or revise skill definition..
State where the skill can be used in
  • personal or out-of-school situations,
  • coursework.

Figure 4.4 A Directive Strategy for Introducing a Thinking Skill or Strategy

5. Find another piece of the data similar to the first.
6. Identify what it is that these items share and state that common feature as the label of a group (category/class).
7. Find all other items in this given information that fit in this group and put them under this label.
8. Repeat the process (Steps 4−7), forming new groups until all data have been placed in appropriate groups.
9. Subdivide some categories into more precise categories and/or combine others into larger, more encompassing categories.

Among the rules that might be pointed out are those about where such a skill can be used—as, for instance, when the data available appear to be disorganized (as in the word list in Figure 4.1) or in an overwhelming amount (as in the list of words in Figure 4.2). Students might also be advised that in encountering data they do not understand, they can put it aside in a category of "other" or "miscellaneous," to deal with after they have classified all other data, another useful rule followed by those experienced in executing this skill.

Next, the teacher should *demonstrate* just how this skill can be employed (Step 3). Using the list of words in Figure 4.1 commonly spoken in New England colonies in 1750 and keeping the list of skill steps projected on the screen, the teacher can walk students through the skill to make several categories of items. Students can volunteer suggestions as they take each step: stating the goal (to find out what life was like in 1750 New England); skimming to report at random some of the words on the handout and stating the meanings of several of these words; selecting one word—any word—and finding another that is, to them, like the word just identified; and so on until a category of words is in place on the chalkboard. The steps can be repeated to make another category of words, if desired—and repeated several more times to make additional groupings. Then the teacher and students can *review* (Step 4) how they executed this skill thus far and how they followed the rules already introduced.

At this point (Step 5) the students can *apply* the skill as demonstrated to complete classifying the words used in the demonstration or to classify the words in Figure 4.2. Working in pairs, perhaps, they can apply the skill as presented and demonstrated to put these words into categories of their own, with the transparency list of steps and rules still projected on the screen to guide them. To conclude the lesson (Step 6), the students can then *reflect* on the steps and rules they used and how they executed them; they can volunteer any other "rules" they seemed to have followed or any additional steps they executed. They need also to revise their definition of the skill to make it more precise or accurate, and they should suggest places in the text or course where they may have used data already classified by the textbook authors.

Finally, to end the class review of the skill, the teacher can present the students a saying or acronym or similar device related to the skill that will help them recall how to do it next time. In this case, the teacher could suggest that whenever it is time to classify data, students should think GROUPS, list these letters down the board (or on a sheet of butcher paper or on a transparency), and then after each letter write or project the step represented in classifying:

G   oal stated

R   ecall meaning of data

O   rganize similar items together

U   use the similarity as the group label

P   lace all other items into groups and label each group

S   ubdivide or combine and relabel groups

Students can copy this list of steps into their notebooks for future reference. If these steps are written on large sheets of paper or on a bulletin board for display, eventually the explanations can be removed, leaving simply the word GROUPS displayed for student reference in future lessons. The homework or seatwork assignment, if one is given, could have students classify the list of words commonly spoken in the Middle Atlantic or Southern colonies around 1750. The substantive flow of the lesson on life in pre-Revolutionary America can thus continue just as in the preceding example.

Reviewing the Strategy

This teaching strategy may be used to introduce any thinking skill or strategy. However, unlike the case of the inductive strategy, in using a directive strategy to introduce a thinking skill or strategy the teacher must know the key attributes of the operation being introduced—and know them well enough to explain and demonstrate them for the students. In using this approach the teacher does not present these attributes as *the only* attributes of the skill. The attributes presented should be offered simply as one way some experts execute the skill—a way that can be used by students and modified by them as they become more proficient with practice in executing the skill. This strategy is most useful when teaching time is scarce and the thinking operation to be introduced is rather complex.

This directive skill-introducing strategy helps students begin to learn a thinking operation in two important ways. It accommodates the need or desire of some students to learn a workable way to do something and "get on with it." Many students have, rightly or wrongly, a low tolerance for ambiguity; trying to figure out inductively how to execute a new thinking operation may prove so frustrating that they simply "turn off" and withdraw or quit. Using this directive strategy thus eliminates or sharply reduces such potential frustration and keeps students engaged in the learning task.

Furthermore, while it may appear that the directive strategy does not allow students to articulate a variety of procedures for doing the new operation, as does the inductive strategy, use of this strategy does in fact quickly lead to such "personalization" of the operation.[7] The initial steps in this strategy do restrict students to one way of executing the new operation; however, at the point of application (Step 5), students frequently execute it *their* ways rather than exactly as demonstrated. Within one or two of the guided practice lessons that follow, students build on the base established by the demonstrated procedure to give their own twists to the skill or strategy being learned. In practice, presentation of a model way to execute any thinking operation as included in this strategy turns out to be just the stimulus or springboard needed by students to engage in a difficult operation with enough insight and confidence to be able to do it—successfully—their ways.

INTRODUCING THINKING SKILLS AND STRATEGIES

Clear, explicit introduction of any thinking operation—whether it be a strategy of decision making or a micro-thinking skill such as classifying—is absolutely essential for helping students understand such an operation and how it might be executed. Either the inductive or directive strategies described in this chapter may be used for this purpose. Figure 4.5 is a lesson plan using one of the two strategies employed in the sample lessons analyzed here. Which of these two skill-introducing strategies does this lesson plan employ?

Review the descriptions of each strategy in the preceding pages. Then study the plan in Figure 4.5. As you read it, fill in each blank down the center of the plan with the name of the step in the strategy that describes the activities listed below that line. Then, on the blank after the title of the plan, write the type of strategy used in this lesson. Answers and a commentary may be found in the notes at the end of this chapter.[8] If you have difficulty deciding which skill-introducing strategy is described in this lesson plan, discuss the sample plan with someone else who has also read these chapters. If you had no trouble identifying the steps in the

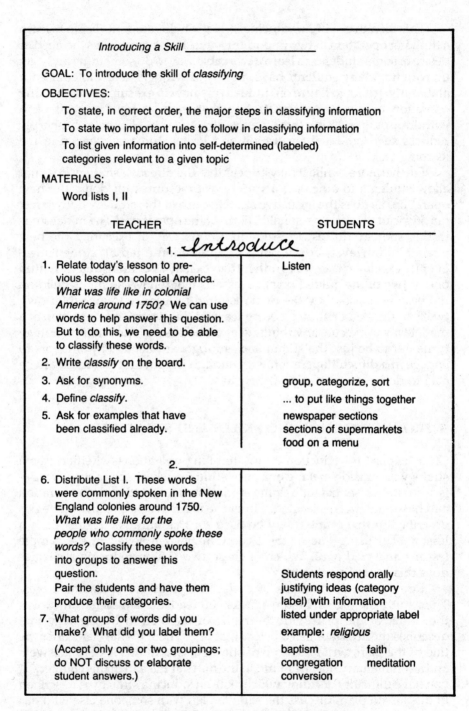

Introducing a Skill _____

GOAL: To introduce the skill of *classifying*

OBJECTIVES:

To state, in correct order, the major steps in classifying information

To state two important rules to follow in classifying information

To list given information into self-determined (labeled) categories relevant to a given topic

MATERIALS:

Word lists I, II

TEACHER	STUDENTS
1. *Introduce*	
1. Relate today's lesson to previous lesson on colonial America. *What was life like in colonial America around 1750?* We can use words to help answer this question. But to do this, we need to be able to classify these words.	Listen
2. Write *classify* on the board.	
3. Ask for synonyms.	group, categorize, sort
4. Define *classify*.	... to put like things together
5. Ask for examples that have been classified already.	newspaper sections sections of supermarkets food on a menu
2. _____	
6. Distribute List I. These words were commonly spoken in the New England colonies around 1750. *What was life like for the people who commonly spoke these words?* Classify these words into groups to answer this question. Pair the students and have them produce their categories.	Students respond orally justifying ideas (category label) with information listed under appropriate label
7. What groups of words did you make? What did you label them? (Accept only one or two groupings; do NOT discuss or elaborate student answers.)	example: *religious* baptism faith congregation meditation conversion

Figure 4.5 A Lesson Plan for Introducing the Skill of Classifying

TEACHER	STUDENTS
3. _____	
8. What did you *do* mentally to classify these words? How did you do it?	State purpose for classifying (To find out ...)
List on the board steps followed.	Tried to find several pieces of information that are alike. Grouped them.
	Put a label on each group ...
	Several different sequences of steps may be offered. Ex.:
9. Help students rearrange steps in order completed—first through last.	1. State purpose/goal. 2. Skim information to note interesting features/items. 3. Take first (or any one "striking") piece of information. 4. Find one more piece like it and put the two together. 5. State—as a label—the feature these two pieces have in common. 6. Add other items like these to this group. 7. Repeat, starting another group with unassigned piece of information until all items are grouped. 8. Combine or subdivide groups.
10. Clarify steps by asking students to tell any rules they followed:	
a) How do you know certain items belong together?	a) They refer to the same things, the same features.
b) How do you know when to stop and start another group?	b) When you can't find any more similar words with ease.
c) When can we classify data?	c) To make sense of it—to handle mixed-up information by reducing it to a few groups of related information.
and so on. Reorder steps if necessary or add steps that should be included.	

Figure 4.5 (*continued*)

TEACHER	STUDENTS

4. _____

11. Distribute List II. Have students alone or in pairs use the rules and steps on the board to classify these words to answer the question: *What was life like in the mid-Atlantic colonies around 1750?* Give help where needed.

Possible categories:

Closed community   *agrarian*

alien	clay
banish	corn
community	fall
congregation	squash
exile	
stranger	

12. Have students report and justify responses. What was life like for people who used these words in everyday life?

5. _____

13. How do you know? Review the *steps* in classifying (*rules, clues*) as you ask:

a) What are the steps?

     a) See responses to #9.

b) When classify data?

     b) When data are mixed up—to reduce them to manageable quanity.

c) What do you do if you can't understand some of the data?

     c) Put them in a "miscellaneous" category.

d) How do you know when to stop and start another group?

     d) When you can't readily find any other data similar.

14. Have students write steps/ rules/clues in notes.

15. Review and revise definitions if necessary. Ask for places or times when this skill could be used in everyday or school life.

assignment

16. Assign List III (words spoken in Southern colonies around 1750). Classify the words to identify what life was like for those people around 1750.

Figure 4.5 *(continued)*

108

lesson, and the strategy used in each step, then write a lesson plan using this strategy to introduce the skill of classifying in *your* favorite subject or class. Check it for accuracy by matching your plan with the appropriate guidelines presented here. This lesson plan and yours can then serve as models of lessons using this strategy to introduce any thinking operation in any subject or class.

Besides the two strategies presented in this chapter, there are, of course, other strategies equally well suited for introducing a new thinking operation. Most of these other strategies consist of some variation or combination of these inductive and directive strategies. One such alternative skill-introducing strategy is described in the next chapter, which then goes on to analyze the essential features of those teaching strategies most effective for introducing any thinking skill or strategy in any subject to any students.

NOTES

1. Ann L. Brown, Joseph C. Campione, and Jeanne D. Day, "Learning to Learn: On Training Students to Learn from Texts," *Educational Researcher* 10:2 (Februrary 1981), p. 16.

2. John R. Hayes, *The Complete Problem Solver* (Philadelphia: Franklin Institute Press, 1981); Michael I. Posner and Steven W. Keele, "Skill Learning," in Robert M. W. Travers, ed., *Second Handbook of Research on Teaching* (Chicago: Rand McNally College Publishing Company, 1973), pp. 808–810, 821.

3. Brown, Campione, and Day, "Learning to Learn," pp. 14, 20.

4. Walter Doyle, "Academic Work," *Review of Educational Research* 53:2 (Summer 1983), pp. 168–170; David Perkins, "Thinking Frames," *Educational Leadership* 43:8 (May 1986), p. 8.

5. Arthur Whimbey, "Teaching Sequential Thought: The Cognitive Skills Approach," *Phi Delta Kappan* 59:4 (December 1977), pp. 255–259; Judith W. Segal and Susan F. Chipman, "Thinking and Learning Skills: The Contributions of NIE," *Educational Leadership* 42:1 (September 1984), p. 86.

6. Brown, Campione, and Day, "Learning to Learn," p. 18; Robert J. Sternberg, "Teaching Intellectual Skills: Looking for Smarts in All the Wrong Places" (Paper delivered at the Wingspread Conference on Teaching Thinking Skills, Racine, May 17–19), 1984, p. 16; Robert J. Sternberg, "How Can We Teach Intelligence?" *Educational Leadership* 42:1 (September 1984), p. 47.

7. Russell Gersten and Douglas Carnine, "Direct Instruction in Reading Comprehension," *Educational Leadership* 43:7 (April 1986), p. 77: Paul Chance, *Thinking in the Classroom: A Survey of Programs* (New York: Teachers College Press, 1986), p. 122.

8. This lesson plan involves students in executing a skill as best they can *before* discussing how it is done. This is the essence of the inductive strategy for introducing any thinking operation. After (1) introducing the operation, the teacher asks students simply (2) to attempt to carry it out. Only after trying it do they (3) reflect on and discuss how they executed it. Discussion focuses on the key

attributes of the operation, especially the major steps through which students go in executing it and any principles or rules that they seem to be following in so doing. Then students (4) apply the operation a second time to new data—but data in the same form as that used in the initial effort, Finally, the students (5) review what they have learned about the operation. In this type of skill-introducing lesson, students do most of the work—they generate most of the substance of the lesson. What they have articulated about the new operation can be fleshed out, modified, and elaborated over the guided practice and other lessons that follow. This particular kind of introduction to a thinking operation is only one of several that could have been employed for this purpose.

What would a lesson plan look like that introduced the skill of classifying by using the other skill-introducing strategy described in this chapter? Figure 4.6 presents such a lesson plan. Read it over to see if it includes the key steps in the directive skill-introducing strategy described in the preceding pages. Label these steps on the lines provided down the center of the plan. If you wish, write a lesson plan using this strategy to introduce the skill of classifying to a class you teach. Check your plan for accuracy against the model plan in Figure 4.6 and against the guidelines for a directive skill-introducing strategy presented in these pages. After you have revised your plan, as necessary, you will have made lesson plans for using two different teaching strategies—an inductive strategy and a directive strategy—to introduce any thinking skill or strategy in any course or subject.

```
┌──────────────────────────────────────────────────────────────┐
│                  Introducing a Skill_____      │
│                                                               │
│  GOAL:  To introduce the skill of classifying                 │
│  OBJECTIVES:                                                  │
│       To state, in correct order, the major steps in classifying information │
│       To state two important rules to follow in classifying information │
│       To list given information into self-determined (labeled) categories │
│       relevant to a given topic                               │
│  MATERIALS:                                                   │
│       Word lists I and II                                     │
└──────────────────────────────────────────────────────────────┘
```

TEACHER	STUDENTS
1._____	
1. Relate today's lesson to previous lesson on colonial America, *What was life like in colonial America around 1750?* We can use words commonly spoken by early settlers to help answer this question. But to do this, we need to be able to classify these words.	
2. Write *classify* on board.	
3. Ask for synonyms. (What is it like?)	categorize/group/sort
4. Define *classify*.	
5. Give examples.	...to put "like" things together
	classify objects in room into people/furniture
	or
	students into boys/girls, short/tall, etc.
Ask for other examples.	sections in newspapers supermarket sections

2._____

6. Explain steps—*list on board*

    Given specific information —

    1. State your purpose: What are you trying to find out?

    2. Skim the information to note what's there.

    3. Take one piece of information and search for one more piece like it. List these together.

    4. State what makes these alike. Write this common feature above them as a label.

Figure 4.6 A Lesson Plan for Introducing the Skill of Classifying

5. Find as many other items as possible that fit this label and add to list.

6. Repeat this process with the next unassigned piece of information until all items are labeled in groups.

7. Combine and/or subdivide groups.

Useful rules to follow:

1. If you do not understand some item, put it in "miscellaneous" category and go on—but come back to it later to try to use it.

2. If a word means more than one thing, it can go in several categories.

3. ...

TEACHER	STUDENTS

3.

7. Distribute List I. These words were commonly spoken in the New England colonies around 1750. *What was life like for the people who spoke these words frequently?*

forests were important	*religious*
ax	baptism
barrel	congregation
clog	conversion
bench	faith
fall	meditation
oak	
saw	
etc.	

8. Walk the class through the steps, classifying items with student help as volunteered. Explain why each step is done as it is executed.

4.

9. Cover up list of steps on board and have students recall what was done and the reasons for doing each step.

As in item 6 above.

5.

10. Distribute List II. These words were spoken frequently in the Middle Atlantic colonies around 1750. *What was life like for the people who spoke these words?* Classify these words to answer this question, using the steps and rules just explained and demonstrated.

Possible categories:

closed community	*agrarian*
alien	clay
banish	cold
community	corn
exile	fall
heresy	harvest
stranger	...
...	

Figure 4.6 (*continued*)

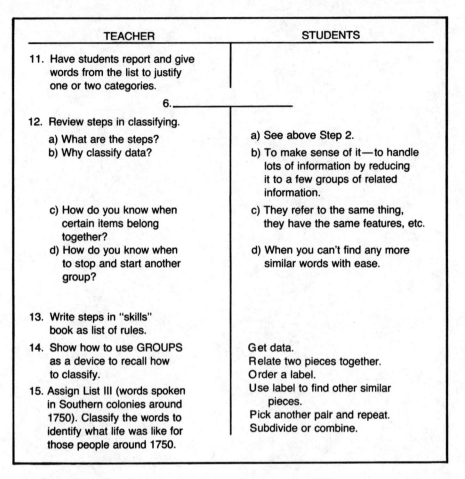

TEACHER	STUDENTS
11. Have students report and give words from the list to justify one or two categories.	

6._____

TEACHER	STUDENTS
12. Review steps in classifying. a) What are the steps? b) Why classify data? c) How do you know when certain items belong together? d) How do you know when to stop and start another group?	a) See above Step 2. b) To make sense of it—to handle lots of information by reducing it to a few groups of related information. c) They refer to the same thing, they have the same features, etc. d) When you can't find any more similar words with ease.
13. Write steps in "skills" book as list of rules.	
14. Show how to use GROUPS as a device to recall how to classify. 15. Assign List III (words spoken in Southern colonies around 1750). Classify the words to identify what life was like for those people around 1750.	Get data. Relate two pieces together. Order a label. Use label to find other similar pieces. Pick another pair and repeat. Subdivide or combine.

Figure 4.6 (*continued*)

Introducing a Thinking Skill—II

The inductive and directive strategies described in the preceding chapter represent two prototypes from a range of strategies that can be used to introduce any thinking operation. Teachers can, of course, devise numerous variations on each of these prototypes. Moreover, the key elements of each can be blended into a third type of strategy that typifies those found midway in this range of strategies. This type of combined strategy can prove very useful with a wide range of students in introducing skills that students may have used earlier but in which they have only limited proficiency, or with skills of a modest level of difficulty, or with skills thought to be at a level of difficulty commensurate with the experience of the students. This skill-introducing strategy is best described as a developmental strategy.

A DEVELOPMENTAL STRATEGY

A developmental introductory strategy puts together the experimenting phase (Steps 1, 2 and 3) of the inductive strategy with the expository phase (Steps 2–6) of the directive strategy. It introduces a thinking operation by, first, involving students in applying it as best they can, knowing that they are likely to be less successful at it than they could be. After discussing with them how they did it and identifying any difficulties they had in engaging in the operation, the teacher then explains and demonstrates those rules or procedures that can be used to eliminate any difficulties encountered by the students. In effect, this strategy creates a discrepancy for the students between what they want or need to do and their current ability to do it and dramatically alerts them to this discrepancy. It then provides information and guided practice for helping them resolve the discrepancy on a need to know basis. Such a strategy incorporates basic principles of Piagetian-based developmental learning theory.[1]

In using this strategy, a teacher organizes the lesson as follows:

1. First, the teacher introduces the new thinking operation, in the context of the subject matter being taught, just as in the inductive and directive strategies.
2. Then the students execute the operation as best they can without any instruction or teacher guidance.
3. The students then review what they have become aware of about the operation and identify places where they encountered difficulties.
4. Next, the teacher explains and demonstrates those procedures or rules that can be used to resolve the difficulties encountered.
5. The students, with teacher guidance as needed, then apply the operation again, incorporating what has been discussed and explained about it.
6. Finally, students and teacher reflect on and review how the operation can be executed and how the attributes given by the teacher make it easier to execute.

By moving through these six steps, the lesson creates a situation that provides its own motivation for learning. It also allows students to build their own representation of the thinking skill or strategy being introduced. Recognizing deficiencies in their knowledge of, or abilities to employ the new skill, they incorporate into their version of it "expert knowledge" that increases their proficiency in its use. Insight into the operation "develops" as the lesson unfolds. Though an introductory strategy of this type often requires longer to execute than either of the strategies described in Chapter 4, it leads perhaps to better initial learning because it helps students resolve a cognitive dissonance that has been allowed to develop and involves inherently satisfying, active learning on their part.[2] Figure 5.1 outlines the major steps constituting this developmental strategy.

STEP 1 *INTRODUCE THE SKILL*

> State that "learning" the skill is today's objective.
> Give the skill label/name.
> Give synonyms.
> State a tentative/working definition.
> State ways the skill can be or has been used:
>
> > • in students' personal experience,
> > • in school activities,
> > • in this course.
>
> Explain how the skill is useful and why it's worth learning.

STEP 2 *EXECUTE THE SKILL*

> Use the skill (as best one can) to accomplish a task.
> Work in pairs, triads, or groups.
> Use subject matter familiar to the students and appropriate to course or from students' experience.

STEP 3 *REFLECT ON WHAT WAS DONE*

> Report what went on in students' heads as they engaged in the skill.
> Identify the steps and rules used and their sequence.
> Clarify procedures or any criteria used.
> Focus on the skill and its attributes.

STEP 4 *EXPLAIN/DEMONSTRATE*

> State any key operations or key rules omitted or misapplied
>   by students.
> Give reasons for using these procedures or rules.
> Demonstrate application of these operations or rules,
>   explaining how and why each is used.

STEP 5 *APPLY THE SKILL TO NEW DATA*

> Use the teacher-introduced procedures and rules with student
>   descriptions of the skill to complete original or another task.
> Students work in pairs or groups.
> Use subject matter familiar to the students and appropriate to course, but in the same structure and media like that used in Step 2.

STEP 6 *REVIEW THE SKILL*

> Report on what was done in students' heads as they applied the skill.
> Review the procedures and rules that seem to constitute the skill.
> State the relationship of this skill to other skills.
> Review or revise the skill definition.
> State where the skill can be used in:
>
> > • personal or out-of-school situations,
> > • coursework.

Figure 5.1 A Developmental Strategy for Introducing a Thinking Skill or Strategy

Applying the Strategy

Rather than using either an inductive or directive strategy, a developmental strategy could have been used to introduce the skill of classifying data into self-identified categories in the imaginary American history class described in the preceding chapter. To do so, in the same topic or subject area as in that lesson, the teacher would begin (Step 1) by setting the subject-matter context exactly as in both the previously explained strategies. Then the teacher could *introduce* in detail the skill to be learned. Writing the label on the board, finding and recording synonyms and a simple definition, and discussing briefly some examples of the skill in use help direct the focus of the lesson to the skill while assisting students to develop the mental set needed to deal purposefully with the skill.

As in the inductive strategy, students then execute the skill (Step 2). Working in groups or with a partner or two, they employ the skill with the same words listed in Figure 4.1 to decide what life was like in the New England colonies around 1750. The teacher may move around the class to provide help with the data, if necessary, or to clarify the task, but should not provide instruction or assistance with the skill itself unless a student is absolutely stuck. In students' *reflecting* (Step 3) on how they actually executed the skill, discussion may well yield two or three different sequences of operations through which various students proceeded. Analysis of these various sequences usually reveals that, as researcher Robbie Case points out, beginners or young students tend to be incomplete or inconsistent in the skill operations they employ rather than to employ incorrect operations.[3] Once the teacher has pointed out these omissions or inconsistencies, the lesson can then proceed—generally with rapt student attention—to how to remedy these difficulties.

By *explanation* and *demonstration* (Step 4) the teacher next can show what students can do to fill in any gaps in the skill or to remedy any inconsistencies. This may require explaining a rule used by experts to execute the skill, a rule that none of the students seemed to employ but one that, if used, makes the skill much more workable. Some youngsters, for example, have a hard time getting started in classifying data. Knowing that they have to match only two items to get underway is a useful "rule" for them. Others often fail to articulate the common feature of any pair of items they spot until after they have tried to collect all similar items; in so doing, they gradually alter or enlarge the initial category to the point where they lose focus and have to recategorize the data. When advised to state the common feature of an initial match of just two items—to make the category label at that point—students then have a specific label to use as a search tool in examining the remaining data. Thus, their search is more efficient and keeps the category with which they are working within reasonable bounds. By becoming aware of these missing rules or operations, students can then incorporate them into their conceptualization of the skill as they apply it once more.

In *applying* (Step 5) their revised descriptions of the skill with another similar data set, as with the words descriptive of life in the Middle Atlantic colonies around 1750 (see Figure 4.2), students come to realize how useful the newly introduced attributes are. In the process, they gain additional insights into the skill. Students can then *review* (Step 6) the key skill attributes thus discovered and tested, revise the skill definition, review synonyms, and discuss examples of how or where the skill has been or can be used in the course. The lesson can conclude with the same assignment as recommended in the sample applications of the inductive and directive strategies described in Chapter 4.

Analyzing the Strategy

Figure 5.2 presents a lesson plan employing this developmental strategy for introducing the skill of classifying within the sample American history lesson just described. This developmental strategy allows students to articulate what they know about this skill and then to become familiar with some of the rules or operations that flesh out their knowledge of it. The teacher's role in such a strategy is to help the students understand why their version of the skill is incomplete or doesn't work, to demonstrate and explain those operations or rules needed to make the skill operable, and to explain the reasons why these added elements are esssential to the skill. The students, on the other hand, then have an opportunity to integrate this new information about the skill into their own understanding of the skill as they apply it in this lesson and in subsequent practice lessons. Both teacher and students need to know something about the skill for this strategy to be useful. The teacher needs to know enough about it to point out those bits of "expert knowledge" that students skip or abuse; students need to be able to engage in the skill to some degree so as to articulate at least a tentative version of it.

This strategy reflects developmental learning theories. The key to such learning consists of making students aware of a gap between what they need or want to do and their present abilities to do it. Learners learn, developmentalists assert, because of their internal motivation to close such gaps, to resolve perceived discrepancies.[4] Thus, thinking operations presented for learning using this strategy must be within the realm of student execution; if not, the resulting discrepancy between desired goal and current achievable goal may be so great as to "turn students off" and close down further learning. While this strategy relies on creating some degree of dissonance and perhaps frustration on the part of students, it can easily result in creating too much. Consequently, teachers

Introducing a Skill: A Developmental Strategy

GOAL: To introduce the skill of *classifying*

OBJECTIVES:

> To state, in correct order, the major steps in classifying information
>
> To state two important rules to follow in classifying information
>
> To list given information into self-determined (labeled) categories relevant to a given topic

MATERIALS:

> Word lists I, II

TEACHER	STUDENTS
Introduce	
1. Relate today's lesson to previous lesson on colonial America. *What was life like in colonial America around 1750?* We can use words to help answer this question. But to do this, we need to be able to classify these words.	Listen
2. Write *classify* on the board.	
3. Ask for synonyms.	group, categorize, sort
4. Define *classify*.	... to put group like things together
5. Ask for examples that have been classified already.	newspaper sections sections of supermarkets food on a menu
Execute	
6. Distribute List I. These words were commonly spoken in the New England colonies around 1750. *What was life like for the people who commonly spoke these words?* Classify these words into groups to answer this question. Pair the students and have them write out their categories.	
7. What groups of words did you make? What did you label them? (Accept one or two groupings; do NOT discuss or elaborate student answers.)	Students respond orally, justifying ideas (category label) with information listed under appropriate label.

Figure 5.2 A Developmental Lesson Plan for Introducing the Skill of Classifying

120

TEACHER	STUDENTS
	example: *religious* baptism faith congregation meditation conversion

Reflect

TEACHER	STUDENTS
8. What did you do to classify these words? How did you do it? List on the board steps followed.	State purpose for classifying (To find out ...) Tried to find several pieces of information that are alike. Grouped them. Put a label on each group ...
9. Help students rearrange steps in order completed—first through last.	Several different sequences of steps may be offered. Ex.: 1. State purpose/goal 2. Skim information to note interesting features/items 3. Take first (or any one "striking") piece of information 4. Find one more piece like it and put the two together 5. State—as a label—the feature these two pieces have in common 6. Add other items like these to this group 7. Repeat, starting another with unassigned piece of information until all items are grouped 8. Combine or subdivide groups
10. Clarify steps by asking students to tell any rules they followed: a) How do you know certain items belong together? b) How do you know when to stop and start another group? c) When can we classify data? and so on. Reorder steps, if necessary.	 a) They refer to the same things, the same features b) When you can't find any more similar words with ease c) To make sense of it—to handle lots of information by reducing it to a few groups of related information

Figure 5.2 *(continued)*

TEACHER	STUDENTS

TEACHER	STUDENTS
11. If students skip an important step or rule or misapply it, point this out and explain how the step or rule should be applied—and why.	Perhaps point out: • usefulness of using a "miscellaneous" category for data not understood (such as "clog") • How to start the skill off by selecting one word at random, searching for another like it, and using the "likeness" as the category label • the importance of stating a group label as soon as two items have been "matched" and then using the label to help find other items that fit the group
12. Demonstrate how these new or corrected rules and/or steps work, using List I.	

Apply

TEACHER	STUDENTS
13. Distribute List II. Have the students in pairs use the rules and steps on the board as well as the new rules and steps to classify these words to answer the question: *What was life like in the Middle Atlantic colonies for the people who spoke these words around 1750?*	Possible categories: *closed community* *agrarian* alien clay banish corn community fall exile squash stranger ... ...
14. Accept one or two groupings suggested by students but do NOT discuss or elaborate on them.	

Review

TEACHER	STUDENTS
15. Review steps and rules in classifying:	
a) What are the steps?	a) See above, Step 9.
b) Why classify data?	b) To make sense of it—to handle lots of information by reducing it to a few groups of related information.
c) How do you know when certain data go together?	c) They refer to the same thing, they have the same features, etc

Figure 5.2 *(continued)*

122

TEACHER	STUDENTS
d) How do you know when to stop and start another group? e) ...	d) When you can't find any more similar words with ease.
16. Write steps and rules in "skills" notebook.	
17. Show how to use GROUPS to recall how to classify data	Get data Relate two pieces together Order a label Use label to find other similar pieces Pick another pair and repeat Subdivide or combine
18. Review and revise definitions if necessary. Ask for, or suggest, places or times when this skill could be used in everyday or school life.	

Figure 5.2 *(continued)*

planning to use the strategy need to be sure that the thinking operation introduced is within the ability level of the students. Often, such a determination can be made only with practice and as a result of a thorough knowledge of the students in a class. As yet, little guidance exists as to which thinking skills are best introduced to which students at what grade levels. Since all individuals engage in thinking to some degree, the key to working with novices or younger students may well be the *type* of things about which we have them think—concrete rather than abstract—rather than the particular skills being taught.

In carrying out this developmental introductory strategy, the teacher conducts the class through the strategy, performing each step much as was done in the corresponding steps of the inductive and directive strategies—with one exception. In explaining and demonstrating the thinking operation being introduced (Step 4), the teacher needs to present only the new step(s) or rule(s). It is not necessary to treat the skill attributes in toto. What proves most useful here is to have the students first report their understanding of the skill attributes (Step 3) as the teacher records them for all to see—lists the procedures that comprise the skill in sequence and also lists any rules followed. Then, in adding new procedures or rules, simply insert these or add these to the appropriate places in what is already written out. Other than this slight change, a teacher can employ the steps in this strategy to introduce any thinking operation just as similar steps in other introductory strategies are carried out. Figure 5.1, as noted above, outlines these steps and can be a guide in preparing any lesson plan for using this strategy to introduce any thinking skill or strategy.

ESSENTIAL FEATURES OF SKILL-INTRODUCING STRATEGIES

The strategies for introducing any thinking operation described in this and the preceding chapter have many similarities. In general, these three strategies employ essentially the same teaching process. Figure 5.3 makes clear these procedural similarities, showing that all of these strategies start with an extended, formal introduction to the thinking skill or strategy being introduced. They then call for students either to execute the operation as best they can or to hear or see how it is executed by someone more expert in it than they are. Next, these three strategies ask students to reflect on or review how the skill was just executed so that they can verbalize its key attributes, especially the steps in a procedure by which it is carried out. After executing the operation a second time, students again review or reflect on its key attributes and attempt to tie the skill or strategy to their academic work and/or their out-of-school experiences. These activities constitute the core of any effective skill-introducing teaching strategy.

The procedures comprising these three introductory strategies incorporate those features of skill teaching that research suggests are most essential to launching effective learning of a new thinking skill or strategy. Understanding the nature of these key features allows a teacher to use these strategies to their maximum potential and to make useful adaptations in these strategies without sacrificing their crucial attributes.

In brief, the inductive, directive, and developmental introductory strategies all:

1. keep the focus on the operation to be learned,
2. model the operation,
3. articulate its key components or attributes,
4. engage students in talking about how they think,
5. provide immediate, guided application of the operation,
6. build in cues useful in transferring the operation,
7. introduce instruction in the operation at a time when the operation is needed to accomplish a subject-matter task,

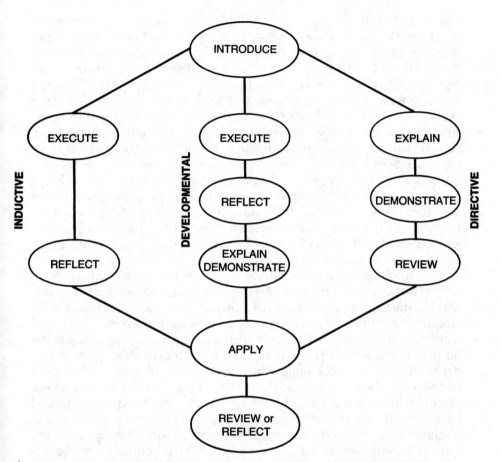

Figure 5.3 Strategies for Introducing a New Thinking Skill or Strategy

8. keep the data and media by which the data are presented the same throughout the introduction, and
9. keep the data or problem relatively simple and short.

Research and thoughtful practice indicate the importance of these factors in teaching and learning any thinking skill or strategy, especially in the initial introductory stages.

Focus on the Operation Being Introduced

In order to make it as easy as possible for students to deal with a newly introduced thinking skill or strategy and thus to enhance the learning of this operation, teachers need to minimize interference from competing input. While teachers may engage in the pursuit of several objectives simultaneously during a lesson, students apparently cannot attend simultaneously to multiple stimuli or inputs and absorb or learn all of them equally well. Multiple inputs in addition to instruction in a new skill can interfere with skill learning. Such interference can be caused by other skills—especially recently introduced ones, by the subject matter being studied or used, and by the emotional content or implications of the subject matter.[5] Thus, a new thinking skill or strategy ought not to be introduced until students have achieved some proficiency in a previously introduced thinking operation. The emotional charge of the content being used or task being undertaken must not be so great as to distract from attention to the new skill. In introducing a thinking skill or strategy, teachers must be sure to eliminate or minimize the effect of other newly learned skills and strategies and the emotional or affective impact or difficulty of the subject matter.

For this same reason so, too, must teachers minimize attention to subject matter in introducing a new thinking operation. As difficult as this may be, the teacher must avoid virtually any discussion of subject matter whatsoever at this point in the teaching framework. Attention to subject matter normally seems to interfere with learning a skill, especially at the introductory stage of skill learning. Left to their own choices, most students elect to focus on subject matter, for after all that is what most teachers talk about, texts present, and classroom tests test! Minimizing or avoiding discussion of subject matter, of course, goes against the natural inclination of most teachers, who care deeply about and feel committed to teaching their subjects. However, for one lesson—this introductory one—it is absolutely crucial to keep any attention to content from interfering with the skill or strategy being introduced. Although students can use subject matter as a vehicle to begin learning about a skill, they should not discuss that subject matter *in this lesson*. For example, to give value to the task assigned the students and to initiate the mid-strategy reflection on or review of the skill (as initially demonstrated or tried in the sample lesson), the teacher can ask students to report briefly on what they found out about the topic (life in New England, in this case). But only two or three items need to be reported, and no discussion or elaboration should follow these reports. Discussion of what students learned about the subject by using the skill—in the case of the example used here, the nature of life in the thirteen colonies around 1750—can be the focus of the next day's lesson. In fact, it is often surprising to see how attention to the new skill in this introductory lesson seems to set up better recall of, and a more sophisticated understanding of, the subject matter in the next lesson.

All three introductory strategies place obvious and continuing emphasis on the thinking operation being introduced. In using any of these strategies, teachers must provide repeated cues to the effect that the new operation is what is to be focused on. In carrying out the introductory step of each strategy (Step 1), for example, the teacher clearly indicates that beginning to learn the operation is the primary objective of the lesson in these ways: by giving explicit attention to defining the operation; by writing its label, synonyms, and definition on the chalkboard or overhead; and by stating or writing this as the objective of the day. *Nothing* to do with subject matter or other thinking skills should be written on the overhead or chalkboard. Rather, the teacher should write three headings on the board—*Steps, Rules, Useful Information*—and, under each, list what students offer as they reflect on or review how they executed the operation. Of course, in explaining how to do the operation for the first time in using the directive strategy, the key steps and rules should be provided to the students via handouts or on the chalkboard or an overhead transparency. And in concluding an introductory lesson, focus should remain on the new operation. Students may need to redefine it or may have recalled synonyms not mentioned earlier. Discussion of examples of where this operation has been applied in the course earlier and where it can be later applied in the course or in daily life helps promote transfer as well as make the operation more relevant to the students. Just as an introductory skill lesson begins by focusing on the thinking operation to be introduced, so too should the lesson end with focus still on that operation.

Model the Thinking Operation

Research indicates that those who achieve a high degree of proficiency in any skill have seen it modeled or demonstrated, often repeatedly.[6] Modeling how an operation works is an extremely useful part of an introduction to any thinking operation because it allows students to actually see and hear how it is executed by someone more competent in it than are they. Such modeling need not be done only by the teacher, however; students good at a thinking operation can demonstrate how they do it. Written descriptions, such as sample problem solutions or narratives, are also useful for this purpose.

The introductory strategies presented all include modeling. In the inductive strategy, students' descriptions of how they engaged in the skill of classifying in effect present the required demonstration. Obviously, the results are by no means prescribed versions of the skill, but they serve as targets and pieces out of which students can construct or modify their own concepts of this skill. Both the directive and developmental strategies also call for demonstration of the operation being introduced—in these instances by the teacher or other "experts."

There is, though, more to modeling a thinking skill or strategy than simply doing something in an expert fashion. Students must be conscious that *someone is modeling* and that a *particular operation* is being modeled.[7] Simply to engage in a thinking task without alerting the students to the fact that execution of the task is being modeled is of little avail. Prior to demonstrating a thinking operation, the teacher needs to point out what is about to happen by explaining some of the key operations to be performed or rules that need to be followed and by alerting students as to what to look for. Before demonstrating the skill of classifying, for example, a teacher would find it useful to explain rules about how to start classifying and what to do in case one encounters troublesome data and to list in proper sequence some of the key elements of the procedure to be performed. As the skill is actually modeled, the demonstrator needs to explain what he or she is doing and why. And, upon concluding the demonstration, students and teacher should discuss what they have seen, especially the steps in the procedure, the sequence in which they were performed, and some reasons and rules for executing them. It is not enough simply to act out a behavior that students are to emulate. It is also important to call to the students' attention—to explain and to discuss with them—what is done, how it is done and why. Thus, demonstration of a thinking operation needs to be closely linked with explanation and discussion of the operation demonstrated.

Articulate Key Components

As a new thinking operation is demonstrated or used or after such demonstration or use, students need to have its major pieces, components, or attributes pointed out to them—or they need to do this themselves if they can. The strategies presented here each offer at least two opportunities to do just this. Novices learning a new operation naturally tend to fragment it and to concentrate on its major components. Allowing students to do this in the introductory lesson builds on a natural way of learning skills and meets very real learner demands regarding "What, exactly do I do?" and "How do I do it?" Discussing the key operations that constitute a skill, the key rules to be followed, and any useful information regarding it accomplishes this goal. While it is not necessary at the introductory stage to discuss every operation, rule, or bit of useful information, attention to the more important major attributes helps students identify these components of the operation and gives them more control over it.[8] Putting these components together and elaborating them follows gradually with guided practice.

Talk About Thinking

Research points out consistently that talking about what goes on in one's mind while engaging in a specific thinking operation or task, and hearing about what others do in their minds assist students in learning the operation.[9] Thinking about thinking—metacognition—is difficult, especially for individuals just being introduced to it. Verbalizing what one thinks, although even more difficult, helps students raise to a level of consciousness what they may intuitively know about the operation. By hearing others describe how they execute it, students discover new ways to engage in the operation. They find, too, that others in fact do similar things or that many people encounter obstacles similar to ones they encountered. Reflection on, and discussion of, what they believe they do or did in executing an operation not only help students isolate key operations but also leads to control of one's thinking. Thus, students find it easier to modify the ways they engage in thinking and to make their use of thinking operations more efficient and effective.

Each of the three strategies provides opportunities for students to talk about what they did as they executed the thinking skill being introduced. Not many students may choose to do so when these strategies are first employed. It is, after all, risky enough to tell what one thinks, let alone how one arrived at those thoughts, especially in situations where the products of thinking—answers—are traditionally judged right or wrong and these judgments are converted into grades with all the attendant consequences. Methods for facilitating student metacognition are described in detail in Chapter 8. They can be employed with students in the introductory lessons right after students try their hands at a skill for the first and second times in the course of these lessons.

In these introductory strategies student discussion of the new operation is as important, if not more important, than their actually executing it. The distribution of time for the various steps in each strategy is a measure of the importance of this step. The introduction to a new operation, Step 1 in each strategy, should require only four to five minutes. Student use of the operation should take up to six or eight minutes, enough to get into it and execute it. The focus here should be on doing the operation, not on completing any substantive task. So, whether or not the students actually process all the data they have been provided is not important at this point. Even less time may be desirable if the operation is particularly difficult or if the developmental introductory strategy is being used. While student levels of frustration at not being able to execute the operation well should not be allowed to reach intolerable or discouraging levels, some degree of frustration may be useful as a device for motivating further learning.

The largest single chunk of time in these strategies should be devoted to student reflection on how they executed the new thinking operation, perhaps fifteen minutes or more, for it is in doing this that they begin to raise to a level of consciousness their understanding of the operation. A second application of the operation can again be allocated six to eight or so minutes, enough time again to work through it at least once. Finally, five to ten minutes or so can be devoted to the review of what has been "discovered" so far about the operation and to making the assignment, if there is to be one. Of course, adjustments in this distribution of time may be required depending on the subject matter, nature of the operation to be introduced, and student abilities. It will require much more time to introduce such complex thinking strategies such as decision making or problem solving than it will to introduce a micro-thinking skill like classifying or synthesizing. But the point to remember is that a significant proportion of whatever time it takes should be devoted to student reflection and discussion of how they executed the operation being introduced.

Guide Application

It proves useful to have students apply a newly introduced thinking operation immediately after discussing a demonstration of it or an initial, unaided try at it. By so doing, students get an opportunity to apply or test out the insights they have gained about it or the procedures just demonstrated; thus, they begin to take ownership of these procedures. By minimizing delay between initial application or demonstration, discussion, and second application, teachers can reduce the impact of potential interference from all types of sources.[10]

In each introductory strategy, in its fourth or fifth steps, students apply (with teacher guidance as necessary) the new operation to, in effect, try or test out what they have heard or seen about it to that point. With such an activity, followed by the ensuing review and discussion, students begin to enter this operation into memory, the first stage in learning a thinking skill or strategy. It is the first of a number of guided applications that they need to achieve proficiency in any thinking operation. When completed as part of an introductory lesson, this activity launches the sequence of skill learning lessons to follow. When the operation is applied to subject matter that is part of the regular course content and to a task that is relevant to the subject, it moves subject-matter learning along toward substantive course goals and satisfies oft-expressed student desires to "get on with it."

Build Cues for Transfer

Contrary to what most educators assume or would like to believe, transfer of thinking skills or strategies from one subject to another or from one context to another is neither automatic nor natural.[11] Most students do not as a matter of course or on their own transfer thinking operations learned in one area to another area. Failure to apply a thinking operation to a new but appropriate setting may, of course, be due to a low level of proficiency in how to engage in the operation. But, in many instances, transfer does not occur because students simply do not know that it is appropriate to use the operation in the new setting—they are not aware of the cues in the new setting that call the operation into play. And sometimes students fail to transfer an operation to a new setting because they do not know how to execute it in that setting.

Part of the task of teaching thinking operations is to teach the cues to setting, media, types of data, and tasks in which a particular thinking skill or strategy can be used. Classifying, for example, is appropriate to undertake whenever a task involves making sense of some data, as in inventing a topic sentence or synthesizing a generalization or conceptualizing or hypothesizing. Teaching students cues to these tasks helps set up transfer. Classifying can be done with numerical data, pictorial or graphic data, and data in forms other than the words used in the introductory lesson for illustrating the introductory strategies presented here. Students need to be alerted to this fact. In introducing a new thinking operation, teachers can move toward transfer by letting students know about or predict where else the new operation can be used other than in the introductory setting itself. The concluding step in each introductory strategy provides an opportunity for teachers to help students begin to bridge, as Reuven Feuerstein calls it, the operation to these other contexts.[12]

Simply talking about additional places where a new thinking skill or strategy is appropriate is, of course, not sufficient to ensure transfer. Skills are very much tied to the information and knowledge contexts in which they are applied. How one goes about classifying graphic data is not precisely the same as how one goes about classifying words. Students need repeated opportunities, with teacher guidance, actually to *apply* a previously introduced thinking operation with new data or new settings—as much to know that the operation is appropriate in these settings as to know how to execute it in these settings. Successful transfer of a thinking operation requires more than an initial introduction to it or discussion of where it can be well used. A start toward transfer can be made at the introductory stage and, by using these strategies presented here, teachers can and should undertake this task. But much more has to be done later for transfer actually to occur.

Introduce the Operation When It Is Needed to Learn Content

Thinking operations are not ends in themselves. They are tools with which individuals make meaning. Although not an inherent part of a skill introducing strategy itself, selecting *when* to introduce a thinking operation is as important as selecting the strategy to use. Introducing a new thinking skill or strategy can be most productive when the students need the operation itself to achieve a subject-matter goal and there is evidence that they are less proficient in the operation than they could be.[13] When introduced at these points in a course, instruction in the operation can move the subject-matter learning along just as the subject matter can serve as a vehicle for beginning to learn the new thinking operation.

In the imaginary lesson illustrating the use of these introductory strategies, the skill of classifying is needed to process the data (words) available for answering the question: What was life like in the thirteen English North American colonies around 1750? The teacher assigns the task, but the students quickly realize that they need some way to make sense out of the assigned data. Learning how to classify these data is entirely appropriate and relevant at this point. In order to get the maximum learning in introducing a thinking operation, teachers need to pick very carefully those places in a sequence of lessons where the operation can best be introduced. Contriving subject-matter tasks that fairly cry out for the use of new thinking skills or strategies provides such places.

Keep the Data the Same

Too often, teachers try to teach a thinking operation by switching too soon the data, task, or context to which it is applied. Because thinking operations are tied closely to the contexts in which they are first introduced, students need to become proficient in them in one context before being confronted with new contexts.[14] It is inappropriate to show students how to do a skill or strategy or to have them try it initially with one data set and then on their next try to give them an entirely different data set in which to apply it. A lesson showing students how to identify a topic sentence cannot be productively followed by a lesson demanding that they write a topic sentence of their own without any instructional guidance at all, for these tasks are two quite different things, though they may both deal with topic sentences.

In the introduction of a new thinking skill or strategy, the data or context needs to remain constant throughout the introduction so that students can focus on the new thinking operation. For example, in the imaginary American history lesson on classifying, the type of data used in both the initial application or demonstration and the second application of the skill was the same in each strategy—words. In subsequent lessons on classifying, until the students demonstrate proficiency in the skill in this context, lists or collections or words should continue to serve as the data for practicing this skill. In order to develop initial proficiency with a thinking operation the kinds of data and media in which it is used must remain the same throughout the introductory lesson, and indeed for the practice lessons immediately following.

Keep the Data Simple and Short

The data to which students apply a new thinking operation initially should be neither voluminous nor too complex. To keep the focus on the operation, the data and task need to be rather straightforward and relatively short, not overwhelming. Excessive data to process get in the way of students' concentrating on how to execute the operation; and data that are too complex to understand turn attention to the data themselves and away from the operation altogether.[15] The data used in the American history lesson on classifying—lists of words—are neither complicated nor unduly long and involved. Students from fourth grade upward who have used these strategies and data are familiar with enough of the data to complete the assigned task without difficulty. The amount of data in each list can be processed in a reasonable time.

The point in an introductory lesson is not to produce fifteen or twenty different categories of words, nor to exercise the new operation repeatedly without interruption. Rather, it is useful to exercise the operation once or twice, or maybe three times—if it is a relatively simple one—and then discuss how it was done. The next application should also be limited to a few tries and then discussed. It is the discussion of how the new operation was executed as much as the actually doing of it that helps students begin to take command of a new thinking skill or strategy.

Figure 5.4 summarizes some basic guidelines for introducing a thinking skill or strategy. These guidelines apply to all three of the introductory strategies. A teacher following these guidelines will be able to help students become acquainted with a new thinking operation.

INTRODUCING THINKING SKILLS AND STRATEGIES

The three introductory strategies presented here prove valuable beyond the fact that they incorporate the findings of research on skill learning. They also meet the criteria of effective teaching identified by researchers and educators such as Walter Doyle, Madeline Hunter, Barak Rosenshine, and Jane Stallings.[16] Each strategy makes the learning objectives public right at the start of the lesson—no surprises with these strategies. All develop set on the part of the students, and all provide instructive input. These strategies not only involve the students in processing data but also provide opportunities to both teacher and students for checking learning. And in all these strategies teachers help students bridge what is being learned to things beyond that particular introductory lesson.

In addition, these three introductory strategies appeal to both teach-

1. Be sure that students understand the lesson objective: learning a thinking skill or strategy.

2. Spend four to five minutes introducing the skill or strategy, including stating synonyms, examples, and a working definition, if possible.

3. Use media and content or subject matter with which students are already familiar, drawn from their own experiences or previously studied. Do *not* introduce a new skill with new data.

4. Keep the application or "doing it" parts of the lesson short — six to eight minutes each, at best

5. Eliminate or at least minimize the interference caused by:
   • other skills or strategies,
   • emotional or value-laden content, and
   • subject matter discussion.

6. Focus on the major components of the skill or strategy being introduced, especially on *how* the operation is executed and *why*.

7. Devote up to one-third of the lesson time to a reflective reporting, discussing and sharing what the students did in their heads to execute the skill.

8. In ending the lesson, involve the students in reviewing the key skill procedures, rules, and criteria identified so far and, if possible, provide a mnemonic device to assist them in remembering these.

9. Help students identify opportunities for using this skill or strategy in their out-of-school activities as well as in their academic work.

Figure 5.4 Guidelines for Introducing a Thinking Skill or Strategy

ers and students. They seem to accommodate different learning styles commonly found among students in most classrooms. The inductive strategy accommodates field-independent learners who often need little instruction to initiate a task and who plunge into a situation focusing more on the whole than on its parts. These students often seem to know almost intuitively how to engage in a skill, even if imperfectly. Using this strategy allows these students to do the operation and then share with others how they did it.

The directive strategy, on the other hand, usually appeals more to field-dependent students who rely on teacher directions and environmental cues to complete a skilled task.[17] It also appeals to those learners characterized by a step-to-step, list-making orientation to remembering and learning. The developmental strategy accommodates those students ready to benefit from instruction in a specific operation by offering them an opportunity to articulate what they can do at the moment; it gives them a reason to want to do it better and then shows them how to do so, thus helping them grow intellectually in the process. Each of these strategies seems to speak to different learning styles.

Of even greater importance, these three strategies are well suited to introducing different types of thinking operations at different points in a students' schooling. The inductive strategy is useful with average to above-average students or with operations about which a number of students in a class may have some knowledge. The directive strategy, on the other hand, appears to be most useful in introducing rather complicated operations to even the most able students or any thinking operations to novices, beginners, or below-average students. The developmental strategy may well be most useful in helping students expand on, elaborate, or apply to new settings thinking operations that they were introduced to earlier or that they have not used for some time.

These introductory strategies also seem to appeal to different types of teachers because of differences in teaching styles. The directive strategy, for example, seems to match the preferred instructional style of an expository teacher. The inductive strategy, on the other hand, appears to suit inquiry-oriented instructors, and the developmental strategy is often the favorite of a constructivist, developmentally oriented teacher.[18] But using only strategies that fit one's teaching preferences is hardly justified considering the variety of thinking operations to be taught and the variety of students in most classrooms.

Even though these strategies may appeal to different teachers for a variety of reasons, any one seeking to teach thinking skills as effectively as possible should be competent in all of them and should employ them as needed according to the substantive task to be undertaken, the abilities and previous skill learning of the students, and the complexity or nature of the operation to be introduced. Any of these may be utilized in deliberately launching a skill lesson or, spontaneously, in the midst of a subject-matter lesson where students are apparently unfamiliar with an operation they are being asked to use. Variety in instruction is also an important consideration. Since all these strategies incorporate the features required of effective introduction to any thinking operation, any of the three can be useful in introducing a thinking skill or strategy. Any teacher should employ all three strategies as appropriate in introducing thinking skills.

As important as is the introductory stage in skill teaching and learning, it is but one of six stages through which students need instruction to achieve a high degree of proficiency in any thinking operation. The skill introducing strategies presented in this and the preceding chapter are very useful in this stage of the teaching of thinking, but they constitute less than 20 percent of what needs to be used to teach a thinking operation to any degree of proficiency at all. It is worth remembering that students do *not* command a thinking operation simply as a result of a single lesson built around one of the strategies. Repeated, follow-up, guided practice in the operation is also required. So, too, is its transfer to new settings and its elaboration in new, more sophisticated dimensions as well as repeated opportunities for its autonomous practice and use. The following chapters present instructional strategies for lessons designed to accomplish these goals.

By using *all* of these strategies in the framework of skill teaching described earlier, teachers can help students become more effective and efficient in thinking skills and strategies.

NOTES

1. Irving E. Sigel, "A Constructivist Perspective for Teaching Thinking," *Educational Leadership* 42:3 (November 1984), pp. 18–22.

2. Sigel, "A Constructivist"; Robbie Case, "A Developmentally Based Theory and Technology of Instruction," *Review of Educational Research* 48:3 (Summer 1978), pp. 439–463.

3. Case, "A Developmentally Based."

4. Sigel, "A Constructivist."

5. Arthur Whimbey, "The Key to Higher-Order Thinking Is Precise Processing," *Educational Leadership* 42:1 (September 1984), pp. 66–70; Michael I. Posner and Steven W. Keele, "Skill Learning," in Robert M. W. Travers. ed., *Second Handbook of Research on Teaching* (Chicago: Rand McNally College Publishing Company, 1973), pp. 808–810; Jane Stallings, "Effective Strategies for Teaching Basic Skills," in Daisy G. Wallace, ed., *Developing Basic Skills Programs in Secondary Schools* (Alexandria, Va.: Association for Supervision and Curriculum Development, 1983), pp. 1–19.

6. Posner and Keele, "Skill Learning," p. 824; David Pratt, *Curriculum Design and Development* (New York: Harcourt Brace Jovanovich, 1980), pp. 312–313.

7. Pratt, *Curriculum*, p. 313.

8. Robert J. Sternberg, "How Can We Teach Intelligence?" *Educational Leadership* 42:1 (September 1984), pp. 38–50.

9. Ann L. Brown, Joseph C. Campione, and Jeanne D. Day, "Learning to Learn: On Training Students to Learn from Texts," *Educational Researcher* 10 (February 1981), pp. 14–21; Sternberg, "How Can We. . . "; Arthur Costa, "Mediating the Metacognitive," *Educational Leadership* 42:3 (November 1984), pp. 58–62.

10. Posner and Keele, "Skill Learning."

11. Bryce B. Hudgins, *Learning and Thinking* (Itasca, Ill.: F.E. Peacock Publishers, 1977), pp. 142–172; David N. Perkins, "Thinking Frames" (Paper delivered at ASCD Conference on Approaches to Teaching Thinking, Alexandria, Va., August 6, 1985); Posner and Keele, "Skill Learning"; Sternberg, "How Can We. . . ."

12. Reuven Feuerstein, *Instrumental Enrichment* (Baltimore: University Park Press, 1980).

13. Carl Bereiter, "Elementary School: Necessity or Convenience?" *Elementary School Journal* 73 (May 1973), pp. 435–446.

14. John McPeck, *Critical Thinking and Education* (New York: St. Martin's Press, 1981); Hudgins, *Learning and Thinking*, pp. 142–172; Posner and Keele, "Skill Learning."

15. Case,"A Developmentally Based"; Perkins, "Thinking Frames"; Alan H. Schoenfeld, "Can Heuristics Be Taught?" in Jack Lochhead and John Clement, eds., *Cognitive Process Instruction* (Philadelphia: The Franklin Institute Press, 1979), pp. 315–336.

16. Walter Doyle, "Academic Work," *Review of Educational Research* 53:2 (Summer 1983), pp. 159–199; Madeline Hunter, *Mastery Teaching: Increasing Instructional Effectiveness in Secondary Schools, Colleges and Universities* (El Segundo, Calif.: TIP Publications, 1982); Barak Rosenshine, "Teaching Functions in Instructional Programs," *Elementary School Journal* 83:4 (March 1983), pp. 335–353; Stallings, "Effective Strategies."

17. Doyle, "Academic Work," pp. 175–178; Peter Martorella, "Cognition Research: Some Implications for the Design of Social Studies Instructional Materials," *Theory and Research in Social Education* 10:3 (Fall 1982), pp. 1–16.

18. Sigel, "A Constructivist."

6

Guiding Practice in and Applying Thinking Skills

Once introduced, a new thinking skill or strategy must be practiced until students can demonstrate proficiency in using it on their own. After the introductory lesson using one of the teaching strategies presented in Chapters 4 and 5, teachers should provide a number of lessons in which students engage in this practice. To be most effective for skill learning, these practice lessons must be of two types. The initial practice lessons should provide instructive guidance along with the student practice of the new operation. Subsequent lessons can then provide opportunities for independent practice of the operation, ultimately in contexts where the students themselves must determine which thinking operations in their repetoire are the most appropriate to apply. These two types of practice lessons carry the teaching of thinking skills and strategies through the second and third stages of the six stage skill teaching framework presented in Chapter 3.

GUIDED PRACTICE

In the practice lessons immediately following the introduction of a new thinking skill or strategy, teacher guidance should accompany student application of the operation being learned. In these lessons students should receive assistance in using the operation, should reflect on what they do as they engage in it, and should discuss its major attributes as well as what goes on in their heads as they execute it. Such activities can precede, accompany, and follow student use of the operation. At this stage of skill learning, students need to be conscious of how they execute the operation and to discuss how it can be executed *each time* they engage in it, if they are to take ownership of it.

A Strategy for Guiding Practice

Teachers can employ a number of strategies to guide student practice in executing a thinking skill or strategy. The key ingredient of any such teaching strategy is instructive guidance in how to carry out the operation being practiced. One basic strategy for providing such guidance consists of these four steps:

1. First, the teacher introduces the operation to be practiced, just as in the lessons employing the introductory strategies described in Chapters 4 and 5.
2. Then students and teacher review the operation to be used by reviewing what they know already about it—its key rules and procedures, and predicting how they will use these procedures and rules in this instance.
3. Next, the students apply the operation, monitoring how they execute it as discussed or planned in the preceding step.
4. Finally, the students reflect on what they did in their minds as they engaged in the operation and summarize what they have learned about it to this point.

This strategy requires about twenty minutes or so in an average subject-matter lesson for a thinking operation of average complexity. This leaves approximately half of a typical forty-five minute class period to then focus on the subject-matter learning that has occurred as a result of applying this operation. This strategy proves especially useful because it builds around what normally goes on in any subject-matter class where thinking operations are used to learn content. Its major step involves applying the operation to achieve a subject-matter objective (Step 3). To this, the strategy adds three activities: a brief introduction to the operation, a preview of it before it is applied, and a follow-up, reflective discussion of it. Each of these three steps takes some time away from direct subject-matter learning; they, in fact, constitute direct *skill* teaching. However, rather than assume students will become proficient in a newly introduced thinking skill simply by using it to learn the subject and to discuss only the product of its use, this teaching strategy allocates some class activities and time to focus explicitly on the thinking operation before turning attention to what was learned about the subject through its use. This modest attention to the new thinking skill or strategy at this point seems to move students toward mastery more quickly than they would move simply if forced to use the skill on their own.

Figure 6.1 outlines in detail what should be done to execute each of the major steps in the practice strategy. This strategy could easily be used to guide practice in any thinking skill or strategy. We can illustrate its salient points by explaining how it could be used to provide guided practice in the skill of classifying information as this skill was introduced in the sample lessons in Chapters 4 and 5.

Once the skill of classifying has been introduced as previously described, the teacher can identify a number of places in a course where it would be useful, for subject-matter learning purposes, to apply it. Almost immediately after studying life in the thirteen colonies, for instance, an American history course normally turns to the coming of the American Revolution. Students thus find themselves studying some laws passed by England to control events and affairs in the colonies. This content offers a good opportunity to practice classifying data. As a preliminary activity, the teacher could have students list the key laws affecting the colonies enacted by the British Parliament after 1690 and identify what they said or did. Then the students would be prepared to classify these laws in order to infer just what England was up to or who in the colonies would be most directly affected by these laws.

Having thus provided a substantive context and purpose for classifying some data, the teacher can launch a guided practice lesson in this skill. To start, the teacher can *introduce* the skill (Step 1) by writing its label—classify—on the board and by having students volunteer synonyms, a working definition, and examples of where the skill can be used and, indeed, was previously used in the course. The skill objective of the lesson needs to be stated explicitly, as does the rationale for using the skill as this point. Such an introduction customarily requires only four to five minutes at most; it serves the same purpose of goal setting and developing set as in the introductory strategies described earlier.

Next, teacher and students can (Step 2) *preview* how the skill is executed and what they need to remember—in terms of operations, rules, and other knowledge—to execute it successfully. This requires a review—what they can recall from their introduction to the skill in the preceding lesson—as well as a prediction of how these attributes can be applied to

STEP 1 *INTRODUCE THE SKILL*

Remind the students that learning the skill is an objective of the course and lesson.

Help the students recall

- the skill label,
- synonyms,
- a simple definition,
- examples of where the skill has already been used.

Discuss the value of the skill.

Point out how use of the skill is helpful here.

STEP 2 *PREVIEW THE SKILL*

Help the students identify key

- rules that direct the skill,
- steps in how the skill works,
- useful information about the skill.

Clarify any obstacles they may anticipate and how to overcome them.

Clarify how to start doing the skill.

STEP 3 *APPLY THE SKILL AND MONITOR*

Have students engage in the skill with reference to what they discussed about it.

Each may work with a partner who checks the executing of the skill.

Teacher provides help as needed.

STEP 4 *REVIEW THE SKILL*

Help the students identify the key attributes of the skill, including its

- rules,
- procedure,
- associated knowledge.

Have the students

- predict where else this skill can be used,
- predict other skills with which this skill can be used,
- identify cues to occasions when it is appropriate to use this skill.

Figure 6.1 A Strategy for Guiding Practice of a Thinking Skill or Strategy

complete the task assigned here. Students should be expected to be the major contributors at this point, but where there is doubt or confusion or error the teacher may also contribute. To aid in this preview, the sequence of skill steps may be mapped or flowcharted or simply listed in sequence on the chalkboard or in student notes. About five to six minutes or so can be allotted to this step, less as students gain experience in applying the skill.

Next the students can *apply* the skill (Step 3) to complete the assigned subject-matter task. They may work alone or in small groups, concentrating on doing the skill, in this case actually grouping the various laws into any categories they choose to answer the assigned question. Or, they might work in pairs, with one student in each pair serving as a process monitor while the other member of the pair executes the skill.[1] The teacher can also provide assistance including demonstrating how to execute one or more of the steps constituting the skill, if necessary. Thus, at this point students execute the skill and monitor how they do it as they proceed.

Finally, students *review* and discuss what they did in their minds as they engaged in the skill (Step 4). With teacher assistance as needed, they can report and discuss the rules, knowledge, and procedures they used, suggesting modifications or additions as appropriate. They can also report obstacles they encountered, offering advice on how to overcome similar obstacles should they arise in future applications of the skill. Again, the teacher may interject suggestions or seek clarification of important steps in the skill procedure or any rules or principles relevant to the skill. This portion of the lesson can conclude with students predicting where else—in this course or elsewhere—use of this skill might be appropriate and the kinds of cues that would so indicate.

At this point, with about twenty minutes or so remaining in the typical class period, the class can turn to the various substantive products generated by the use of the skill. In terms of this illustrative lesson on English colonial laws after 1750, students could report the various ways they categorized the laws—in terms of the area of life each dealt with, as economic, political, and so on, or in terms of region affected, as the frontier, tidewater, and so on. They could also explain the insights inferred from the categories they made as they seek to answer the assigned subject-matter questions. And the class can then proceed to its study of the subject, to undertake another guided practice lesson in classifying data two or three days hence. Thus, in employing this particular teaching strategy, a teacher devotes about half of the lesson time to the thinking skill or strategy being practiced, with the remainder devoted to subject matter. Learning both the thinking operation and subject matter are legitimate goals of such guided practice lessons. Pursuing each goal explicitly and in sequence, however, is much more useful than in pursuing both simultaneously, with skill learning assumed to be implicit in a discussion of the subject at hand. Figure 6.2 presents a lesson plan useful for carrying out the guided practice strategy described here.

This strategy for guiding practice offers three opportunities for students to deal explicitly with any thinking operation—twice before they apply it (Steps 1 and 2) and once afterward (Step 4). Any of a number of

GUIDING PRACTICE IN A SKILL

GOAL: To guide practice in the skill of classifying

OBJECTIVES:

To state the major steps in a procedure for classifying data into self-invented categories.

To state two important rules to follow in classifying data.

To apply the skill of classifying to identify which colonial groups were most affected by British laws 1690–1775.

MATERIALS:

List of laws

TEACHER	STUDENTS
1. Relate this lesson to previous lesson on British laws. Now that we know what they said, we can classify these laws to determine which groups in the colonies were most affected by them.	

Introduce

TEACHER	STUDENTS
2. Write *classify* on board.	
3. Ask for synonyms.	group, categorize, sort ...
4. Define *classify*	to put like things together
5. Ask for examples ... • out of school	sections of a newspaper sections of a supermarket
• from previous classes.	listing of types of colonial governments determining lifestyles in the colonies

Preview

TEACHER	STUDENTS
6. What do we do mentally to *classify* data? What steps can we follow?	One procedure: 1. State our goal in classiffying. 2. Scan the data. 3. Find two pieces of data that are alike. 4. State the common feature as a category label. 5. Find other data that fit this label. 6. Repeat steps 3–5 for new categories of data. 7. Combine/subdivide categories.

Figure 6.2 A Lesson Plan for Providing Guided Practice in the Skill of Classifying

TEACHER	STUDENTS
7. What *rules* are useful to follow?	To start, take the first piece of these data and find another just like it ...
8. What is it helpful to know to to classify data?	Some possible categories such as economic, political, religious, and so on ... or occupations or types of government, and so on. If you don't understand some data put them in "miscellaneous" category
9. What kinds of obstacles could occur in classifying, and how would you overcome them?	If all data go in one category, —we need new category system.

Apply

10. Have students, in pairs, put the laws into categories to answer the question: Which groups in the colonies were most affected by British laws?	

Review

11. Go over the steps, rules, and knowledge that consti-tute *classifying*. • When is it useful to classify data? • What obstacles keep cropping up? How can we handle them? • What steps can we follow?	See items 6–9 above.
12. Make any needed changes or additions to skill attributes in notes.	

Content Discussion

13. Now that we have classified these laws, let's find out who was most affected by them and why.	
14. Continued discussion of content ...	

Figure 6.2 *(continued)*

techniques may be used to conduct these reviews. Before students apply the skill, they can preview—or review—it in any of the following ways:

1. Recalling from memory the key attributes of the operation.
2. Referring to the steps and rules of the operation previously copied into their notebooks.
3. Reviewing the topic in which the operation was most recently used and recalling how they applied it in that case, listing what they did, in what sequence, and why.
4. Giving examples of where the operation could be used and explaining how they could execute it.
5. Responding to a scrambled list of key steps to be put into correct order.
6. Matching a list of rules to the appropriate steps.

To conclude any guided practice strategy, a teacher could also use one of the above activities or any of the following, in which students could:

1. Make a mobile depicting the key attributes of the operation.
2. Write a set of directions (in a paragraph, flowchart, or list) to younger students, telling them how to execute the operation.
3. Make a map or other type of diagram showing the key attributes of the operation and how they relate to one another.
4. Identify where else in their study of the subject or in their daily out-of-school life use of this operation might be appropriate.

These latter techniques could even become the basis of an additional lesson. Some students could produce products to be displayed around the room for others to use in subsequent applications of the operation. All these techniques or activities involve students in recalling and otherwise processing what they have learned to that point about a particular skill or strategy. Teachers can vary their use of these in order to fit activities to the ability levels of their students and to the complexity of the thinking skill or strategy being studied as well as simply to bring variety to these steps of skill instruction.

This guided practice strategy could also extend over several class lessons with an intervening homework assignment. A teacher could introduce and have students review a thinking skill to be practiced and then let them apply it as homework, monitoring it as they work. To start the next class, students can review how they executed the skill and what they learned about it in so doing. Then they can turn to discussion and processing of the subject matter being studied, as outlined above.

The strategy described here can be modified in any number of ways as long as the essential introduction to the thinking skill and discussion of how it works are included. As a substitute for either the preview or review step, for example, a teacher might have students work in pairs, having one partner serve as the monitor, while the other actually executes the skill; in this arrangement it is the monitor's task to provide corrective guidance in how to carry out the operation as the partner actually executes it.

As students become experienced in employing the new thinking skill or strategy through repeated guided practice in applying it, the teacher can shorten and eliminate any of these "guidance providing" steps until the students simply engage in the operation without any explicit attention to it or any guidance at all. For instance, after several lessons employing all four steps of this strategy, the teacher might elect to shorten and then eliminate the introduction to the operation. After noting which operation is to be used and getting a definition of it from the class, the teacher moves the students immediately to executing it. After several additional guided practice lessons organized in this fashion, the teacher might even eliminate the follow-up discussion of how students executed the operation—save for discussion of any obstacles encountered in its use—and proceed immediately to discussion of the subject matter. In a later practice lesson the teacher might shorten and then eliminate the pre-discussion of the operation to be used altogether. By this time the students will have achieved the ability to use it autonomously. Gradually, over a number of guided practice lessons, the teacher can reduce the amount of explicit guidance or attention given the thinking operation. Thereafter, students use it without any guidance at all.

Key Features of Guided Practice

The guided practice strategy described here incorporates the major features of effective skill teaching also included in the introductory strategies described earlier. This strategy keeps the students focused on the thinking skill or strategy being practiced during the initial part of the lesson; provides opportunities for them to articulate its essential attributes; involves them in talking about and reflecting on what goes on in their minds as they apply it; and bridges the operation to other settings. In addition, the skill is used when appropriate to substantive learning objectives and when the kinds of data—in the case of the example here, lists of items— are identical to those used in its introduction. To minimize interference, all guided practice lessons in the weeks following introduction of a new thinking skill or strategy should use only the kind of data used in the introductory lesson. Modeling, it should be noted, is not an essential part of practice at this stage, although a teacher can choose to demonstrate or have a student demonstrate any attribute of the new operation wherever necessary. Modeling might be especially appropriate, however, if the lesson were one of the first guided practice lessons in the operation following its introduction.

Research indicates that for practice to be most beneficial in learning thinking skills and strategies it should be frequent, intermittent, in small chunks, and accompanied by immediate feedback.[2] Translated into the framework for teaching thinking operations presented here, this means that at this second stage of the framework—that of guided practice— students must engage in a number of guided practice lessons spaced out over a period of several weeks following the introduction of a new thinking operation. How frequent such lessons should be is not known for certain. Certainly such frequency depends on the degree of student proficiency sought, the complexity of the skill, the abilities of the students, and the kinds of data and tasks with which the operation is used. It varies for each operation and for each student or group of students. But it is clear from skill teaching research and experience that the initial guided practice lessons should follow the introductory lesson closely, perhaps spaced over every three lessons or days for a week or two.[3] Relatively close spacing enhances recall of what was introduced. Subsequent practices might be spaced out over greater intervals with more intervening days or lessons devoted to other subjects or tasks. Guided practice lessons need to be scheduled until students demonstrate the level of continued proficiency that the teacher seeks. More intermittent spacing of skill practice serves to maintain skill proficiency better than does practice massed into a rapid-fire series of lessons right after a new skill or strategy is introduced.

For example, an American history teacher who has introduced the skill of classifying data into self-invented categories (as in the sample lesson in the preceding chapters) could plan a number of guided practice lessons in this skill over the weeks immediately following the introductory lesson, as data and tasks suitable for classifying occur. Such places might include study of the laws regulating colonial life between 1750 and 1776 and subsequent study of colonial reactions to these laws and to British reactions to colonial reactions, points of view regarding the relationship of the colonies to Britain, and battles fought during the American Revolution. Other opportunities also exist for students to classify information for better understanding the subject being studied in such a course. The point is that any thinking skill or strategy once introduced needs to be practiced or applied relatively frequently thereafter, with appropriate guidance and with the intervals between practices gradually lengthened as students begin to "get the hang of it."

No specific guidelines exist for the most appropriate length of any practice application of a thinking skill. Again, the length of such lessons will depend on student abilities, the subject-matter task, and complexity of the operation to be learned. Experience suggests, however, that practice applications should be relatively short, requiring twenty to thirty minutes or so for students in the intermediate grades upward. Students, of course, need time to reflect on and discuss how they execute a skill, but that portion of the lesson requiring use of the operation itself should not require prolonged exercise of it. What is needed as much as executing the operation are opportunities to discuss how it can be or was done. Those strategies that are most useful for guiding practice in a thinking operation are those that, in the space of a forty–fifty minute lesson, allow time to *carry out* the operation, to reflect on and *discuss* it, and also to *discuss what was learned about the subject* as a result of employing it.

Feedback is absolutely essential during this stage of skill learning. At this point students are still learning the new operation, so instruction in how to do it rather than testing how well students do it must remain the primary goal of any such lesson. This feedback can be provided in a variety of ways. It can, for example, be "feedforward." Research on effective problem solving indicates that individuals considered to be excellent problem solvers spend considerable time planning how to go about solving a problem before they actually engage in trying to solve it.[4] Planning how to execute any thinking skill or strategy actually makes its execution much more efficient and the effort much more productive. Consequently, instructive guidance in any thinking operation can be provided *before* students actually engage in it. This guidance feeds information about the operation forward and informs its application, while discussion of it after execution only informs its application next time—if the information can be remembered that long.

Instructional feedback may also occur while the thinking operation is being used as the teacher or a student's partner observes a student using it and provides immediate comments regarding omissions, inconsistencies, or errors the student makes. Or feedback may also follow the application of the operation as students report and discuss how they executed it, any rules that proved useful, particular operations they found useful, or anything that gave them difficulty and how that was handled.

By having students recall what they know about a thinking skill or strategy *before* they try to apply this skill or strategy and by helping them plan what they will do to execute it *before* they do it, teachers can provide the guidance necessary to make practice of a newly introduced thinking operation a learning rather than testing experience. By providing confirming or corrective feedback *during* and *after* application of a skill or strategy, students can sharpen their execution of it and deliberately attend to how it is carried out. The whole purpose of such feedback or feedforward is to help students become more conscious of how they engage in thinking so that they can take deliberate command of their mental abilities when they so desire. *Guided* practice helps accomplish this goal.

Any number of strategies may be used to structure guided practice in any thinking operation, so long as these strategies include the key ingredients of such practice—an introduction focused on the skill, feedback, and feedforward instruction and reflection on how the operation was executed—and are used frequently and in small doses. Arthur Whimbey's Thinking Aloud Paired Problem Solving strategy, for instance, can be well used in this stage of teaching thinking operations.[5] In this strategy students work in pairs to execute the skill. One student carries out the skill, reporting aloud what he or she is doing and why, while the second student checks the extent to which the first is executing the key operations of the skill. After discussing what was done, the students can read, view, or listen to how an expert executed the same skill, compare that to how they did it, and then, switching roles, apply the skill again to a new set of identical data. This process can be repeated with teacher guidance as appropriate, until students demonstrate the degree of proficiency desired at this stage of the learning process.

An introductory lesson followed by a number of guided practice lessons using the strategies described here can move students toward mastery of any thinking operation. As students become increasingly proficient in executing an operation, the teacher can gradually shorten and then eliminate the amount of guidance provided. When, in the teacher's judgment, students have achieved the desired level of proficiency in an operation, they should be provided a number of opportunities to apply it independently—first, on command, and eventually without any cues or guidance from the teacher. Such autonomous use of the skill will complete the initial stages of skill teaching in which a thinking skill or strategy has been explicitly introduced and students have received repeated, guided practice in using it.

INDEPENDENT APPLICATION

The major goal of teaching any thinking skill is self-initiated and self-directed student use of the skill. No actual instruction is involved. The activities at this point in the instructional sequence assume that students have some degree of competence in the skill and can execute it without any teacher guidance. This third stage of skill teaching consists essentially of repeated, individual application of a skill to achieve substantive, subject-matter related learning goals.

Skill Using Activities

For purposes of skill learning, independent practice should take at least two forms. Initially, the kinds of opportunities provided ought specifically and rather obviously to call for use of the skill on which teaching has been focused. Thus, at this point in teaching the skill of classifying data, for example, an American history teacher who has been teaching this skill as described in the preceding pages can provide periodic writing, debating, ditto worksheets, discussion, and reporting tasks that require students to classify information in order to complete them. Cues to the skill to be used should be rather explicit, presented within the task by directions specifying a specific skill, as, for example, "Classify the data below to determine which side had the most advantages over the other in. . . ." This type of lesson should emphasize how well the students can execute a "given" operation on their own more than which operation is to be employed.

The second type of independent practice should provide opportunities for more autonomous use of a thinking skill or strategy where there are not instructor-provided cues as to which particular operation(s) should be employed.[6] Since proficiency in a thinking operation consists as much of knowing when or where to use it and being willing to do so as well as being able to execute it rapidly and accurately, teachers must create opportunities for students to learn how to make these choices, too. Activities of this type embed the operation completely in the task or subject matter and do not cue the students specifically to employ a particular thinking skill. In the case of classifying, for instance, tasks that require students to write paragraphs or short essays justifying given or self-invented hypotheses or conclusions, also involve classifying. In executing tasks such as these, students should classify the data they work with. Emphasis in such activities should be as much on whether the students choose to use the appropriate thinking operation as on how well they execute it.

As was pointed out in the Prologue, many teachers customarily provide students opportunities to practice thinking skills and strategies without guidance or follow-up instruction. Tasks involving the use of ditto worksheets or textbook end-of-chapter exercises containing questions above the level of simple recall; paragraph or essay writing; completion of puzzles; debates; simulations; and other similar activities serve as useful vehicles for carrying out lessons at this third stage of teaching thinking skills. These tasks all exercise certain thinking skills. In using these techniques, however, the thinking skill(s) to be exercised must actually be required to complete the assigned task. If the task can legitimately be completed without using a skill that the teacher would like students to use, such practice activities prove of little use as far as this stage of skill learning goes.

Teacher Questioning

Questioning is one of the most popular of all techniques that teachers use for skill exercising and thus deserves some attention here. Although many teachers use questioning well for a variety of instructional purposes, they frequently misuse it as a technique in the teaching of thinking.

Many educators have long asserted that asking students questions sequenced or keyed to increasingly complex or higher levels of cognition actually teaches students how to think at these levels. These educators assume a direct relationship between the asserted level of a question and the presumed level of thinking in which a student must engage to answer it. The validity of this assumption is doubtful, however. Research on questioning provides little convincing support for this claim.[7]

This is not to say that questioning does not encourage or stimulate thinking. In many cases it does. However, as R. T. Dillon and other researchers have pointed out, such types of questioning may inhibit as well as encourage thinking. High-level questions may actually shut down thinking on the part of many students.[8] Nor is this to say that the effort to answer questions does not stimulate thinking. Students who respond to such questions *do* think, but in many instances they are clearly not engaged in the level or type of thinking intended by the questioner. When one might intend that a question required analysis to answer, a student may, in fact, respond simply on the basis of recall—and be judged correct in his or her answer. That question-asking may *exercise* thinking skills seems quite clear. That question-asking *teaches* anyone how to engage in any specific skill better than they otherwise could is, however, suspect.

There can be little doubt, nevertheless, that questions requiring more than simple recall are essential for exercising or stimulating thinking. Teachers wishing to ask questions as a way of providing opportunities for students to practice thinking operations can do a number of things to ensure that such practice occurs. Many of the activities useful in independent practice of thinking skills and strategies are cast in the form of such questions. Educator Hilda Taba pioneered in showing teachers the importance of levels and sequencing of questions for this purpose.[9] Taba stressed the importance of asking, first, questions requiring recall of information, followed by questions requiring the processing of that information (by classifying, comparing, contrasting, or judging it), and finally by questions requiring students to apply what they were learning to develop generalizations or similar kinds of knowledge. Such structured hierarchies of questions—either text or teacher provided—can be very useful to students—in practicing various kinds of thinking operations. But more than simply sequencing and asking different levels of questions are required to guarantee that students take advantage of the opportunities for thinking they present.

To ensure that students actually engage in thinking, teachers can do at least three things other than ask different levels of questions. They can (1) use *their responses* to student answers to encourage or direct thinking. They can (2) employ questions explicitly designed to elicit specific types of thinking. And they can (3) teach students how to ask their own questions. Use of these techniques makes questioning more likely to provide practice in thinking than does simple manipulation of the presumed levels of questions.

How teachers respond to student answers can shape or at least stimulate additional student thinking.[10] For example, one teacher response can be silence. Leaving a longer period of silence after a question has been asked proves to be an extremely useful technique. Research indicates that simply allowing more time for students to respond to a question than is normally allowed may stimulate students to think beyond the level of recall.[11] The average "wait time" for teachers— time elapsing between when a teacher asks a question and the time a student response is acknowledged—is 1.3 seconds. When teachers wait a little longer (for up to 3 seconds, for example) before responding, students appear to continue to think more about their answers. They often give reasons to support their answers (frequently because they assume teacher silence is a sign that they have erred) or give longer answers in complete sentences, both of which behaviors some researchers interpret as evidence of more complex thinking.[12]

To further stimulate thinking, educator Arthur Costa recommends that, in responding, teachers accept student answers, than paraphrase them or have other students paraphrase them to stimulate additional student processing or reasoning. Teachers also can respond by requesting clarification or elaboration by the respondent or other students. Or teachers can probe a response for evidence and reasoning in support or contradiction of the response. Teachers can also provide students additional data that challenge their answers and require some accommodation by the students. Getting students to elaborate on, justify, or clarify answers rather than judging the accuracy of an answer may make teacher questioning more effective as a stimulant to more complex levels of thinking than does simply asking different levels of questions in and of itself. Teacher responses that are carefully chosen may actually direct students into the use of specific thinking skills.

Historian Allan O. Kownslar suggests one way questions might elicit use of specific kinds of thinking skills more explicitly than is often customary.[13] He suggests use of questions similar to the following to initiate student use of specific thinking skills:

1. What is a *verifiable fact*?—a *value claim*? What verifiable facts does (this source) contain? What value claims does it contain?
2. What does *relevant* mean?—*irrelevant*? What statements or information in (this source) are relevant to the main topic of or claim made in (this source)?

3. What is *bias*? What are some clues to bias? Does (this source) show bias? How can you tell?
4. What is an *unstated assumption*? What unstated assumptions can you find in (this source)? Justify your selections.
5. What is a *logical fallacy*? What, if any, logical fallacies are in (this source)? Explain the reasons for your selections.
6. What makes a source *credible*? How credible is (this source)? Justify your judgment.

To answer each of these questions, students must recall what they know about a particular thinking operation, then engage in that operation and be prepared to explain how they did it. If such questions were put on a handout for students to keep, teachers could then simply assign students certain questions by number for any specific assignment. Similar kinds of questions could be provided to students for each of the major steps in a problem-solving or decision-making process or for purposes of analysis, synthesis, or evaluation. The explicit reference in these questions to the type of skill sought from the student targets thinking more directly than does providing different levels of questions, especially where these levels of questions are not clear to the students or go unannounced.

Student Questioning

If teachers really wanted to teach students how to engage in thinking, rather than ask questions of the students, they would teach students how to ask their own questions. Using teacher-asked questions as the major device for guiding student practice in or use of thinking skills contradicts a major goal of the teaching of thinking—making students independent learners—because teacher-asked questions keep students dependent on someone else to initiate and direct thinking. An active, thinking student ought to be able to generate and direct his or her own thinking. Learning how to invent one's own questions enables students to achieve this goal.

Some years ago educator Francis Hunkins suggested a number of strategies for helping students learn how to invent their own questions and to become more independent thinkers.[14] These questioning strategies require students (1) to plan a series of questions to ask and then (2) to answer these questions, (3) to assess their results and the questions they used to get these results, and (4) to review their questioning strategy and articulate principles implicit in that strategy. One strategy based on his suggestions requires students to:

1. PLAN
   a. Pick a topic.
   b. Brainstorm questions.

    c. Evaluate the questions, in terms of
        low/high cognitive level,
        focusing/expanding on/from the topic,
        information/feeling,
        preferred/not preferred,
        other criteria.
    d. Select a given number of questions.
    e. Sequence them in some order.
    f. State the goal to be achieved.
    g. Revise the list of questions.
2. ANSWER
    a. Answer the questions.
    b. Add new questions, if necessary, and answer them.
3. ASSESS
    a. Evaluate the content results in terms of the goal.
    b. Evaluate the questions (and the sequence) in terms of the goal.
4. REVIEW
    a. Modify the questions and/or the sequence.
    b. Identify the main principles implicit in the questioning strategy used.

In the planning stage of the PAAR strategy, students select or are given a topic and then (in groups, pairs, or alone) brainstorm a number of questions, usually ten or so, the answers to which may help them learn about that topic. They then evaluate each question as to whether it is low level—requires recalling or collecting data—or high level—requiring processing or analyzing, synthesizing or evaluating data; whether it focuses on the topic or expands beyond the topic; whether it deals with information about the topic or feelings/attitudes related to the topic; whether it strikes their fancy or does not appeal to them; or whether it meets any other set of criteria they or the teacher suggest. This can be done using a matrix as shown in the sample questioning worksheet in Figure 6.3. It proves useful to require students to use the four criteria shown in this figure for all activities in which they invent their own questions. They can insert additional teacher-given or other criteria of their own selection in the untitled columns under *Other*.

Once students have evaluated each of their questions, they then can select those that appear most useful. At this point the teacher may specify a minimum number of questions and their distribution as, for example, directing students to select "any six questions, with no more than two of these being in the 'low' category." Such directions prevent students from giving in to the temptation to select all low-level, fact-gathering, or regurgitating questions. The specific limitations on which kinds of questions can be chosen may vary from assignment to assignment.

QUESTION-ASKING GUIDE

1. TOPIC:
2. QUESTIONS (ten minimum):

	Low	High	Focus	Criteria Exp.		(Other)	

3. Pick six of the above questions and write on the line to the left of each a number indicating the order in which you will answer them, starting with number one for the first to be answered.

4. State (in the space below) the GOAL you expect to achieve by answering these questions:

5. Rewrite, revise, or add any questions.

6. Answer your questions, recording your answers on a separate page.

7. Assess the quality and thoroughness of
   • your responses
   • each question
   • the sequence of questions

8. To what extent did the answers to these questions achieve your goal?

9. What other important things did you learn by answering these questions?

10. Review your questioning strategy to:
   a) modify (rewrite) any questions so they would have been more useful.
   b) add any questions you should have asked to achieve your stated goal.
   c) Renumber the questions to indicate the order in which the revised list of questions should be asked if used again.
   d) List any rules, guidelines or principles that tell how and why you selected and sequenced the questions as you did or would do again.

Figure 6.3 A Question-Asking Guide

After selecting questions they wish to answer, students complete the planning process. They sequence the questions in any order that appears to them to make sense by numbering them on the lines on the worksheet. Having thus developed a sense of direction or focus for their inquiry, they can then better articulate a goal that answering these questions will probably accomplish, a goal that may have been only implicit or vague to this point. They may here wish to revise some questions, eliminate several, and/or add several new ones that will enable them to really accomplish their now-stated goal—or to change the goal that seemed to guide their original selection of questions.

In carrying out a question-generating activity such as that described here, for example, one junior high school earth science class brainstormed the following list of questions about the topic *climate*:

Climate		Low	High	Focus	Exp.	Info.	Attitudes
1	What is it?	✓		✓			
4	How does it affect people?		✓		✓		
	How many kinds are there?	✓		✓			
5	Can climates be altered?		✓	✓			
6	How?		✓	✓			
3	What causes climates?	✓		✓			
2	What do climates consist of?	✓		✓			
	Where are there different climates?	✓			✓		
	Have they always been the same?		✓		✓		
	How is climate different from weather?		✓	✓			
7	Which climates do most people like? Why?		✓		✓		✓

Evaluation of these questions led these students to select six as indicated on the lines in front of each question above. Their goal, they then decided, was "to explain how people and climates affect each other." Although they didn't have to, they added question 7 to their list after stating their goal, because they felt it would be interesting to answer.

The next task for a student using this technique is, of course, to answer the questions and to record or report their answers in some form assigned by the teacher or selected by the students. Students can submit lists of answers, an essay or some type of written report, maps or charts or graphs, notes for an oral report or debate, or whatever type of communication seems appropriate given the teaching/learning objectives of the activity.

Finally, after answering the questions and reporting their findings, students can assess what they have done and review their question-asking strategies. They can judge how well their responses and questions—and the sequence of questions—helped them achieve their stated goal. In so doing, they can judge the thoroughness of their responses as well as of their questions and the value of the sequence of their questions. They can also indicate any other substantive learning they developed by answering these questions, looking especially for unanticipated things they might have found out about their topic and question-asking. By reviewing their assessment, they can then modify the questions they used by rewriting any into more effective forms, adding more useful ones, and eliminating those that proved useless. The reasons for revising and ordering their questions can then be written out to serve as guidelines or rules to be followed in the future.

Teachers can teach or use any number of variations of this particular question-asking strategy. One such variation is illustrated in Figure 6.4. A question-planning guide such as this could be used by students virtually any time, once they had been introduced to and practiced how to invent, evaluate, and sequence questions as described above. After brainstorming questions and listing them under item 1, students can determine their functions and then judge the direction in which they lead and their usefulness in getting information. Once the questions have been evaluated, students can choose the questions they wish to answer and write the goal of their inquiry—where the questions will lead them. After adding new or revised questions under item 3, students can number the questions they have chosen in the order that they will ask them, modifying them or continuing to add others as they proceed. Once students have completed this, they can proceed with the task of answering and assessing their questions, reflecting on how they went about the task and what they learned by so doing.

Engaging in question-asking as described here can be a group, class or an individual activity. It can be taught like any skill. A teacher can introduce the skill using the directive strategy (Chapter 4), and students can receive guided practice in using it through the worksheet in Figure 6.3. Periodically, the teacher can have students report to the rest of the class, discussing what they have done to that point, and why, and even suggesting to one another questions or ideas that may be helpful. Such reporting, sharing, and revising is very appropriate midway in the planning step and at the conclusion of each of the other steps. Of course, as students become more proficient in executing this skill, the reporting may be shortened and eventually eliminated; the worksheet in Figure 6.4 may

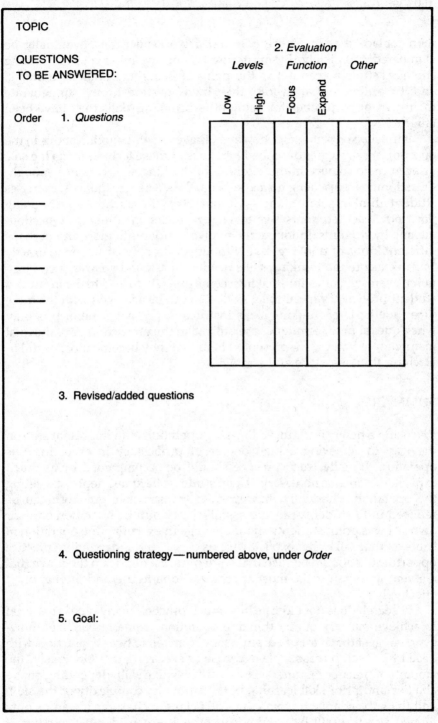

Figure 6.4 A Question-Planning Guide

then replace that in Figure 6.3; and a worksheet may eventually be eliminated completely. By mastering this or any other question-asking strategy, students can get to the point of being autonomous thinkers; and, by asking and answering their own questions, they can generate their own opportunities for using other thinking skills they have been taught.

It must be remembered, however, that even with modifications in the questioning strategies described here, use of these techniques as the sole or even major device in the teaching of thinking simply is not enough. Questioning by teachers, no matter what the student responses, exercises student thinking, but alone—without other instruction—questioning does not teach students *how* to engage better in thinking. Question-making by students undoubtedly involves students in more and perhaps different kinds of thinking, but without additional instruction in exactly *how* to execute the thinking skills needed to ask and answer such questions, even such question-making seems unlikely to lead to the improved student proficiency in thinking skills that can be achieved with the more direct methods of thinking skills instruction presented here. It is only when questioning techniques are utilized in the practice stage of the total instructional framework presented here that they become most useful in teaching thinking skills and strategies.

SUMMARY

Practicing a newly introduced thinking operation is an important step on the way to achieving a high degree of proficiency in executing this operation. Initially, such practice should be accompanied by as much explicit guidance as necessary to help students become adept at executing the operation. Gradually, however, such instructive guidance can be reduced until students can successfully carry out the operation on their own. At this point students should engage in executing the operation in contexts that call rather explicitly for its use. Later, independent practice opportunities should be such that students must decide on their own that a given operation is the most appropriate one to use and then apply it effectively.

Research does not indicate how much practice of any type is required to achieve mastery of any thinking operation. Some researchers, however, suggest that it may take anywhere from ten to twenty practices with a skill to develop reasonable expertise at executing it.[15] Obviously, the amount of practice required will vary from skill to skill, depending on the abilities and prior skill learning of the students, complexity of the skill, and the subject area in which the skill is taught. In some instances only limited practice will be required; in others, a considerable number of practice lessons will be required to develop the desired level of student proficiency. A teacher will know, by the performance of students, when guided practice can give way to independent but explicitly cued practice and when students are then proficient enough to engage in even less directed, independent use of the skill. Once students have been able to demonstrate such proficiency, a teacher can move on to help them generalize the skill to the point of using it on their own initiative in settings or contexts beyond which they have been learning and applying it. Teaching thinking skills and strategies to transfer is the focus of the following chapter.

NOTES

1. Arthur Whimbey, "Teaching Sequential Thought: The Cognitive Skills Approach," *Phi Delta Kappan* 59:4 (December 1977), pp. 255–259.

2. Barak V. Rosenshine, "Teaching Functions in Instructional Programs," *Elementary School Journal* 83:4 (March 1983), pp. 340–343, 345–348; Michael I. Posner and Steven W. Keele, "Skill Learning," in Robert M. W. Travers, ed., *Second Handbook of Research on Teaching* (Chicago: Rand McNally College Publishing Company, 1973), pp. 816, 809–823; Jane Stallings, "Effective Strategies for Teaching Basic Skills," in Daisy G. Wallace, ed., *Developing Basic Skills Programs in Secondary Schools*, (Alexandria, Va.: Association for Supervision and Curriculum Development, 1983), pp. 1–19; Bryce B. Hudgins, *Learning and Thinking*, (Itasca, Ill.: F. E. Peacock Publishers, 1977), pp. 92–98.

3. Posner and Keele, "Skill Learning"; Hudgins, *Learning and Thinking*, pp. 96–98.

4. Benjamin S. Bloom and Lois J. Broder, *Problem-solving Processes of College Students* (Chicago: University of Chicago Press, 1950).

5. Whimbey, "Teaching Sequential Thought."

6. Carl Bereiter, "How to Keep Thinking Skills from Going the Way of All Frills," *Educational Leadership* 42:1 (September 1984), pp. 75–78; Rosenshine, "Teaching Functions," pp. 345–348.

7. Meredith D. Gall, "The Use of Questions in Teaching," *Review of Educational Research* 40:5 (December 1970), pp. 707–721; Philip H. Winne, "Experiments Relating Teachers' Use of Higher Cognitive Questions to Student Achievement," *Review of Educational Research* 49:1 (Winter 1979), pp. 13–49; Doris L. Redfield and Elaine Weldman Rousseau, "A Meta-Analysis of Experimental Research on Teacher Questioning Behavior," *Review of Educational Research* 51:2 (Summer 1981), pp. 237–245; R. T. Dillon, "The Multi-Disciplinary Study of Questioning," *Journal of Educational Psychology* 74:2 (April 1982), pp. 147–165.

8. David McNamara, "Teaching Skill: The Question of Questioning," *Educational Research* 23:2 (February 1981), pp. 104–109; Dillon, "Multi-Disciplinary."

9. Hilda Taba, "Implementing Thinking as an Objective in Social Studies," in Jean Fair and Fannie R. Shaftel, eds., *Effective Thinking in the Social Studies: 37th Yearbook* (Washington: National Council for the Social Studies, 1967), pp. 25–49.

10.   Arthur L. Costa, "Teacher Behaviors That Enable Student Thinking," in Arthur L. Costa, ed., *Developing Minds* (Alexandria, Va.: Association for Supervision and Curriculum Development, 1985), pp. 125–128, 131–135.

11.   Mary Budd Rowe, "Wait-Time and Rewards as Instructional Variables," *Journal of Research in Science Teaching* 11:2 (1974), pp. 81–94.

12.   Costa, "Teacher Behaviors."

13.   Adapted from Allan O. Kownslar, "What's Worth Having Students Think Critically About?" *Social Education* 49:4 (April 1985), pp. 304–305.

14.   Adapted from Francis P. Hunkins, *Involving Students in Questioning* (Boston: Allyn and Bacon, 1976).

15.   Bruce R. Joyce and Beverly Showers, *Power in Staff Development Through Research on Training* (Alexandria, Va.: Association for Supervision and Curriculum Development, 1983).

7

Transferring and Elaborating Thinking Skills

To be proficient in a thinking skill or strategy means to be able to use that operation effectively and efficiently on one's own in a variety of appropriate contexts. To develop such proficiency requires more than simply introducing the thinking skill or strategy and practicing it in a single context.[1] It also requires instruction and guided practice in how and when to transfer the thinking skill or strategy from the context in which it was initially learned to the widest variety of contexts possible. The final three stages of the thinking skill teaching framework presented here focus on this crucial task.

TEACHING FOR TRANSFER

To transfer a skill means essentially to be able to apply it effectively in a setting or with data other than the setting or data in which it was originally learned or experienced. Specialists in cognition, such as David Perkins, point out that transfer is of two kinds.[2] One, called "high road" transfer, consists of applying a skill learned in one setting to another quite different setting. The other—called "low road" transfer—consists of applying a skill learned in one setting to other rather similar settings. While "low road" transfer is the more likely to occur with minimum effort, neither kind of transfer occurs automatically.[3]

Thinking skills and strategies fail to transfer readily for several major reasons. The first has to do with the user's lack of knowledge about and expertise in the skill or strategy being employed. Thinking operations are very much tied to the contexts, subjects, and types of data with which they are initially used or experienced. Unless they are repeatedly applied—with reflection—in additional contexts or with other kinds of data, they are not likely to be generalized to the point of even appearing to be useful or applicable in a variety of contexts.

Thinking skills and strategies, for example, are often shaped by the media to which they are applied.[4] While their general procedures may remain substantially the same regardless of the media with which they are used, their knowledge components often differ. Ignorance of these varying knowledge components often inhibits effective application of the skill. For instance, detecting the bias of a newspaper or magazine differs considerably from detecting bias in a document such as a letter or speech or single article. While the procedure for detecting bias is generally the same in both instances, the clues one looks for differ because of differences in the media. In a newspaper, for instance, position on a page, size of the headline, and type of graphics associated with the articles are critical clues to bias, often moreso than the kinds of language used within any article. Unless one knows that these clues are important to look for in this instance, using this analytical skill may not be as productive as it otherwise could be.

Thinking skills and strategies are also very much shaped by the subject matter, disciplines, or content with which they are used.[5] Classifying biology data differs significantly from classifying historical data or parts of speech, not so much in the procedure employed as in the kinds of category systems most likely to yield useful insights about these different bodies of content. Knowledge of appropriate category systems in these instances is influenced more by knowledge of subject matter than by knowledge of the skill itself.

Thinking operations often fail to transfer for yet another reason. Many students fail to learn the cues that make use of a particular skill appropriate to different situations. Part of teaching and learning thinking operations involves identifying those cues or signals in a wide variety of situations that call for using particular skills or strategies. Again, this is essentially a matter of knowledge or information. In learning a thinking skill or strategy, students should explicitly deal with those elements in a number of settings that call for the use of the thinking skill or strategy they seek to master.

No thinking operation remains static, in the form in which it was initially used or learned. Like virtually all skills, thinking skills and strategies—or knowledge of and proficiencies in applying them—change and develop over time as individuals become more experienced in using them for a variety of purposes in a variety of contexts. In order to understand the utility of any particular thinking skill or strategy in a number of contexts, students must have generalized and elaborated its attributes. Generalizing a skill consists essentially of taking it beyond the specific parameters of the setting in which it was initially experienced.

As students apply a newly learned thinking skill or strategy, with reflection, to a number of new settings, they elaborate its key attributes. That is, they add to their knowledge of the cues that call it into use, of the criteria it might employ, of rules or principles specific to certain kinds of data, or even of certain procedural features to which one must attend under certain special circumstances. Elaborating thinking operations beyond their initial attributes helps students to understand some of the more complicated nuances of these operations, those not dealt with in the initial stages of learning these operations. As individuals elaborate a new skill or strategy, they begin to generalize its key attributes beyond specific cases or contexts to classes and categories of contexts. Those thinking operations most thoroughly generalized and elaborated are most likely the ones students can and will transfer on their own.

Teaching thinking skills and strategies to transfer thus involves showing students (1) how to apply these operations in a variety of contexts—personal life experience contexts as well as academic subjects, (2) why it is appropriate to do so, and (3) the cues signaling that use of these operations is appropriate. To accomplish this, the thinking skill or strategy needs to be applied in new contexts where students can be introduced to attributes of it with which they are as yet unfamiliar.[6] Furthermore, this "reintroduction" needs to be followed by guided practice in applying the elaborated version of the operation in each of these new contexts and forms, and then by opportunities for its independent application in a number of different contexts. In effect, this instructional sequence repeats the first three stages of the skill teaching framework presented in Chapter 3. Every time a previously introduced and practiced thinking skill or strategy is to be transferred, or elaborated, either in terms of its application or its attributes, it must be reintroduced, receive guided practice, and have independent practice in its new context or form.

Transferring and Elaborating

Teachers can launch their efforts to help students develop facility in transferring a thinking skill or strategy by conducting a single thirty to forty minute lesson similar to that used to introduce it. The strategies useful in introducing a new thinking skill—as illustrated in Chapters 4 and 5—can easily be adapted for organizing such a lesson. All that is required is to add a new step early in each strategy, a step in which teacher and students review what they already know about the skill *before* they apply it in a new context or explore new attributes. For example, the inductive introductory strategy, as described in Chapter 4, consisted of these five steps:

Introduce

Execute

Reflect

Apply

Review

In following these steps, students can begin to articulate a beginning version of any thinking skill. However, by adding a *review* step between introducing and executing of the skill, this same strategy allows students to go over what they know about the skill in one context before they try to apply it in a new setting or add new attributes to it. Thus, an inductive strategy for initiating elaboration or transfer of a previously introduced thinking skill becomes:

1. Introduce
2. *Review*
3. Execute
4. Reflect
5. Apply
6. Review

By carrying out each of these *six* steps, students can begin to learn new aspects or applications of a thinking skill or strategy to which they have been introduced earlier.

The *review* step added to this transfer/elaboration teaching strategy consists essentially of three tasks:

1. Students recall attributes of the skill or strategy as learned thus far, including:
   • its procedure
   • rules used
   • useful information about it.

2. Students describe how to execute the operation.
3. Students identify potential obstacles to smooth operation of the skill and possible ways to overcome the obstacles.

By having students complete this review before attempting to transfer or elaborate a previously introduced thinking operation, a teacher can help students develop the referents and set needed to facilitate such additional learning.[7]

Figure 7.1 outlines in some detail how the inductive skill introducing strategy described in Chapter 4 works when modified to initiate transfer or elaboration of any thinking operation. This outline may be used as a guide for preparing lessons to launch any such effort with any previously introduced thinking skill or strategy. The essential difference between this version of the inductive strategy and the original version, it should be noted again, is simply the addition of a new second step wherein students review what they already know about the operation being used *before* they apply it or receive new information about it.

The directive and developmental strategies for introducing a thinking operation may also be altered, just as the inductive introductory strategy has been altered, for use in initiating the transfer or elaboration of any thinking skill or strategy. Figures 7.2 and 7.3 outline both strategies modified by the inclusion of the new step of *review*. Like the outlines of similar skill teaching strategies in this book, these outlines, too, may be used to prepare or conduct lessons to initiate transfer or elaboration of any thinking operation.

It seems unnecessary to illustrate the use of all these skill transfer/elaboration strategies here. However, the following brief explanation of how one of them might work in practice will clarify how all three can be successfully employed. A lesson using the directive strategy for transferring/elaborating a skill may best serve this purpose.

Suppose, as a continuation of the lessons on the skill of classifying used in the preceding chapters, an American history teacher wished to help students transfer this skill from use with written data to use with another medium. By this time in this history course, students may be studying the period midway between the War of 1812 and the Civil War, a period known to historians as the Middle Period! Numerous paintings by many famous artists of the period are available and can be used to develop insights into this period of America's past. Working with these paintings also offers an excellent opportunity to apply the skill of classifying, which the students, as a result of their preceding skill lessons, have generally mastered when applied to written data. A lesson initiating the transfer of this skill to a new medium is thus most appropriate at this point.

After establishing the subject-matter context of this lesson, the teacher can pose a significant question about America in the Middle Period and then point out that some paintings displayed at the front of the room or in

STEP 1 *INTRODUCE THE SKILL*

State that "learning" the skill is today's objective.
Give the skill label/name.
Give synonyms.
State a tentative/working definition..
State ways the skill can be or has been used:

  • in students' personal experiences,
  • in school activities,
  • in this course.

Explain how the skill is useful and why it's worth learning.

STEP 2 *REVIEW THE SKILL*

Students recall attributes of the skill as learned thus far:

  • operations,
  • rules used,
  • useful information about the skill.

Students describe how to execute the skill.
Students identify potential obstacles to smooth operation of the skill and
  ways to resolve the obstacles.

STEP 3 *EXECUTE THE SKILL—DO IT*

Use the skill (as best one can) to accomplish a task.
Work in pairs, in triads, or groups.
Use subject matter familiar to the students and appropriate to the course (or,
  if necessary, from students' experience).

STEP 4 *REFLECT ON WHAT WAS DONE*

Report what went on in students' heads as they engaged in the skill.
Identify the steps/rules used and sequence of each.
Clarify the procedure or any criteria used.
Focus on the skill and its attributes.

STEP 5 *APPLY SKILL TO NEW DATA*

Use what has been discussed about the skill to complete a second task.
Work in pairs, triads, or groups.
Use subject matter appropriate to the course and familiar to the students and
  in same structure and media as in Step 3.

STEP 6 *REVIEW THE SKILL*

Report on what students did in their heads as they applied the skill.
Review the steps/procedures that seem to constitute the skill.
Review the rules that direct use of the skill as well as when it is to be used.
State the relationship of this skill to other skills.
Review or revise the skill definition.
State where the skill can be used in personal or out-of-school situations.

Figure 7.1 An Inductive Strategy for Initiating Transfer/Elaboration of a Thinking
Skill or Strategy

STEP 1 *INTRODUCE THE SKILL*

    State that "learning" the skill is today's objective.
    Give the skill label/name.
    Give synonyms.
    State a tentative/working definition.
    State ways the skill can be or has been used:

        • in students' personal experience,
        • in school activities,
        • in this course.

    Explain how the skill is useful and why it's worth learning.

STEP 2 *REVIEW THE SKILL*

    Students recall attributes of the skill as learned thus far:

        • operations,
        • rules used,
        • useful information about the skill.

    Students describe how to execute the skill.
    Students identify potential obstacles to smooth operation of the skill and ways
        to resolve the obstacles.

STEP 3 *EXPLAIN THE SKILL*

    State any new procedures constituting the skill in step-by-step sequence,
        explaining what one does and why for each step.
    State new rules and "things to know" about the skill.

STEP 4 *DEMONSTRATE THE SKILL*

    Lead the class step-by-step through the skill:

        • state the goal,
        • refer to each step in the procedure,
        • give reasons for doing each step.

    Show how the rules are carried out.
    Use subject matter familiar to the students.

STEP 5 *REVIEW WHAT WAS DONE*

    Review the procedures and rules.
    Review the reasons for each (as illustrated in the demonstration).

STEP 6 *APPLY THE SKILL*

    Execute the skill with teacher guidance.
    Work in pairs, triads, or groups.
    Complete material used in demonstration or use new but same kind of
        data/media.
    Use course subject matter familiar to students but in same structure and
        media as in Step 4.

STEP 7 *REFLECT ON THE SKILL*

    Review the steps comprising the skill and the rules guiding its use.
    Reflect on ways in which the skill is used and when it is appropriate to use.
    State the relationship of this skill to other skills.
    Review or revise skill definition.
    State where the skill can be used in:

        • personal or out-of-school situations,
        • coursework.

Figure 7.2 A Directive Strategy for Initiating Transfer/Elaboration of a Thinking Skill or Strategy

STEP 1 *INTRODUCE THE SKILL*

State that "learning" the skill is today's objective.
Give the skill label/name.
Give synonyms.
State a tentative/working definition.
State ways the skill can be or has been used:

- in students' personal experience,
- in school activities,
- in this course.

Explain how the skill is useful and why it's worth learning.

STEP 2 *REVIEW THE SKILL*

Students recall attributes of the skill as learned thus far:

- operations,
- rules used,
- useful information about the skill.

Students describe how to execute the skill.
Students identify potential obstacles to smooth operation of the skill and ways
  to resolve the obstacles.

STEP 3 *EXECUTE THE SKILL—DO IT*

Use the skill (as best one can) to accomplish a task.
Work in pairs or in groups.
Use subject matter appropriate to course and familiar to the students.

STEP 4 *REFLECT ON WHAT WAS DONE*

Report what went on in students' heads as they engaged in the skill.
Identify the steps and rules used and their sequence.
Clarify operations or any criteria used.
Focus on the skill and its attributes.

STEP 5 *EXPLAIN/DEMONSTRATE*

State any key operations or key rules omitted or misapplied by students.
Give reasons for using these operations or rules.
Demonstrate application of these operations or rules, explaining how and why
  each is used.

STEP 6 *APPLY THE SKILL TO NEW DATA*

Use the teacher-introduced operations and rules with student descriptions of
  the skill to complete another task.
Students work in pairs or groups.
Use subject matter familiar to the students and appropriate to course but in
  same structure and media as in Step 3.

STEP 7 *REVIEW THE SKILL*

Report on what was done in students' heads as they applied the skill.
Review the operations and rules that seem to constitute the skill.
State the relationship of this skill to other skills.
Review or revise the skill definition.
State where the skill can be used in

- personal or out-of-school situations,
- coursework.

Figure 7.3 A Developmental Strategy for Initiating Transfer/Elaboration of a
Thinking Skill or Strategy

170

a text can be used to help answer this question. The skill of classifying can be used to help make sense of these paintings as they might apply to the question at hand. So, to launch this transfer lesson, the teacher can (Step 1) *introduce* this skill. Because students have been practicing this operation for some time, they will be relatively quick to provide synonyms, a working definition, and examples of how or where this skill has been used previously, outside of class as well as in. This same type of introduction launched the original introduction to the skill and many of the follow-up guided practice lessons in this skill. Like these introductions, this *re*introduction clearly establishes this skill as the major learning goal of this particular lesson while helping the students retrieve whatever they know about it so they can proceed to execute it with confidence.

However, before students try to apply this skill as they understand it to this new medium—paintings—they should *review* what they know about the skill already (Step 2), how to execute it, and any useful rules to follow. At this point, they can also predict any obstacles that might arise to its effective application and suggest ways to overcome these obstacles. This review of the skill is especially appropriate here because it focuses student attention on the basic procedure and rules constituting the skill; thus, it provides some guidance for executing it even in a new context. And by discussing obstacles that may arise in carrying out the skill and recalling or suggesting how to overcome them, students can be prepared for difficulties they may encounter in this new application.

Now the teacher can proceed to show students how to carry out this skill in a context in which they have not yet applied it. The teacher can point out and *explain* (Step 3) how this skill may have to be executed somewhat differently in applying it with a new medium. In this particular instance, the skill procedure remains essentially the same as when used with written data, but the features of the new medium to be classified—paintings—differ. Certainly the students can classify paintings in terms of their "content"—the kinds of people depicted, the landscapes, buildings, and so on—essentially the same type of attributes useful in dealing with words used in earlier classifying lessons. But paintings have their own attributes that also can be used to form categories, attributes related to composition, the use of color and perspective, figure-ground relationships, texture, and so on. Becoming aware of these aspects of the new medium will help students execute this skill better than if they remained ignorant of them. And so the teacher needs to explain some of these things about painting that will enable students to classify paintings more effectively. *Demonstrating* with some paintings (Step 4) exactly how one could classify these paintings, using such domain-specific knowledge, can alert students to the ways this information can shape the skill's execution.

After briefly *reviewing* (Step 5) key steps in classifying and any rules to follow in carrying out these steps, students can then classify additional paintings to answer the question at hand (Step 6). When finished, they can *reflect* (Step 7) on and report what they did in their heads as they adapted their understanding of the skill of classifying to this new situation. A revised description of important steps in executing the skill can be listed for all to copy, or several different descriptions may be listed. Any new rules "discovered" in the process may also be discussed and recorded, as may information about paintings that affect the use of this skill with them. Problems or obstacles seemingly peculiar to applying this skill with paintings can be explored, too. To conclude the lesson, students and teacher can then generalize about the skill and about those context cues, both written and visual, that may shape its execution. By so doing, students can begin to broaden their awareness of where this skill can be applied and how it might work in another setting. Follow-up guided practice in applying this skill with additional paintings and other visuals will further generalize the skill and facilitate its transfer to still other settings later.

Figure 7.4 presents a lesson plan employing the directive transfer/elaboration strategy illustrated by the preceding lesson description. This lesson plan incorporates the essential features of the strategy outlined in Figure 7.2. Interestingly, this directive strategy for initiating transfer or elaboration of a previously introduced thinking operation proves extremely effective, especially for average to below-average students.[8] Many of these students find it frustrating and extremely difficult to "discover" inductively time after time how a particular skill can be successfully applied in a new context or with new data sets. Other, more able or experienced students also seem to prefer lessons employing this strategy at this point in learning a thinking operation; many of them, too, resent being asked continually to "discover" or invent everything they are expected to learn. In elaborating a skill, students seem to be more attentive and motivated when new attributes of the skill are explained and demonstrated or when the teacher demonstrates at the beginning the nuances of executing it in a new context. Even in applying the skill as demonstrated, the students often begin to adapt it so that such a presentation does not necessarily lead simply to mimicking or copying someone else's way of doing it.

As do the other skill introducing strategies presented here, these strategies initiating transfer incorporate attributes of effective skill teaching and learning explained in Chapter 5. Each of these three transfer/elaboration strategies keeps the focus of the lesson strictly on the skill being used; subject-matter products of this skill use can be the subject of the lesson immediately following. Each strategy includes modeling the new attributes of the skill: in the inductive strategy by "expert" students—in the other two by the teacher or other "experts." In each strategy students are given opportunities to see and hear the new attributes of

TRANSFERRING/ELABORATING A SKILL

GOAL: To initiate transfer of the skill of classifying.

OBJECTIVES:

    To state in correct order the main steps in a procedure for classifying data.

    To list at least three rules to follow in classifying paintings.

    To apply the skill of classifying to state two features of a given set of paintings.

MATERIALS:

    Three sets of paintings (six each).

TEACHER	STUDENTS
1. Relate this lesson to the preceding lesson. What do these paintings suggest about American culture in the Middle Period?	
2. We can classify these paintings into different categories to answer this question.	
Introduce	
3. Write *classify* on the board.	
4. Ask for synonyms.	categorize, sort, group
5. Ask for definition of *classify*.	to put like things together
6. Ask for or give examples of things already classified:	
• in out-of-school life,	newspaper sections types of cars seasonal clothing
• in this course to date.	lists of explorers life in the 1750s laws favored by different sections
Review	
7. Go over one or two procedures for classifying data—focus on steps and rules to follow *Procedures*:	One procedure: 1. State the purpose of classifying. 2. Scan the data. 3. Find two items that have the same feature. 4. State the common feature as a label for these two. 5. Find all other data that fit under this label. 6. Repeat Steps 3–5 until all data are in groups. 7. Combine or subdivide groups.

Figure 7.4 A Directive Lesson Plan for Initiating Transfer/Elaboration of the Skill of Classifying

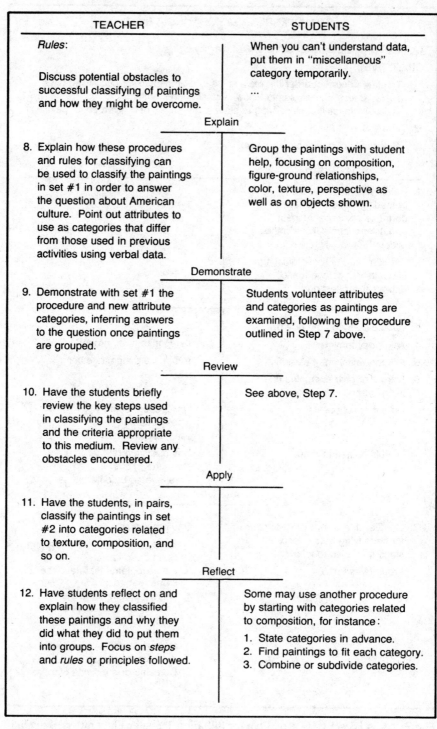

TEACHER	STUDENTS
Rules: Discuss potential obstacles to successful classifying of paintings and how they might be overcome.	When you can't understand data, put them in "miscellaneous" category temporarily. ...

Explain

8. Explain how these procedures and rules for classifying can be used to classify the paintings in set #1 in order to answer the question about American culture. Point out attributes to use as categories that differ from those used in previous activities using verbal data.	Group the paintings with student help, focusing on composition, figure-ground relationships, color, texture, perspective as well as on objects shown.

Demonstrate

9. Demonstrate with set #1 the procedure and new attribute categories, inferring answers to the question once paintings are grouped.	Students volunteer attributes and categories as paintings are examined, following the procedure outlined in Step 7 above.

Review

10. Have the students briefly review the key steps used in classifying the paintings and the criteria appropriate to this medium. Review any obstacles encountered.	See above, Step 7.

Apply

11. Have the students, in pairs, classify the paintings in set #2 into categories related to texture, composition, and so on.	

Reflect

12. Have students reflect on and explain how they classified these paintings and why they did what they did to put them into groups. Focus on *steps* and *rules* or principles followed.	Some may use another procedure by starting with categories related to composition, for instance: 1. State categories in advance. 2. Find paintings to fit each category. 3. Combine or subdivide categories.

Figure 7.4 *(continued)*

TEACHER	STUDENTS
13. Review steps in different procedures, any rules followed, types of categories that prove useful ...	
14. Suggest other kinds of media with which this skill can be used and unique criteria that need to be applied.	

Figure 7.4 *(continued)*

the skill articulated and to discuss what they did in their minds as they executed the skill. And each strategy provides for a second application of the skill immediately following discussion of how to make the skill work in the new setting or form. If properly used, each strategy also concludes with attention to transfer—to where else the skill has been or might be employed.[9] Figure 7.5 summarizes the three different strategies presented here for reintroducing a thinking skill to initiate transfer or elaboration of that skill. Using one of these strategies enables teachers in a single thirty to forty minute lesson to launch transfer of a thinking skill or strategy learned in one context to another context and thus begin to help students elaborate or generalize it.

As noted above, the key ingredient in the strategies presented here for launching transfer or elaboration of a skill is the review (Step 2) of what the students know about the skill *before* they attempt to adapt it to a new setting or task or receive a demonstration and explanation of how to make the adaptation. This attention to the key attributes of the skill on the part of the students *before* they consider any modifications in its attributes or use not only makes them more confident of their ability to execute the skill but also helps them recall and make conscious the key operations they can use in employing the skill. This step, in effect, provides a starting place for modifying the skill. These strategies are a natural extension of the strategies previously used by the teacher to introduce any thinking skill or strategy.

Guided Practice

To complete the transfer of a skill to a newly introduced context or to assimilate the newly introduced or refined attributes of a thinking operation requires frequent, repeated, guided practice.[10] Initial practice of the operation in its elaborated form or new context must be accompanied by

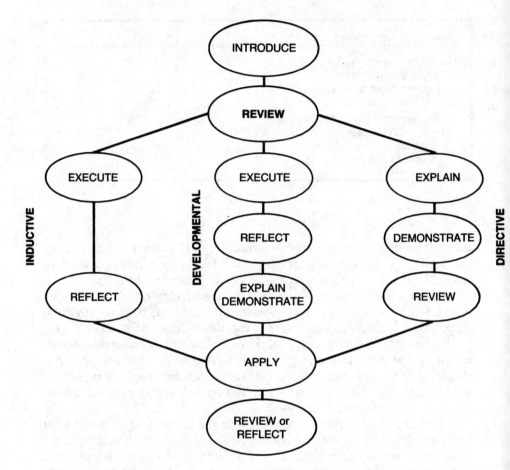

Figure 7.5 Strategies for Initiating Transfer or Elaboration of a Thinking Skill

instruction and guidance. Teachers can use the general strategy for guided practice described in Chapter 6 to conduct these lessons and can carry out the strategy exactly as described there. This strategy, it will be recalled, involves (1) introducing the operation just as in each teaching strategy described here, (2) previewing how to execute it, (3) applying the operation, having students monitor their work as they proceed, and (4) having students review how they executed the operation. A good portion of any lesson using this strategy, it should also be remembered, can then be devoted to the subject to which the thinking skill or strategy has been applied. As with any new thinking skill, students may need three or four or even more of these guided practice lessons in order to achieve some degree of competence in this new form or application of the skill.

Autonomous Practice and Application

As students demonstrate increasing proficiency in executing a thinking skill or strategy in its elaborated form or new context, the amount of instruction and guidance can be reduced. After two or three guided practice lessons in the operation using all steps in this teaching strategy, the teacher might shorten, then drop, the preview step. Then, after several more practice lessons in it, the review step could be shortened, then dropped, with only the introduction and active monitoring of the skill as it is used serving as guidance. As students approach the desired level of proficiency, the teacher might even intersperse practice lessons in using the skill being learned in its original form or setting with continued but autonomous practice in the skill as elaborated. Eventually, students should get to the point of being able to execute the skill in its new form without any guidance or instruction at all.

Independent application of any thinking operation in many contexts is an important part of teaching a skill to transfer. In mastering a thinking skill or strategy, students must make decisions about which operations to use and under what conditions. At this final stage in the teaching of thinking, students need frequent opportunities to consider applying the operations being learned to a variety of contexts, some of which may not require using the operations and some of which may require using a number of other skills and strategies as well. Repeated practice in "exercises" obviously requiring use of the same skill is not enough to help students generalize and transfer a skill. For any thinking operation to become an integral part of a student's repertoire, students must have practice, with and without guidance, in deciding whether or not it is appropriate to use the operation in different contexts, as well as practice in actually applying the skill in these contexts.[11]

Teaching thinking operations to transfer is, thus, not something that can be completed in one lesson or probably even in one course. Rather, it requires attention over a sequence of lessons and courses. To help students transfer or elaborate a skill or strategy even into settings similar to that in which it was introduced requires repeated guidance in these settings. Thus, a skill like detecting bias in data, if introduced in a language arts context, needs to be elaborated by guided practice in social studies, journalism, science, and other settings. When initially teaching a thinking skill, a teacher must help students become aware of the cues they can look for in related settings that will call out the skill. In courses where students encounter these settings, teachers must also alert students to the presence of these cues as they provide reinforcement, transfer, and elaboration of the thinking skill introduced earlier.

To teach for "high road" transfer, teachers should help students generalize consciously and deliberately from the context in which the skill or strategy was originally developed, the cues and attributes of settings where the operation may be appropriately used. This can be accomplished by explicitly reintroducing the operation in such settings and providing instruction and guidance in how to apply it in some of these settings, by teaching generalized cues to such settings, and by showing students—and by giving them practice—in how to predict and monitor the application of the operation in novel settings. Teachers in a variety of subject areas thus need to combine efforts in introducing a thinking skill, teaching it to some degree of proficiency and then elaborating it in and transferring it to differing settings and to more sophisticated levels of operation.

TEACHING THINKING SKILLS AND STRATEGIES

It takes more than a single lesson to "teach" any thinking skill or strategy to some degree of proficiency. In order for students to become proficient in a thinking operation, they must have repeated, instructive practice in it in a variety of contexts and media. Chapter 3 outlines one useful framework for teaching thinking operations in this manner. Teachers seeking to help students become proficient in any thinking operation—whether it be problem solving, syllogistic reasoning, decision making, analyzing for bias, or any other similar operation—can organize their teaching over a semester, year, or sequence of semesters to provide such lessons in that operation. Figure 7.6 outlines the six stages in this framework and summarizes some of major teaching strategies for use in each of these six stages. Mastery of these strategies and their use at appropriate points in teaching a thinking operation can lead to the highest possible degree of student proficiency in thinking.

Applying the Skill Teaching Framework

A social studies teacher responsible for teaching the skill of classifying can, for example, use this framework to plan a sequence of lessons in this skill that can help students become proficient in it. There can be, first, an introductory lesson early in the course where the subject matter lends itself to classifying data—as when the students have many explorers or colonies to learn about. Such a lesson might employ one of the strategies presented in Chapter 4 and 5. Guided practice lessons could follow at appropriate intervals and at places where there are data that can be classified (as in the kinds of laws governing life in the colonies, battles in the Revolution, people on different sides of the independence question, reasons for moving westward into the Louisiana Purchase territory and so on) until students evidence some ability to execute the skill rapidly and

INTRODUCING			TRANSFERRING/ELABORATING		
INTRODUCTION	GUIDED PRACTICE	APPLICATION	REINTRODUCTION	GUIDED PRACTICE	AUTONOMOUS USE

Inductive
Introduce
Execute
Reflect
Apply
Review
 	
Directive
Introduce
Explain
Demonstrate
Review
Apply
Reflect
 	
Developmental
Introduce
Execute
Reflect
Explain/Demonstrate
Apply
Review
	General
	Introduce
	Preview
	Apply/Monitor
	Review
		Activity or ditto
		  work sheets
		Answering textbook
		  questions
		Teacher-asked
		  questions
		Discovery or
		  inquiry teaching
		Classroom discus-
		  sion
		Debates
		Writing
		Challenging
		  assignments
		Student-asked
		  questions
			Inductive
			Introduce
			Review
			Execute
			Reflect
			Apply
			Review
			
			Directive
			Introduce
			Review
			Explain/Demonstrate
			Review
			Apply
			Reflect
			
			Developmental
			Introduce
			Review
			Execute
			Reflect
			Explain/Demonstrate
			Apply
			Review
				General
				Introduce
				Preview
				Apply/Monitor
				Review
					Activity or ditto
					  work sheets
					Answering textbook
					  questions
					Teacher-asked
					  questions
					Discovery or
					  inquiry teaching
					Classroom discus-
					  sion
					Debates
					Writing
					Challenging
					  assignments
					Student-asked
					  questions

Figure 7.6 Strategies for the Direct Teaching of Thinking

accurately on their own. The practice strategies presented in Chapter 6 would be appropriate for these lessons.

If introduced with written data, this skill could next be transferred and elaborated with data displayed in graphic form. A transfer lesson, using one of the strategies outlined in this chapter, would be required to help students see how to make the transfer. Such a lesson might use graphs depicting population distribution in the early national period, for example. Additional lessons offering guided practice in classifying graphically displayed data could then be scheduled for appropriate places, not too far apart from one another, in subsequent topics such as early elections, the development of new transportation routes, and so on. If the teacher wanted to introduce a new dimension of the skill such as the multivariable classification of data, another transfer lesson would be needed to help students understand how to do this. Several more lessons offering guided practice would then be required—perhaps using data relevant to pre-Civil War political and economic conditions. Finally, lessons requiring independent use of the skill of classifying could be provided for students to apply the skill on their own as they also apply other previously learned thinking skills and strategies. Figure 7.7 diagrams a sequence of lessons for teaching any skill through the various stages of the instructional framework as described here.

Regardless of the subject or grade level being taught, a teacher should remember that the teaching strategies and skill teaching framework outlined here can be employed spontaneously in the midst of any lesson or teaching process. Of course, specific skill teaching lessons can be planned in advance for use in any recitation or discussion or even discovery-teaching process at points where a teacher feels students will need to learn a new thinking operation. However, a teacher sensing, in the midst of any ongoing lesson or teaching process, that students are unable to execute a particular thinking skill needed at that point, can also interrupt the lesson or process to introduce the needed skill, using one of the skill introducing strategies described in Chapters 4 and 5. Once this introductory lesson has been conducted, the regular lesson can be resumed. Thereafter, the teacher can provide periodic guided practice, transfer, and elaboration of the skill as opportunities to use it arise in the context of the overall teaching process or subject matter, regardless of whether the process is built around questioning strategies, discussion—including dialogical discussion—recitation, or discovery/inquiry teaching. The skill teaching framework and direct teaching strategies presented in these pages can readily be infused on a pre-planned or spontaneous basis into any teaching process or subject or grade level to teach specific thinking skills and strategies.

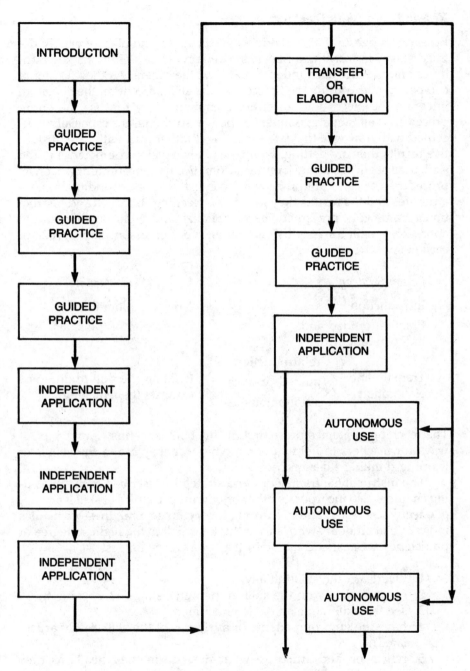

Figure 7.7 A Sequence of Lessons for Teaching a Thinking Skill or Strategy

Research and Skill Teaching

Research suggests that individuals go through a number of clearly defined stages in learning a new skill. Initially, they identify its key attributes and practice each independently of the others. As they feel more competent in executing the "pieces" of the skill procedure, they begin to integrate the pieces into an entire operation. They practice the entire procedure—all steps in sequence, but in so doing are especially concerned with how well they are executing it rather than with the substantive results they are getting. Finally, as they develop competence in the skill, they begin to execute it rather automatically, concentrating not on its procedures or rules but on how the context shapes or conditions these attributes and the results they get.[12] The teaching strategies and instructional framework presented there capitalize and build on this natural approach to skill learning by employing types of lessons appropriate to each stage:

Lesson Strategy	*Stage of Skill Learning*
Introduction	Novice exploration
Practice, guided and independent	Integration of the skill
Transfer and elaboration $\Big\langle$ reintroduction, guided practice, autonomous use $\Big\rangle$	Relating the skill to different contexts (generalizing)

The teaching strategies presented in this book are thus simply explicit ways for teachers to help students wherever they are in the stages of learning thinking skills and strategies.

The instructional framework and strategies described in the preceding chapters also incorporate other important principles of skill learning, of effective teaching, and of learning theory. In general, these principles indicate that students who learn a thinking skill to the highest degree of proficiency soonest and maintain that proficiency longest:

1. Overlearn the skill initially,
2. focus explicitly on the skill in the initial stages of learning it,
3. see the skill modeled or demonstrated,
4. have the key components or attributes of the skill clearly articulated,
5. reflect on and articulate what they do in their heads as they execute the skill,
6. engage in frequent, intermittently spaced, guided practice requiring small chunks of time and providing immediate instructive feedback, and

7. transfer and elaborate the skill, with instructional guidance and autonomous practice to contexts (data or media) other than that in which it was initially introduced and practiced.[13]

The direct teaching of thinking incorporates these principles into continuing classroom instruction. Research suggests that, to maximize results, such instruction should come at a time when students recognize a need to learn the thinking operations in order to accomplish subject matter-related objectives.[14] However, just because one has not yet formally introduced a thinking operation to students does not mean that they cannot be expected to engage in it. Even the youngest students can evaluate or infer simple relationships or engage in most cognitive operations, not as well as experts obviously, but well enough to get on for the time being. But they usually skip or ignore important steps and rules that experts have found to be of critical importance to effective use of these skills or strategies.[15] Instruction in thinking skills and strategies seeks to introduce and teach these operations and rules and to help students learn how to employ them effectively in a variety of settings. Such instruction is best initiated when students are ready for it and when they perceive that mastering the operation is useful for accomplishing a substantive or personal objective. Subject-matter courses offer excellent arenas for such skill teaching.

Subject Matter and Thinking Skill Teaching

The subject matter in which a thinking operation is introduced and initially practiced is important for reasons other than motivation. Thinking skills and strategies often differ in their execution depending on the subject matter to which they are applied. Usually these differences lie in the subject-related knowledge used in executing the skill, but occasionally the skill itself is modified as it is applied to different bodies of content. Subject matter informs how thinking skills and strategies are applied and serves as a vehicle for learning and practicing these operations. Thus, tying thinking operations to specific subject-matter contexts not only enhances subject-matter learning but also develops facility in skill use.[16]

It should be noted here that the subject matter selected for teaching a skill can, in effect, hinder as well as enhance skill learning. If too much content is provided, students and teacher usually get sidetracked into covering the content instead of keeping their focus on the skill. Attention to content rather than skills also usually results when the subject matter is complex, or terribly new, or charged with emotion. If the subject matter used to initiate instruction in thinking skills and strategies is not in the same form that students have been using with the skill up to that point, this, too, can detract from skill learning. Being familiar with the content enables students to focus exclusively on the thinking operation being taught. This reduces interference and promotes learning the skill. For best results in terms of skill learning, the subject matter of an introductory or guided practice lesson must be short, relatively straightforward and uncomplicated, and in the same form as in preceding lessons.[17]

During the introduction of a thinking skill or strategy the information or subject matter used should not be gathered by the students as part of the lesson itself. Data gathering is a skill of its own. Data for use in learning other skills should either be provided by the teacher or gathered by students in the preceding class or for homework prior to the class. Thus, if a teacher wanted students to produce the list of items that would be classified in a lesson introducing the skill of classifying, these items should be brainstormed or copied from texts the day or lesson before this introduction. If a teacher foresees student difficulty with terms or words to be used in a skill lesson, the teacher should provide definitions for them, or the students should search out such definitions in the lesson preceding the use of these terms or phrases. The flow from introduction to application and discussion of a new skill in an introductory lesson should not be interrupted by the use of other new skills.

Moreover, in the initial stages of learning a new skill the examples relevant to the skill ought to be relatively obvious. More subtle, less obvious examples are appropriate only after students have developed some degree of proficiency and confidence in executing the skill. For instance, in introducing the skill of analyzing to identify unstated assumptions, several examples of these assumptions should fairly leap from the page or other media used. More subtle or complicated examples can be used at later stages in teaching the skill.[18]

It is not always advisable to step out of the subject matter of a course for subject matter with which to introduce a new skill. Certainly, using content from a student's life experience or from a school event experienced by all students in a class is useful at times to introduce a skill because use of such familiar content then allows students to focus on the unfamiliar skill as much as possible. But consistent introduction of a skill using non-course-related matter merely gives the impression that one cannot use this skill in the subject. Such practice also leads to problems with transfer. Generally, it is possible to introduce a skill using the subject matter of the course in which the skill is to be introduced and advisable to do so, in part, because this enhances motivation for learning the skill. More importantly, this procedure maintains the subject-matter continuity of the course and advances the learning of the subject while facilitating the introduction of the skill.

The way in which students execute a thinking skill or strategy, especially in their initial tries with it, often shapes the effectiveness of such teaching. Experience suggests that it is best to have students apply a skill for the first few times with a partner, as part of a triad, or in a small group. Such arrangements minimize student risk, encourage peer teaching and learning, and help students to improve thinking about and articulating their thinking.

Common Problems in Teaching Thinking Skills

The direct teaching of thinking is not always easily launched. Problems occasionally crop up, especially for those just learning the skill teaching framework and strategies presented here. However, these problems, inherent in the task of learning any new approach to teaching, can be overcome with patience and reflective practice. The following discussion of several common problems may alert teachers to them and thus eliminate them as obstacles to effective teaching of thinking.

Some problems are essentially teaching problems, such as failing to carry a lesson through all its major steps. This failure detracts from the value of any thinking skill lesson, especially the failure to include a final review of what the students have learned about the skill being studied and an effort to bridge or set a skill up for transfer to other settings. However tempting, it is not useful to conclude a class by telling students, "Today, class, we learned . . .!" No teacher knows conclusively what was learned. Students do, and they should report it. If they can't report anything, that in itself is a powerful clue to the impression made on them by the lesson—and an indicator of what should be done, or redone, better in the next lesson!

Slipping from focus on the skill being taught into discussion of subject matter for the sake of learning subject matter is also a common problem for teachers. It is a natural slip. But in the initial stages of skill teaching and learning, focus must stay as explicitly and deliberately as possible on the skill being introduced. Discussion of substantive insights or products produced by the use of the skill can come in the next lesson, if the skill lesson is an introductory lesson, or after the students have reviewed the skill in a guided practice lesson.

This problem often arises out of a well-intentioned effort to fit the skill lesson into something that the teacher wants to do with the strategy or lesson as a whole. Because of conventional teaching assumptions, there is a tendency in teaching a thinking operation to forget that *the thinking operation* is, in fact, the subject matter of the lesson—at least in the introductory, guided practice and transfer lessons. These lessons should focus explicitly on the skill. They should have no other major goal. Teachers need to exercise special caution to ensure that in lessons teaching any thinking operation to the stage of independent use they keep the focus explicitly, directly, and continuously on the skill.

Failing to distinguish student descriptions of the physical actions in which they engage while thinking—listing data, writing a conclusion, and so on—from their descriptions of cognitive acts is another common, but natural, problem in teaching thinking. Too often teachers accept descriptions of physical behaviors rather than thinking behaviors in discussing with students what they do in their heads as they engage in a thinking skill or strategy. While understandable and quite acceptable for elementary age students or complete novices, such descriptions offered by average students at the middle school ages and beyond are not useful in developing thinking.

This particular problem often results from other problems arising in the course of teaching that relate more to teacher knowledge of the skills being taught than to proficiency in teaching methods or strategies. One of these problems arises from teachers not understanding the attributes of the skills they are asked to teach. Few teachers have studied thinking skills in any depth; few, if any, have ever taken a college or inservice course in thinking; few have engaged in appropriate self-study in informal logic, problem solving, decision making, conceptualization, or any other cognitive skills of significance. The wide range of terminology found in thinking skills literature and training programs compounds this situation. Many teacher, thus, do not know whether a procedure they are trying to teach is a reasonably accurate or complete description of the thinking operation or not.

What teachers know about the thinking skills they are trying to teach is as important to effective teaching and learning of these skills as is knowledge and mastery of strategies appropriate to this task. Chapters 1 and 2 addressed these important aspects of thinking skills and strategies selected for teaching.

Guidelines for the Teaching of Thinking

Problems such as the above can be eliminated—or their effects ameliorated—by observing the following guidelines for the teaching of any or all thinking skills and strategies:

1. Start with a simplified version of the skill and build it gradually in subsequent semesters or courses.
2. Minimize interference from subject matter, emotion, and other skills; keep the focus on the skill.
3. Teach for metacognition; help students think about their own thinking.
4. Maximize generalizability of the skill; teach for transfer.
5. Keep the content used—at least initially—short and simple.
6. Clarify the attributes of the skill and their interrelationships.
7. Model the skill and explain what is being done and why.

8. Introduce instruction in a skill when it is needed to achieve a subject-matter objective.
9. Teach specific skills in the context of major thinking processes or strategies in order to give these skills functional meaning and purpose.[19]

Teaching thinking skills, in sum, to be most effective, should be direct, purposeful, and developmental. For each major skill or strategy teachers should provide lessons that move from introduction through guided practice to independent use and then through elaboration and more guided practice to autonomous use. At most of these stages, teachers should employ strategies that teach rather than that simply exercise the skill. Such teaching can use subject matter as a vehicle for learning the skill—and can use application of the skill to learn more about subject matter. Teaching thinking skills and a subject should complement each other. Finally, skills should build on one another, each growing out of previously learned skills and each setting up more complex skills and strategies. From a simple introduction to a basic, unrefined version of a skill, instruction should provide increasingly more sophisticated understanding of the skill. It should also move from teacher-directed explicit attention to the skill to student-initiated and directed autonomous use of the skill. Learning a thinking skill should not be treated as an end in itself. It is when a skill is used to construct new meaning, find new relationships, or invent new insights that is has proved worthwhile. The strategies and techniques suggested here serve to accomplish this goal.

SUMMARY

Improving student thinking takes more than practice. It requires teaching, too—a considerable amount of it. The most effective teaching of thinking consists of direct instruction in the major skills and strategies that constitute thinking and in the dispositions that support it. Direct instruction in thinking skills means, first and foremost, organizing skill learning through a sequence of lessons over an extended period of time. It also means employing teaching strategies that show students how to use these thinking operations and that provide instructive practice in and transfer of them.

Direct instruction in thinking skills also means two additional things. It means continued teaching for metacognition so that students can take conscious command of the skills they seek to employ when thinking. It also means teaching continuously the attitudes and values that support and motivate thinking. Without helping students take ownership of the thinking skills they are being taught, use of the teaching strategies and instructional framework presented here will fall short of its potential. Chapter 8 focuses on these two important aspects of all thinking skill lessons.

NOTES

1. John McPeck, *Critical Thinking and Education* (New York: St. Martin's Press, 1981), p. 78.

2. David N. Perkins, "Thinking Frames" (Paper delivered at ASCD Conference on Approaches to Teaching Thinking, Alexandria, Va., August 6, 1985), pp. 14–15.

3. Bryce B. Hudgins, *Learning and Thinking* (Itasca, Ill.: F.E. Peacock Publishers, 1977), pp. 142–172; Herbert J. Klausmeier and J. Kent Davis, "Transfer of Learning," *Encyclopedia of Educational Research* (New York: Macmillan, 1969), pp. 1483–1495; Robert J. Sternberg, "How Can We Teach Intelligence?" *Educational Leadership* 42:1 (September 1984), p. 52.

4. Neil Postman, "Critical Thinking in the Electronic Era," *National Forum* 65:1 (Winter 1985), pp. 4–8, 17.

5. McPeck, *Critical Thinking*; Edward Feigenbaum and Pamela McCorduck, *The Fifth Generation: Artificial Intelligence and Japan's Computer Challenge to the World* (Reading, Mass.: Addison-Wesley Publishing Company, 1983), pp. 38, 56, 76–77; Walter Doyle, "Academic Work," *Review of Educational Research* 53:2 (Summer 1983), p. 168.

6. Doyle, "Academic Work," pp. 175–178; Hudgins, *Learning and Thinking*; Michael I. Posner and Steven W. Keele, "Skill Learning" in Robert M. W. Travers, ed., *Second Handook of Research on Teaching* (Chicago: Rand McNally College Publishing Company, 1973), pp. 816–823.

7. Posner and Keele, "Skill Learning," pp. 809–811, 821–822.

8. Doyle, "Academic Work," pp. 175–178; Peter Martorella, "Cognition Research: Some Implications for the Design of Social Studies Instructional Materials," *Theory and Research in Social Education* 10:3 (Fall 1982), pp. 1–16.

9. Posner and Keele, "Skill Learning," pp. 805–831; Doyle, *op. cit.*, pp. 159–199; Sternberg, "How Can We . . .," pp. 38–50; Jane Stallings, "Effective Strategies for Teaching Basic Skills," in Daisy G. Wallace, *Developing Basic Skills Programs in Secondary Schools* (Alexandria, Va.: Association for Supervision and Curriculum Development, 1983), pp. 1–19.

10. Doyle, "Academic Work"; Posner and Keele, "Skill Learning"; Stallings, "Effective Strategies."

11. Carl Bereiter, "How to Keep Thinking Skills from Going the Way of All Frills," *Educational Leadership* 42:1 (September 1984), pp. 75–78.

12. Hubert L. Dreyfus, "Expert Systems Versus Intuitive Enterprise" (Paper delivered at George Mason University, Fairfax, Va., May 29, 1984).

13. Posner and Keele, "Skill Learning," pp. 805–831; Doyle, "Academic Work," pp. 159–199; Stallings, "Effective Strategies," pp. 1–19; Barak Rosenshine, "Teaching Functions in Instructional Programs," *Elementary School Journal* 83:4 (March 1983), pp. 335–353.

14. Carl Bereiter, "Elementary School: Necessity or Convenience?" *Elementary School Journal* 73:5 (May 1973), pp. 435–446.

15. David N. Perkins, "Thinking Frames," *Educational Leadership* 43:8 (May 1986), p. 8; Hudgins, *Learning and Thinking*; Sternberg, "How Can We. . . ."

16. McPeck, *Critical Thinking*.

17. Posner and Keele, "Skill Learning," pp. 805–831; Alan H. Schoenfeld, "Can Heuristics Be Taught?" in Jack Lochhead and John Clement, eds., *Cognitive Process Instruction* (Philadelphia: The Franklin Institute Press, 1979), pp. 335–336.

18. Schoenfeld, "Heuristics."

19. Doyle, "Academic Work"; Hudgins, *Learning and Thinking*; Posner and Keele, "Skill Learning"; Rosenshine, "Teaching Functions"; Stallings, "Effective Strategies"; Sternberg, "How Can We. . . ."; Norman Frederiksen, "Implications of Cognitive Theory for Instruction in Problem Solving," *Review of Educational Research* 54:3 (Fall 1984), pp. 363–407.

8

Helping Students
Control and Direct
Their Own Thinking

Those who are most effective at thinking are not simply skilled at the
various cognitive operations that constitute thinking. They also consciously direct their own thinking. Because the teaching of thinking seeks
to develop effective thinking, such teaching involves more than developing technical proficiency in a number of cognitive operations. It also
involves helping students become independent thinkers, proficient at
self-initiated and self-directed thinking. Consequently, the teaching of
thinking consists of teaching students to think about their own thinking,
consciously and deliberately, while engaged in thinking for functional
purposes. And it also consists of helping students develop those dispositions or habits that both support and drive skillful thinking. This chapter
focuses on these remaining two dimensions of the teaching of thinking.

TEACHING FOR METACOGNITION

Thinking becomes more effective and efficient when we think about how
we are thinking as we think! This thinking about thinking is called

metacognition. Metacognition consists of standing outside of one's head and directing how one is going about executing a thinking task. It involves planning how to carry out the task and carrying it out. It involves, in addition, monitoring one's progress, adjusting one's actions to the plan, and even revising both plan and actions in the process. Metacognition is difficult to learn and to execute because it involves thinking about how to accomplish a thinking task—tasks like resolving a problem, classifying data, creating a hypothesis and so on—while actually executing that thinking task. This, in effect, means doing two kinds of thinking at once. The ability to engage in metacognition thus develops slowly in individuals. However, because metacognition is so important to skillful thinking, most experts agree that any serious effort at teaching thinking skills must also help students develop their skills of thinking about thinking.[1]

Helping students think about their own thinking is one of the key ingredients in each of the introductory, guided practice and transfer/elaborating strategies for teaching thinking skills described in the preceding chapters. Each of these strategies explicitly attends to helping students reflect on, talk about, and hear others talk about what they do in their minds as they engage in the thinking skill or strategy they are learning. By repeated attention to the key operations which one could—and should—execute when thinking about his or her own thinking, teachers can help students develop the inclination and skills necessary to engage in metacognition whenever they have thinking tasks to perform.

The Nature of Metacognition

Some researchers describe metacognition as the highest, most sophisticated level of thinking.[2] Many conceive of it as the executive function of the mind, that function by which individuals manage and control how they go about using their minds.[3] Figure 8.1 identifies what is involved in the major metacognitive operations of planning, monitoring, and assessing. Although these operations may appear to be sequential, in practice they are not strictly linear but recursive. In executing any thinking skill or strategy, effective thinkers customarily start by planning how they will go about doing it and then continuously refer to that plan in carrying out the operation. Then, in executing the plan, they assess the extent to which the plan is working and may revise the plan or even perform unplanned operations as a result of this continuing assessment.[4] Teachers can use the key operations of metacognition described here as a structure or guide for helping students to think about their own thinking as they learn how to do it better.

Before jumping into a thinking task, effective thinkers plan just how they are going to carry it out and why they propose to do it that particular way. Such anticipatory thinking not only eases the actual execution of the

I. PLANNING

    Stating a goal
    Selecting operations to perform
    Sequencing operations
    Identifying potential obstacles/errors
    Identifying ways to recover from obstacles/errors
    Predicting results desired and/or anticipated

II. MONITORING

    Keeping the goal in mind
    Keeping one's place in a sequence
    Knowing when a subgoal has been achieved
    Deciding when to go on to the next operation
    Selecting next appropriate operation
    Spotting errors or obstacles
    Knowing how to recover from errors, overcome obstacles

III. ASSESSING

    Assessing goal achievement
    Judging accuracy and adequacy of the results
    Evaluating appropriateness of procedures used
    Assessing handling of obstacles/errors
    Judging efficiency of the plan and its execution

Figure 8.1 Key Operations in Metacognition

thinking operations employed but also makes it more likely to achieve the desired goal and to produce a substantive product of quality. Such planning usually involves three major tasks: setting a clear goal, laying out a strategy or plan for achieving that goal, and anticipating potential roadblocks to successful execution of the plan.

After stating and clarifying what needs to be accomplished—a goal—an individual selects the most appropriate thinking operations to perform—whether to identify the types of data needed, search for common characteristics in these data, or whatever—and then arranges these in a sequence that gives promise of accomplishing that goal. This operation usually includes attempts to identify any obstacles that may arise—such as the absence of some data that may be needed—or errors that could be made—and to plan right then how to overcome such obstacles or correct or avoid the errors. These acts require recalling past experience with the particular operations chosen or data to be used and predicting on the basis of similar past experiences. Finally, by predicting the desired and anticipated results of the plan, the individual can keep a focus on the goal in executing the thinking plan just devised.

In executing the plan that has been devised, the individual then consciously checks or monitors what he or she is doing mentally to ensure executing the task as envisioned, to avoid skipping or using incorrectly any steps or rules, and to see if the operations are producing the desired results. As educator Arthur L. Costa notes, monitoring thinking involves both looking backward to the plan and looking ahead to anticipate appropriate future moves.[5] It also requires attending very carefully to what is going on at the moment. Juggling all three types of operations requires considerable mental effort and involves, in effect, the ability to deal with different levels of abstractions.

Monitoring any act of thinking consists essentially of keeping one's place in a sequence of planned operations and applying criteria of effectiveness and accuracy to each procedure used. These operations help in assessing when a subgoal has been achieved and in deciding when it is appropriate to move on to the next procedure that carries out the thinking strategy. This involves recalling what has occurred thus far. The individual must also assess the reasonableness and accuracy of the results obtained as of the moment, as well as compare the current status of the act with similar efforts performed in the past and with results anticipated in the earlier planning of the process. Such mental manipulations do not come easily to novices.

All of this requires the individual continuously to keep the goal in mind—a forward-looking task—so as to anticipate what is likely to or should happen next. To do so one must recall the sequence of planned operations remaining to be used. One must also remain alert to possible obstacles and errors likely to be encountered down the line so as to minimize the likelihood they will crop up or be ready to handle them if they do occur. This means that the individual must be alert to feedback of various types and must know the kinds of information needed from it. In essence, monitoring a thinking act consists of being conscious of what one is doing, where it fits in a planned sequence of steps, and what ought to occur next even as one is actually engaged in the thinking act itself.

The third and final major step in metacognition consists of assessing both the process employed in achieving the goal and the product of this process. Having completed a thinking task, an individual should assess the entire operation. This requires attending to three things: the quality of the product, the quality of the procedures used to generate the product, and the way in which any obstacles were handled. The individual assesses the reasonableness and accuracy of the substantive product generated by the thinking skill or strategy in which he or she has been engaged—the solution, the decision, the classification scheme, for example—to determine the extent to which the goal was achieved. The process itself and the operations of which it consisted are also evaluated to determine the extent to which they proved useful and efficient in achieving the desired goal and any subgoals along the way. As part of this process, one also reflects on the obstacles or errors encountered to determine how well they were anticipated and handled, as well as whether they could have been avoided altogether or handled differently. Finally, the individual usually judges how efficient the overall plan was and modifies it for future use on similar occasions before storing the entire experience in long-term memory.

These various stages of metacognition are comparable to what teachers usually do as they plan and execute daily lessons. Before teaching a lesson, a teacher decides on its goal and selects a variety of techniques to achieve this goal—perhaps a pop quiz, a mini-lecture, discussion of the quiz, student work on a ditto to apply the lesson ideas, a review, and an assignment—and sequences these techniques. The teacher also tries to anticipate any obstacles to a smooth-running lesson. What, for example, if there is a fire drill in the middle of the quiz—or if students fail to bring pens or pencils—or if students forget their texts? Contingency plans will be made to handle any such occurrence.

A teacher also carefully monitors the lesson as it is carried out. In so doing, the teacher remains alert to the time used up, to indications that the students are ready for the next task specified in the plan, to feedback suggesting that the plan should be amended to take advantage of an unexpected but useful "teachable opportunity" or to repeat something that is apparently not clear, and to any obstacles that might crop up. On completion of the lesson, the teacher assesses the extent to which the various techniques used proved effective and efficient in achieving the stated goal, as well as to any unanticipated results of the lesson. By attending to planning, monitoring, and assessing a lesson, teachers engage in the same kind of mental activity as in metacognition except that they are focusing on an activity rather than on any thinking operation such as problem solving or judging the strength of a claim or argument.

The description of metacognition presented here represents a rather idealized conception of what happens in one's mind when engaging in thinking most effectively and efficiently. It is not something that one should expect young students to be able to do on first try or to do well even on fourth try. Indeed, it is doubtful that most older students will engage in metacognition by the time they leave school. Metacognition abilities develop slowly, beginning around the age of five and blossoming around ages eleven to thirteen and thereafter.[6] Because thinking about thinking in effect involves engaging in abstract processing or other rather abstract processes, it is tied closely to the development of an individual's stage of formal abstract thinking, which in many instances does not mature until after students leave high school. As surprising as it may seem, for example, while 68 percent of high school freshmen are at the concrete operational stage of cognitive development, about 66 percent of our students are still at this same stage upon graduation from high school three years later, even though more of them are making significant movement in this direction by that time.[7] Learning how to engage in metacognition thus comes slowly even for many older students. Teachers—especially in the elementary grades—should not thus expect students to develop much proficiency at thinking about their own thinking. Yet teachers at all levels can nevertheless do a number of things to facilitate developing this ability and the inclination on the part of students to engage in it.

Developing Readiness for Metacognition

Teaching for metacognition means helping students slow down their own thinking and raise that thinking to a level of consciousness so that they can take deliberate control of it, reproduce it on their own initiative, and modify it as they use it. Because, however, the cognitive abilities that undergird metacognition are slow to develop, it appears most useful to come at metacognition indirectly until the junior high school years. The direct teaching of metacognition can then follow. Teaching metacognition in the elementary grades can thus focus on developing readiness for metacognition rather than on trying to show students how to engage in any particular metacognitive skills. This enables teachers and students at this level to attend exclusively to learning specific thinking skills without competition from another type of thinking skill—metacognition. Such an approach might consist largely of engaging students in thinking, first, about physical activities and then in extending their metacognitive thinking to single acts of thinking.

Teachers can do a number of things to facilitate the development of metacognition at a readiness level. Educators Elizabeth Bondy and Arthur L. Costa, among others, suggest that these activities include the following:[8]

1. *Conscious choosing*
   Whenever students have an opportunity to make a choice—determining what to do next in class or what to do for recess, and so on—have them identify at least two options and then identify some possible consequences of each option. By then reflecting aloud on the consequences, students can articulate criteria for making the choice and extend their thinking beyond the here and now to the anticipation of future events or ideas.
2. *Categorizing with multiple criteria*
   Whenever students have an opportunity to discuss their actions or choices, have them make at least two categories, such as useful/not useful or like/not like or fun/not fun, and so on. Like the

preceding activity, this activity extends student thinking and requires thinking about another thinking act.

3. *Paraphrasing what is heard*

   Have students restate, put in their own words, or elaborate one another's plans and actions as they engage in them or observe their peers engaging in them. This may take the form of having students state goals, suggest ways to accomplish them, and try to outline exactly what would have to be done to carry out their "plan." They can also restate or paraphrase directions, or rate and discuss their own understandings of something.

4. *Reflecting on how an answer was derived*

   Have the students, on occasion, stop in the middle of a thinking task to discuss whether they are doing it correctly, exactly where they are in the process, whether they skipped anything and/or what to do next (and why) once they resume the process. Students can also predict the results of a thinking task and, when finished with it, reflect on and discuss the extent to which their prediction was accurate, whether or not anything occurred to alter it, and so on.

5. *Engaging in "I think" writing*

   After or before engaging in a thinking task, students can write a short paragraph describing how they were thinking about it. At first such writing may be a disjointed stream of consciousness, but students can focus eventually on reporting how and why they did or planned to do a task a specific way.

6. *Making plans*

   Students can plan classroom activities and assignments in terms of goals, sequence of activities, and anticipated obstacles; list the plan on the board; and refer to it as they engage in the planned activity—in effect, monitor their plan as they execute it. Upon concluding the activity or assignment, they can evaluate their plan as well as the success of their activity. Thus, students can go through the essential steps of metacognition early on but in terms of specific physical or concrete tasks rather than in terms of thinking tasks. The idea behind this and all these activities is to get young students to extend their thoughts beyond the immediate present and to stay alert to what they are doing. Having done these activities, the jump to doing this about thinking is less difficult than it otherwise might be.

Although none of the above activities actually teaches how to engage in metacognition, they develop students' readiness to do so; and developing readiness is one important function of formal schooling.[9] These activities move students toward being able to engage in metacognition by giving them opportunities to plan, monitor, and assess their activities, even if physical rather than cognitive. Through repeated opportunities and guidance in how to step outside of any task and reflect on how they are executing it, students can develop readiness to apply these same procedures to thinking tasks. Sharing their thoughts with others and hearing others articulate their own thoughts about similar activities help students develop the procedures they can apply to thinking as they are able to do so.

As students advance into the intermediate grades, teachers can have them engage in various "think aloud" activities about the thinking or physical tasks in which they are engaged or are about to engage or have just completed.[10] Students can check their progress in any task by periodically assessing the results they are getting, perhaps by answering these questions posted on butcher paper or on a bulletin board: What is my goal? Does this make sense so far? Is my plan working? Am I accomplishing my goal? Another set of questions might be used to help students plan a thinking activity: What do I already know about this? What do I want to know about it? What do I *need* to know about it? What things are worth knowing? Also useful as a follow-up to a task is still another series of questions:

What did I do first to accomplish this task? . . . next? . . . next?

What did I know that enabled me to do these things?

How did I know I was doing it correctly or well?

What kinds of obstacles did I encounter? How did I deal with them?

In checking a student or group engaged in a thinking activity, a teacher could ask (and have students stop and discuss) other kinds of questions, too, such as these:

1. What am I doing?
2. Why?
3. What other way can I do it?
4. How does it work? Can I do it again— or another way?
5. How would I help someone else do it?[11]

Many other activities similar to these can be devised. Rather than teaching students how to plan, monitor, and assess a thinking task, teachers can, by the questions they ask or activities in which they engage students, guide them in their planning, monitoring, and assessing and provide opportunities to reflect on, articulate and hear others discuss their own thinking. At this stage, a teacher will probably have to be content with descriptions of physical behavior much more often than with mental behaviors. Many novices in reporting their thinking about even a thinking task tend to report nonthinking behaviors at first such as: "I got my paper. Then I found a pencil. Then I looked at the board. . . ." Elementary students or even adults just beginning to learn how to engage in metacognition are more accustomed and able to deal with physical things around them than with anything going on inside their minds. With practice, however, this tendency disappears. Gradually they begin to talk about and even try to explain some thinking action. By helping students set goals, plan a way to accomplish them, predict the outcomes of their plans, check their progress as they work out the plans, and then assess the procedure used and the results they get, teachers can help individuals develop readiness to benefit from more explicit instruction in metacognition later.

Teaching of Metacognition

In the junior high school years teachers can begin more direct teaching for metacognition. They can start by teaching the three major parts of the metacognitive process—planning, monitoring, and assessing—and then focus on some specific operations constituting each part. And students can apply these to thinking tasks. Initially, teachers can *model* the overall process and involve students in their modeling. In directing the execution of a variety of metacognitive tasks, they can use the same instructional strategies described in the preceding chapters, sequenced from introductory lessons through guided practice, independent application, elaboration, and continued guided practice to autonomous use. By the tenth grade, students should be able to engage in metacognition even if it is a rather simplified and sometimes superficial in nature.

Modeling can be one useful technique for helping students to learn how to think about thinking. But modeling—enacting a specific behavior—must be accompanied by explanatory commentary if it is to be of most instructive value.[12] While engaging step-by-step in working through a problem, a teacher must explain how and why each step was executed as it was. This could be done, for example, by demonstrating for students how the teacher solved a problem such as deciding what kinds of activities to include in a specific class or why a particular homework assignment was made—by stating the teacher's goal(s) and then telling how the goal was accomplished and the reason for each step taken in so doing. If not knowing (or not wanting to provide) an answer to a question from the class, for example, the teacher can describe a plan for getting the answer—and then actually carry it out, explaining how and why he or she is executing the plan.

A teacher can also demonstrate metacognitive operations and, in so doing, discuss them with the class. In working a problem, for instance, the teacher can introduce the appropriate procedure by (1) stating the goal, (2) selecting and explaining the operations to perform, (3) outlining the rules that need to be followed, and (4) predicting what obstacles are likely to crop up. Then he or she can execute the procedure, explaining decisions made along the way. As this is done, students can be invited to work the problem along with the teacher and periodically to report and discuss as a class where they are in the process, how they got there, how they dealt or could deal with any problems encountered along the way, and what they could do next. To conclude, the students and teacher together can reflect on and assess how well the goal was achieved by using the procedures selected and what might have been done differently or better to make the procedure more efficient or to produce better results.

It is an easy jump from such teacher-modeled activities in metacognition to the paired problem-solving techniques popularized by Arthur Whimbey and Jack Lochhead.[13] As described in the preceding chapter, the procedure requires students to work in pairs to engage in thinking tasks, with one student doing the work and reporting aloud what he or she is thinking while the other student checks the process, trying to ensure that the partner does not skip any steps or violate any rules. As students engage in this process over and over again, switching roles each time, they engage in an increasingly sophisticated way in most of the operations constituting metacognition.

Teachers can also provide direct instruction in metacognition by offering a series of lessons just like these described above for teaching classification. In one lesson, for instance, they could introduce the overall strategy, using perhaps the directive introductory strategy. Then, whenever students have an opportunity to apply a previously introduced and practiced thinking skill, they can be guided in applying the operations in the metacognitive strategy as they relate to that specific skill. Metacognitive skills can later be elaborated to use with a variety of thinking skills and tasks.

Teacher or student-made "thinking guides" may also be useful for developing student proficiency in metacognition. Figure 8.2 presents one such metacognitive thinking guide. In this sample guide, students complete the items in the left-hand *planning* column before beginning the assigned thinking task. Here they write their goal and the steps they intend to go through—in sequence—to achieve that goal. They also anticipate obstacles or errors that could arise and list ways to overcome these. Then, as students carry out their plan, they can *monitor* it by checking off (in the middle column) the various components of their plans as they complete or encounter them. Referring to this guide and actual checking as they go help students keep track of what they are up to,

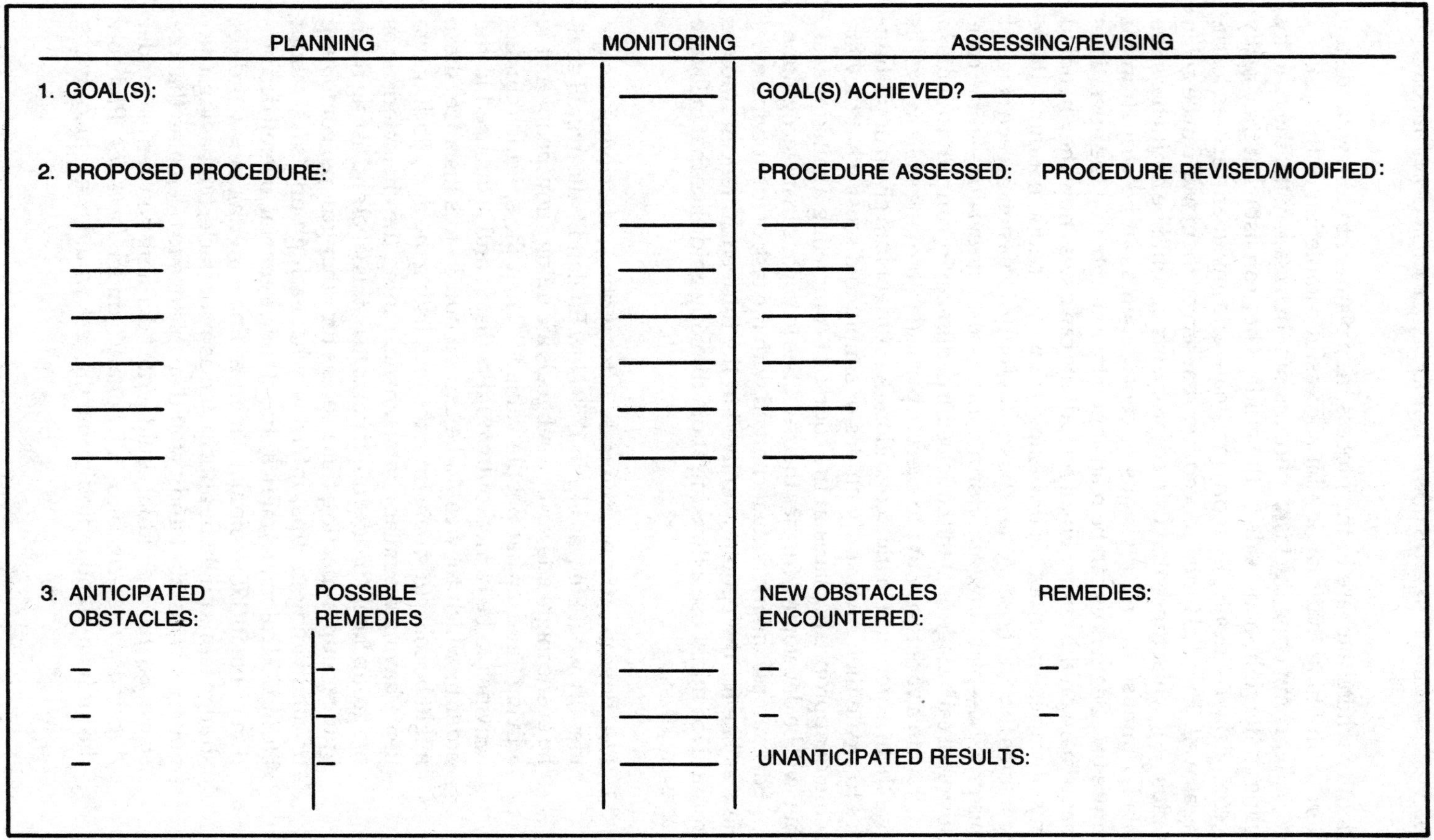

Figure 8.2 A Guide for Thinking about Thinking

identify where they are in the process they planned to follow, and stay alert to anything that may inhibit successful completion of the task.

After completing the task, students can then *assess* what they did by filling in the right-hand side of the guide. They can list what they really accomplished—ideally, their original goal—and any unanticipated learning as well. Those planned procedures that served them well can be given a plus (+), while those that caused problems or could be omitted can be rated a minus(−), and revisions or replacements can be written in for future use. Sequences can be rearranged by renumbering the operations that remain on the guide. Finally, students can assess how they handled any obstacles or errors, listing suggestions for better handling those problems that did arise. A class or small-group discussion of each stage of this process—planning, monitoring, and assessing/revising—at the conclusion of each stage or at the conclusion of the activity can put students in touch with a variety of ways to execute particular thinking skills as well as give them experience in metacognition. As students are given opportunities to create their own study guides or simply to discuss what they are doing at appropriate places in the course of completing a thinking task, they will be developing further their abilities to engage in metacognition.

For example, an individual charged with the task of identifying what life was like for the people who lived in the thirteen American colonies around 1750 might use a thinking about thinking guide like that in Figure 8.2 as follows:

1. *Plan* how to carry out the task. After writing "classifying data to identify what life was like in 1750 New England," the overall goal, he or she might add several subgoals including "how people made a living" and "what people valued." Then the specific thinking activities to be carried out would be listed and sequenced in the order in which they could be carried out. In this instance, these might be collecting data from the text, listing the data, finding two items having a similar characteristic, stating the characteristic as the group label, finding other items to fit this label and listing them in the group, repeating this process for other groups, combining or subdividing groups, inferring what each group "says" about life in 1750 colonial America, and stating a general, overall description of life in 1750 colonial America. Encountering new words or strange terms might be anticipated as an obstacle, but having a dictionary or glossary handy would enable one to overcome that obstacle. So this individual could write "defining new terms" under *Anticipated Obstacles* and "dictionary" under *Remedies*. Probably the individual could predict that this task would result in knowing

something about the economic, social, and political conditions of the period, and could enter these items under *Predicted Results*.

2. *Monitor the procedure* as it is executed. Keeping the goal and subgoals clearly in mind while working through these procedures, this individual could put a check in the middle column of the guide after completing each part of the procedure. It might even be appropriate to add something to the procedure, as the task is executed.

3. *Assess/revise* what was learned about life in 1750 colonial America as well as about the procedure used to develop this knowledge. What was actually learned about life in 1750 could be written in the space under goals in the right-hand column and be judged in terms of reasonableness and accuracy. Is this accurate? Does it reasonably relate to the goal? The steps in the procedure that worked satisfactorily could be marked with a +; any that proved to be less than useful could be crossed-off. Procedures that should have been used could be written in under *Procedure Revised/Modified*. Any new obstacles that were encountered would go under the appropriate label, with ways they were or could have been overcome written next to them. Finally, anything unexpected that was learned-about either the topic or the procedures employed to deal with it—or both—could be written under *Unanticipated Results*. Discussing the completed guide could lead to further changes under the various headings. The guide can be kept in a student's notes for reference at the time another similar task is encountered.

The activities and techniques outlined here can be used with the strategies described in preceding chapters for providing use in the introduction, guided practice, and transfer/elaboration of thinking skills or strategies. What is important to remember is that use of these techniques does not actually teach students how to engage in metacognition. It does, though, provide opportunities for them to do so and encourages—indeed in some instances, requires—them to do so. It is not productive to teach two sets of skills simultaneously. While teaching how to engage in metacognition—as a skill—can be taught like any other thinking skill using the instructional framework and strategies presented here, it should not be taught directly until students have shown a readiness to profit from such instruction and even then not in competition with new cognitive skills or strategies. The actual teaching *of* metacognition might best be reserved for the last few years of high school or the first years of college. By then most students have been introduced to, and have been practicing, the important thinking operations for some time; they then have the time, the intellectual power, and the need to learn how best to make these operations work for them.

Teaching about Metacognition

Teachers can also teach about metacognition by giving students opportunities to analyze how experts engage in various kinds of thinking operations. Here the subject of a lesson is someone else's thinking. Students can view, listen to, or read such examples or case studies of thinking in action, and with teacher assistance they can identify the kinds of thinking strategies and skills employed and the key attributes of each. Many sources of such examples are readily available.[14] Others may be located or created by teachers. Figure 8.3 presents one classic example of an expert engaged in problem solving. This story is about a Talmudic scholar en route from a large city in southeastern Europe to a small Jewish community, or sthetl, in the late nineteenth century. A brief explanation of how it can be analyzed will illustrate how students can use it and others like it to think about thinking.

Read the story in Figure 8.3 twice. First, read it simply to understand the story. Then read it again to identify the main operations this scholar performs as he seeks to resolve the problem identified at the beginning of the story. It may help, as you read, to write in the margin of the story a(n):

P   next to each line in which the scholar states a problem or asks a question;

H   next to each line in which he states an hypothesis;

T   next to those sections where he tests an hypothesis;

C   next to those lines where he states a conclusion;

    and any other symbols suitable for indicating other thinking skills or rules he seems to be employing.

What does this scholar do as he thinks through the problem that attracts his attention?

Identifying a Problem

To our scholar, the facts just don't seem to make sense. There seems to be a gap between what he knows about Marmaresch and what he knows about people dressed like the stranger. Why would a person like this be going to a place like that? (What image do you have of Marmaresch as a result of reading this story?) Certainly such a well-dressed, obviously well-to-do man has no business going to Marmaresch, or so our scholar

A Talmudic scholar from Marmaresch was on his way home from a visit to Budapest. Opposite him in the railway carriage sat another Jew, dressed in modern fashion and smoking a cigar. When the conductor came around to collect the tickets the scholar noticed that his neighbor opposite was also on his way to Marmaresch.

This seemed very odd to him.

"Who can it be, and why is he going to Marmaresch?" he wondered.

As it would not be polite to ask outright he tried to figure it out for himself.

"Now let me see," he mused. "He is a modern Jew, well dressed, and he smokes a cigar. Whom could a man of this type be visiting in Marmaresch? Possibly he's on his way to our town doctor's wedding. But no, that can't be! That's two weeks off. Certainly this kind of man wouldn't twiddle his thumbs in our town for two weeks!

"Why then is he on his way to Marmaresch? Perhaps he's courting a woman there. But who could it be? Now let me see. Moses Goldman's daughter, Esther? Yes, definitely, it's she and nobody else ...! But now that I think of it—that couldn't be! She's too old—he wouldn't have her, under any circumstances! Maybe it's Haikeh Wasservogel? Phooey! She's so ugly! Who then? Could it be Leah, the money-lender's daughter? N—no! What a match for such a nice man! Who then? There aren't any more marriageable girls in Marmaresch. That's settled then, he's not going courting.

"What then brings him?

"Wait, I've got it! It's about Mottell Kohn's bankruptcy case! But what connection can he have with that? Could it be that he is one of his creditors? Hardly! Just look at him sitting there so calmly, reading his newspaper and smiling to himself. Anybody can see nothing worries him! No, he's not a creditor. But I'll bet he has something to do with the bankruptcy! Now what could it be?

"Wait a minute, I think I've got it. Mottell Kohn must have corresponded with a lawyer from Budapest about his bankruptcy. But that swindler Mottell certainly wouldn't confide his business secrets to a stranger! So it stands to reason that the lawyer must be a member of the family.

"Now who could it be? Could it be his sister Shprinzah's son? No, that's impossible. She got married twenty-six years ago—I remember it very well because the wedding took place in the green synagogue. And this man here looks at least thirty-five.

"A funny thing! Who could it be, after all ...? Wait a minute! It's as clear as day! This is his nephew, his brother Hayyim's son, because Hayyim Kohn got married thirty-seven years and two months ago in the stone synagogue near the market place. Yes, that's who he is!

"In a nutshell—he is a Lawyer Kohn from Budapest. But a lawyer from Budapest surely must have the title 'Doctor'! So, he is Doctor Kohn from Budapest, no? But wait a minute! A lawyer from Budapest who calls himself 'Doctor' won't call himself 'Kohn'! Anybody knows that. It's certain that he has changed his name into Hungarian. Now, what kind of name could he have made out of Kohn? Kovacs! Yes, that's it—Kovacs! In short, this is Doctor Kovacs from Budapest!"

Eager to start a conversation the scholar turned to his travelling companion and asked, "Doctor Kovacs, do you mind if I open the window?"

"Not at all," answered the other. "But tell me, how do you know that I am Doctor Kovacs?"

"It was obvious," replied the scholar.[15]

Figure 8.3 Problem Solving: A Case Study[15]

thinks, anyway. He seems to know enough about this little town to assume that only some very special occasion could be calling this gentleman there. The scholar is curious, "Who can it be . . .?" His problem statement is simple and direct.

Breaking the Problem into Subproblems

Our scholar doesn't jump to any hasty conclusions. Nor does he tackle the entire problem all at once. Although he seeks primarily to determine the identity of the stranger, he breaks this problem into a number of subordinate problems in order to make it manageable. The solution to each subproblem will, he hopes, lead him to an answer to his major question. He elects first to figure out why this man is going to Marmaresch, thinking perhaps that if he can determine this, he will have some clues to the man's identity. So the immediate problem becomes ". . .why is he going to Marmaresch?"

Hypothesizing and Testing Hypotheses

Our scholar again studies the subject of his curiosity—reviews his data— and notices that he is well dressed and modern. From the stranger's behavior and appearance he infers the man is reasonably wealthy. The scholar then attempts to recall data—information about the town—that might suggest something important enough to bring a man like this to Marmaresch. As he does, he suddenly comes up with a possible reason— the town doctor's wedding. However, examination of additional recalled information about the date of the wedding and the apparently sleepy, dull nature of the community itself suggests that this hypothesis is unacceptable. He reasons that a successful businessman like this stranger would not waste his time for two weeks waiting for a wedding! So the scholar concludes by rejecting this as "the answer" and returns to the problem once again.

"Why then is he on his way to Marmaresch?"

Courtship! A second hypothesis. So he dredges up some more information relevant to this guess:

> . . . Moses Goldman's daughter, Esther? Yes, definitely, it's she and nobody else . . .! But now that I think of it—that couldn't be! She's too old—he wouldn't have her, under any circumstances! Maybe it's Haikeh Wasservogel? Phooey! She's so ugly! Who then? Could it be Leah, the money-lender's daughter? N--no! What a match for such a nice man! Who then? There aren't any more marriageable girls. . . .

Again, analysis of the evidence fails to yield anything that would lead one to believe that this gentleman could be courting a girl from the town, so our scholar concludes that this hypothesis, too, is inaccurate. Thus he discards it.

"What then brings him?"

Our scholar states the problem for a third time! Suddenly he recalls more information about events in the town that appears to offer a reasonable explanation. Bankruptcy! This becomes his third hypothesis:

"Wait, I've got it! It's about Mottell Kohn's bankruptcy case!"

Concluding

At this point the scholar concludes about his first subproblem. He does not discard the idea of bankruptcy, but accepts it as the reason for this stranger's trip to Marmaresch. He does so because all other reasonable explanations simply don't make sense in terms of all the information available to him. As the last remaining "big event" in the community that he can imagine or recall, Mottell Kohn's bankruptcy seems to be the only thing important enough to bring an individual like this to Marmaresch. So for our scholar, at least, part of the original problem is now resolved— even if only tentatively. The stranger is going to Marmaresch because of a bankruptcy!

Defining a New Subproblem

The main problem still remains, however, "Who can it be. . .?" Having decided why the stranger is on his way to Marmaresch, the scholar now attempts to determine the man's possible connection with the bankruptcy case. He asks himself "What connection can he have with that?" A new problem! If our scholar can figure out this connection, he will be another step closer to knowing the man's identity!

Hypothesizing and Testing the Hypothesis

Once again he guesses at an answer:

. . .Could it be that he is one of his creditors? Hardly! Just look at him sitting there so calmly, reading his newspaper and smiling to himself. Anybody can see nothing worries him! No, he's not a creditor. . . .

Creditors, he assumes, would not be too happy or calm about the prospects of receiving only part instead of all of what Kohn might owe them. So that hypothesis is discarded, and our scholar posits a new line of inquiry. What other kinds of people are usually involved in bankruptcy cases?

> Wait a minute, I think I've got it. Mottell Kohn must have corresponded with a lawyer from Budapest about his bankruptcy.

Concluding

This makes sense! Now our scholar thinks he is on the right track. His traveling companion must be a lawyer. He is another step closer to resolving his original problem: "Who can it be. . .?"

Problem-Hypothesis-Test-Conclude

Our scholar now turns to two other subproblems. His perception of human nature apparently leads him to assume that people, if possible, do not expose their personal affairs to strangers or to the public in general. He also seems to know Mottell Kohn quite well, or at least he thinks he knows him. So, he immediately discards the possibility of this individual being a total stranger. That hypothesis, he believes, is untenable. Now the alternative appears to be relatively easy:

> But that swindler Mottell certainly wouldn't confide his business secrets to a stranger! So it stands to reason that the lawyer must be a member of the family.

All the scholar needs to do now is figure out which relative it could be. First, he states the problem again. Then he hypothesizes. He rejects his initial hypothesis because the available data—the date of the marriage and the apparent age of the man in question—do not support it. But then, suddenly, everything seems to fall into place:

> Now who could it be? Could it be his sister Shprinzah's son? No, that's impossible. She got married twenty-six years ago—I remember it very well because the wedding took place in the green synagogue. And this man here looks at least thirty-five.
> A funny thing! Who could it be, after all. . .? Wait a minute! It's as clear as day! This is his nephew, his brother Hayyim's son, because Hayyim Kohn got married thirty-seven years and two months ago in the stone synagogue near the market place. Yes, that's who he is!
> In a nutshell—he is Lawyer Kohn from Budapest.

And so the scholar arrives at an answer to the problem regarding the stranger's relationship to Kohn. Thus, he stated and answered—to his satisfaction—four major questions, each of which has been designed to help him determine the solution to the major problem "Who can it be. . .?" Now he has a conclusion.

Stating a Conclusion

A conclusion? Possibly, but not quite. For even though the scholar now believes that he knows the man's identity, one other minor problem remains to be dealt with:

> But a lawyer from Budapest surely must have the title "Doctor'! So, he is Doctor Kohn from Budapest, no? But wait a minute! A lawyer from Budapest who calls himself "Doctor" won't call himself "Kohn"! Anybody knows that. It's certain that he has changed his name into Hungarian. Now, what kind of name could he have made out of Kohn? Kovacs! Yes, that's it—Kovacs! In short, this is Doctor Kovacs from Budapest!"

Using his knowledge of the culture in which he lives, the scholar finally voices a conclusion, a solution to the original problem of "Who can it be. . .?" Of course, this man must be Dr. Kovacs! Our scholar has gone as far as he can go on his own. He has stated the solution to the problem that launched his inquiry.

Applying the Conclusion to New Data

Because our scholar is human, however—because he, too, can tolerate only so much ambuiguity—he wants to know if he is correct. He could ask the man "Are you Dr. Kovacs?" but the situation or his own norms of behavior or the culture does not permit this. Instead, he assumes that the man is Dr. Kovacs—that his own solution is correct—and applies it to the situation. Turning to his traveling companion, he asks:

> "Doctor Kovacs, do you mind if I open the window?"
> "Not at all," answered the other. "But tell me, how do you know that I am Dr. Kovacs?"
> "It was obvious," replied the scholar.

Such is a strategy of problem solving. Figure 8.4 summarizes the strategy employed by the scholar. Student or student and teacher analysis and discussion of this case study or others engages students in thinking about and discussing thinking and can even help them sharpen their own skills at thinking. Such an approach to teaching for metacognition helps and encourages students in thinking about their own thinking.

MAIN PROBLEM—WHO CAN IT BE?

1. *Subproblem #1*   *... why is he going to Marmaresh?*

   Hypothesize   he's on his way to the ... wedding. ...
   Test
   Conclude   No. ...

   Hypothesize   ... he's courting. ...
   Test
   Conclude   No. ...

   Hypothesize   it's about ... bankruptcy. ...
   Test
   Conclude   Yes. ...

2. *Subproblem #2*   *... something to do with bankruptcy?*

   Hypothesize   ... a creditor. ...
   Test
   Conclude   No. ...

   Hypothesize   ... a lawyer. ...
   Test
   Conclude   Yes. ...

3. *Subproblem #3*   *... stranger or relative?*

   Hypothesize   ... a stranger. ...
   Test
   Conclude   No! ... a family member!

4. *Subproblem #4*   *... which relative could it be?*

   Hypothesize   ... sister Shprinzah's son. ...
   Test
   Conclude   No. ...

   Hypothesize   ... brother Hayyim's son. ...
   Test
   Conclude   Yes. ...

5. *Subproblem #5*   *What is his exact name?*

   Hypothesize   ... must have the title Doctor. ...
   Test
   Conclude   Yes. ...

   Hypothesize   ... changed his name to Kovacs. ...
   Test
   Conclude   Yes. ...

CONCLUSION
In short, this is Dr. Kovacs from Budapest!

Then this conclusion is applied to new data to help
make sense out of the situation—and to satisfy the
scholar that his inquiry really is accurate!

Figure 8.4 Analysis of Problem Solving: A Case Study

TEACHING THINKING DISPOSITIONS

Like functional thinking, metacognition is hard work. To engage in either requires effort and attention as well as expertise in executing the skills of which each is comprised. Both functional thinking and metacognition also require a willingness to engage in such thinking, a disposition to stay at it until the goal has been achieved, and an awareness—almost a faith—that, by skillful use of one's mind, one can achieve the established goal. These additional elements of thinking represent an affective dimension of thinking. They support and drive thinking. Developing these and related dispositions is closely related to developing one's metacognitive abilities and basic thinking skills and strategies.

Experts identify a number of dispositions that undergird effective thinking. These include a respect for, and a desire to seek and give, reasons, a willingness to suspend judgments, a desire to consider other points of view on a topic, a desire to identify and judge a number of alternatives before making a choice, and a willingness to revise one's opinion in light of new evidence. Figure 8.5 lists some of the more significant thinking dispositions as suggested by educators Robert Ennis, David Krathwohl, and others.[16] Individuals considered to be effective at thinking are consistently disposed to behave in ways that evidence the attitudes and values implicit in these dispositions.

Dispositions such as those noted here do not necessarily develop on their own. They, too, must be taught. These dispositions are *not*, however, taught in exactly the same ways as are the skilled operations of thinking. Teaching them takes much longer than does teaching a specific skill and requires use of direct as well as indirect teaching techniques and strategies.

Teachers can use at least four techniques to foster development of attitudes associated with thinking:

1. *Model behaviors that demonstrate the desired dispositions.*
   Teachers, in their teaching, should suspend judgments until they have as much relevant information as possible and should make deliberate, explicit efforts to secure such information. They should deliberately seek out a variety of points of view on an issue or topic. They should articulate a number of alternatives in decision-making situations before considering any and making choices. They should give their reasoning for their assertions and decisions. In so doing, teachers should explain to their students why they are doing these things, and they need to be sure that students recognize this demonstrating of important aspects of thinking.
2. *Insist on student behavior that reflects the dispositions sought.*
   Teachers should require students to exhibit behaviors demonstrat-

1. Seek a clear statement of a problem, a thesis, a question.
2. Deliberately examine a variety of viewpoints.
3. Seek to be well informed.
4. Use credible sources.
5. Seek a number of alternatives.
6. Seek/give reasons.
7. Seek/provide evidence.
8. Be open-minded.
9. Be willing to change a position/judgment when evidence and reasons are sufficient to do so.
10. Judge in terms of situations, issues, purposes, and consequences (not in terms of fixed, dogmatic precepts or emotional, wistful thinking).
11. Persist in carrying out a thinking task.
12. Be slow to believe—be skeptical.
13. Be objective.
14. Suspend judgment when appropriate/sufficient evidence and reasoning are lacking.

Figure 8.5 Selected Thinking Dispositions

ing the dispositions indicative and supportive of effective thinking, just as they do. Students should be required to give reasons for their claims and decisions and to ask others to do the same, to generate alternatives before making choices, to seek out and explore a variety of points of view, to withhold judgment, and so on. Practice of such behaviors, even if at the insistence of a teacher, can, in time, lead to internalization of the values implicit in these behaviors.

3. *Engage students in repeated activities that require use of these disposition-based behaviors.*

Learning activities must consistently and continuously require students to exhibit behaviors related to effective thinking. One or two cases, instances, or opportunities to do so over the course of a semester or year are not sufficient even to begin to develop such dispositions. Teachers must design and carry out activities in which students repeatedly seek out and discuss a variety of points of view, collect additional data, suspend judgment, and choose from a number of alternatives. These and related behaviors must be practiced in appropriate places over and over again across many grade levels and in many subjects.

4. *Reinforce behaviors that demonstrate the appropriate dispositions.*
   Behaviors illustrative of effective thinking can be reinforced by
   explaining and demonstrating their value as well as by offering
   praise, grades, and other reinforcements for them. Teachers need
   to take care in so doing, however, to ensure that their reinforcements clearly relate to the behavior, not to the students(s) exhibiting it. Few, if any, students can be or even may wish to be like
   another individual, but all can exhibit a valued behavior.

Other techniques can also be employed to help students develop
dispositions supportive of skillful thinking. But there is more to
developing such dispositions than the use of certain techniques.
When these techniques are used is equally important. For attitudes,
values, and dispositions are formed early in life. Indeed, in most
cases they are established rather firmly by the time youngsters enter
their junior high school years.[17] The implications of this situation are
thus very significant for the development of these dispositions that
guide and support skillful thinking. Schools must start as early as
possible to develop these dispositions if youngsters are to develop
the affective support system requisite for effective use of the training
skills and strategies teachers also seek to teach.

This suggests that the teaching of thinking cannot be limited to
the secondary grade levels. If it is in the elementary grades that basic
attitudes and dispositions are nurtured and developed, then a considerable effort should be made to teach thinking dispositions in the
elementary schools. Teachers in these grades can use many of the
techniques outlined here to develop the dispositions listed in Figure
8.5. In fact, these techniques should be used consistently across all
elementary and secondary grades to develop and reinforce these and
similar dispositions.

Many of the dispositions that support and drive effective thinking, it
should be noted, run counter to the natural inclinations of novice thinkers
and students of all ability levels. For students who find thinking difficult
or who seem to abhore academic work of any kind, efforts to seek out
additional data beyond those already in front of them or to seek alternatives beyond the first one that pops up are simply "too much work." And
these students are quick to point out they did not sign up for such work!
Other students, often those categorized as academically talented, frequently find winning in argumentation or essay writing preferable to
finding the "truth." They prefer to use their thinking skills to persuade
others of the validity of a particular personal opinion rather than to
establish what is true or accurate in as objective terms as possible. Re-
specting others, examining alternative viewpoints, analyzing data that
challenge a preconception, and judging on the basis of evidence and

reasoning rather than on the basis of dogma or personal bias often run counter to their preferred forms of behavior.

There is no magic formula for helping students such as these develop the dispositions supportive of effective thinking outlined in this chapter. Yet this is an important part of the teaching of thinking. Initiating efforts to develop these dispositions at the earliest stages—in preschool programs, or by the latest, in the primary grades—certainly would help accomplish this goal. Providing instruction in appropriate thinking skills and strategies and offering opportunities to develop these operations in subject matter of immediate interest to these students may also underscore the value of such skills and dispositions. A teacher contributes to development of these dispositions by patiently explaining the long-range implications of sloppy "one-sided" thinking, of failing to use all the data available, or of not considering a variety of alternatives. This can also be accomplished by providing lessons where the results of such thinking can be examined by the students. Certainly, modeling and insisting on student behaviors that illustrate these dispositions will help, too. Developing dispositions supportive of effective thinking clearly is a challenge requiring a continuing and long-range effort by teachers, parents, and students alike.

Effective student thinking is not likely to develop if teachers concentrate on teaching skills and techniques without attention to the affective dimension as well. And skillful student thinking is not likely to develop if schools delay attention to developing these disposition until after the elementary school years. Considered attention to this aspect of the teaching of thinking is as important as is attention to metacognition and to systematic teaching of thinking of specific thinking skills and strategies, if students are to become as proficient as possible in thinking.

TEACHING FOR INDEPENDENT THINKING

Helping students learn how to control and direct their own thinking and developing the dispositions that support and motivate thinking are essential aspects of the teaching of thinking. Without the ability to engage in metacognition or lacking the dispositions that drive skillful thinking, individuals are not inclined to use to full potential the thinking skills and strategies they are learning. Metacognition and thinking dispositions and skillful functional thinking are closely interrelated.

According to educational researcher and reading specialist Ann Brown, teaching thinking skills without attention to metacognition results in little more than "blind training."[18] Unless students are helped to become conscious of their own thinking, keep track of what they are doing when they engage in thinking, and assess the effectiveness of what they do, they cannot take control of their own thinking and become self-directed thinkers. They will simply remain blind to how they engage in thinking. Without such conscious control of their own thinking, they cannot transfer thinking skills from one setting to another without the greatest of difficulty. Teaching for metacognition helps students become conscious of how they think so that they can control it to increase the efficiency and effectiveness of their thinking.

Teaching those dispositions supportive of skillful thinking helps develop the willingness to engage in thinking and standards for guiding such thinking. Valuing the use of credible sources; valuing sufficient information, other points of view, and careful reasoning; and valuing the deliberate search for alternatives motivate and drive thinking and enhance its potential effectiveness. Individuals holding these and similar values deliberately engage in those thinking behaviors typical of skilled thinking.

Teaching for metacognition and teaching the values that underlie dispositions supportive of effective thinking are very much related. Being able to engage in metacognition and being disposed to think skillfully enhance one's self-concept. And a positive self-concept expresses itself in higher achievement, in school and out.[19] For a variety of reasons many students commonly believe that they are at the mercy of their own minds; they often see themselves as victims rather than as directors of their own thinking. Being able and inclined consciously and deliberately to control their own thinking—and knowing from training and experience that they can do so—encourages them to take control of their thinking and to employ it willingly at their own initiative. Such behavior increases their chances of success at thinking. Success begets self-confidence, and self-confidence enhances self-concept. Enhanced self-concept finds expression in greater achievement in academic study as well as in out-of-school endeavors. Attention to both metacognition and thinking dispositions are thus critically important in the teaching of thinking.

NOTES

1. Ann L. Brown, Joseph C. Campione, and Jeanne D. Day, "Learning to Learn: On Training Students to Learn from Texts," *Educational Researcher* 10:2 (February 1981), pp. 14–21; Robert J. Sternberg, "How Can We Teach Intelligence?" *Educational Leadership* 42:1 (September 1984), pp. 38–50; Raymond S. Nickerson, David N. Perkins, Edward E. Smith, *The Teaching of Thinking* (Hillsdale, N.J.: Lawrence Erlbaum Associates, 1985), pp. 100–109.

2. Robert J. Sternberg, *Beyond Intelligence: A Triarchic Theory of Human Intelligence* (New York: Cambridge University Press, 1985).

3. Brown, Campione, and Day, "Learning to Learn"; Judith W. Segal and Susan F. Chipman, "Thinking and Learning Skills: The Contributions of NIE," *Educational Leadership* 42:1 (September 1984), p. 86.

4. Arthur Whimbey, "Students Can Learn to Be Better Problem Solvers," *Educational Leadership* 37:7 (April 1980), pp. 560–565; Ann L. Brown, "Knowing When, Where and How to Remember: A Problem of Mega-cognition," in Robert Glaser, ed., *Advances in Instructional Psychology* (Hillsdale, N.J.: Lawrence Erlbaum Associates, 1978).

5. Arthur L. Costa, "Mediating the Metacognitive," *Educational Leadership* 42:3 (November 1984), pp. 57–62.

6. Ibid, p. 57.

7. H.T. Epstein, "Growth Spurts During Brain Development: Implications for Educational Policy and Practice," in J.F. Chall and A.F. Mirsky, eds., *Education and the Brain* (Chicago: University of Chicago Press, 1978), pp. 343–370; Martin Brooks, Esther Fusco, and Jacqueline Grennon," Cognitive Levels Matching, *Educational Leadership* 40:8 (May 1983), pp. 4–5.

8. Costa, "Mediating"; Elizabeth Bondy, "Thinking About Thinking," *Childhood Education* 17:2 (March/April 1984), pp. 234–238.

9. Jerome Bruner, *Toward A Theory of Instruction* (Cambridge, Mass.: Harvard University Press, 1966), p. 29.

10. Bondy, "Thinking."

11. Harold Berlak, "The Teaching of Thinking," *School Review* 73:1 (Spring 1965), pp. 1–13.

12. David Pratt, *Curriculum Design and Development* (New York: Harcourt Brace Jovanovich, 1980), p. 313; Michael I. Posner and Steven W. Keele, "Skill Learning," in Robert M. W. Travers, ed., *Second Handbook of Research on Teaching* (Chicago: Rand McNally College Publishing Company, 1973), pp. 820–823; Ann Marie Palincsar and Ann L. Brown, "Reciprocal Teaching of Comprehension-Fostering and Comprehension-Monitoring Activities," *Cognition and Instruction* 1:2 (Spring 1984), pp. 117–175.

13. Arthur Whimbey, "Teaching Sequential Thought: The Cognitive Skills Approach," *Phi Delta Kappan* 59:4 (December 1977), pp. 255–259.

14. Arthur L. Costa, "How Scientists Think When They Are Doing Science," in Arthur L. Costa, ed., *Developing Minds: A Resource Book for Teaching Thinking* (Alexandria, Va.: Association for Supervision and Curriculum Development, 1985), pp. 114–117; Carol Madigan and Ann Elwood, *Brainstorms and Thunderbolts: How Creative Genius Works* (New York: Macmillan, 1983).

15. Reprinted from *A Treasury of Jewish Folklore* by Nathan Ausubel, Copyright©1948, 1976 by Crown Publishers, Inc. Used by permission of Crown Publishers. By permission of Schocken Books, Inc. from *L'Chayim*, by Immanuel Olsvanger. Copyright©1949, by Schocken Books, Inc.

16. Robert H. Ennis, "Rational Thinking and Educational Practice," in Jonas F. Soltis, ed., *Philosophy and Education: 80th Yearbook* (Chicago: National Society for the Study of Education, 1981) and "A Logical Basis for Measuring Critical Thinking Skills," *Educational Leadership* 43:2 (October 1985), p. 46; David R. Krathwohl et al. *Taxonomy of Educational Objectives—Handbook II: Affective Domain* (New York: David McKay, 1964), pp. 181–185.

17. Bruce R. Joyce, "Social Action for Primary Schools," *Childhood Education* 46:5 (February 1970), p. 135.

18. Brown, Campione, and Day, "Learning to Learn," p. 15.

19. William Purkey, *Self-Concept and School Achievement* (Englewood Cliffs, N.J.: Prentice-Hall, 1970).

9

Assessing Student Thinking

"Will it be on the test?" Of all the student-asked questions heard in classrooms, this one may be the most common. For many students what is worth attending to and trying to learn is determined primarily by whether or not a teacher tests it. If topics or skills "covered" in class do not show up on end-of-chapter, unit, semester and/or final exams, students assume that they simply are neither important nor worth trying to learn. One way to give value to the instruction in thinking provided by the teaching strategies described in the preceding pages, while also diagnosing teaching and learning, is to devote a significant portion of school and classroom teaching to assessing student proficiency in the thinking operations being taught.

Two types of assessment are useful for this end. Teachers can include on their major paper-and-pencil tests items specifically directed at thinking skills and strategies and evaluated as such. And they can also use observational techniques to assess student thinking. Both methods provide data useful to making judgments about the quality—and changes in quality—of student thinking. By incorporating such practices into their testing procedures, teachers can gain valuable evidence not only about the learning of their students but also about the quality of their own instruction. What is even more important, such deliberate and publicly affirmed attention to thinking skills can provide significant additional motivation for students to attend to learning the thinking operations teachers seek to teach.[1]

PAPER-AND-PENCIL TESTS

Unfortunately, formal paper-and-pencil assessing of student proficiency in thinking is not a normal part of most classroom practice. Research suggests that less than 10 percent of most teacher-made classroom tests measure student performance above the level of simple recall.[2] Two reasons may account for this. First, most teachers view their primary function as teaching subject matter and simple subject-matter related skills. Second, since many teachers believe that students learn thinking skills automatically while processing subject matter, they assume that correct answers to subject-matter test questions indicate that students have mastered the thinking skills that teachers believe they have been teaching. This assumption is highly suspect.

Most teacher-directed classroom testing explicitly assesses subject-matter learning. Objective tests measure recall and recognition of facts and related information. Even essay tests—which some teachers claim to use as measures of thinking—commonly measure only subject-matter learning. Most teachers evaluate student essays on the basis of the kinds, amounts, accuracy, and relevance of information given as evidence in support of a claim, the number and kinds of sources cited, and the number and accuracy of the specific facts given, rather than on the basis of any discernible reasoning, critical thinking, or other thinking operations used. The message to students is thus quite clear: facts, generalizations, and information are what count. Although one may use certain thinking skills and strategies to learn information, learning these skills themselves is hardly important, they presume.

If students are to develop more proficiency in thinking than they normally do, teachers must test directly—and appropriately—the thinking skills they teach.[3] Teachers can incorporate test items to measure student proficiency in thinking skills into every unit, mid-semester, and final exam they construct. In most cases, but not always, these tests consist largely of objective test items. To assess the thinking operations being taught in a course, a teacher can simply include with the subject-matter items on their regular tests a number of other objective items specifically dealing with thinking skills and strategies. These items can use the subject matter of the course. They can be mixed throughout a test or collected together in one section of the test so that students can clearly see the importance attached to learning the operations being taught. Such items can be objective types (multiple choice or completion or matching) as well as essay questions. They can include items about the skill or strategy—when it is to be used, rules that guide its use, and so on—as well as items that require students to execute it.

Any instrument developed to assess student proficiency in one or more thinking operations should be a challenge to students, but, as psychologist Robert Sternberg writes, it should be "a surmountable challenge."[4] That is, the task should stretch the student's thinking but not be impossible to complete successfully. And, as Sternberg cautions, the challenge itself should be in the thinking required to complete the item rather than in the knowledge needed to do so.

Test Formats for Newly Introduced Skills

For greatest impact on student learning, it may be best initially to cluster in a special section of a unit or semester test all questions assessing performance on a skill or strategy that has been the subject of considerable classroom attention. Not only will this format underscore for the students the importance of the specific thinking skills or strategies that have been taught, but it also reaffirms skill learning as an important continuing goal of learning in the class. Once a teacher has "caught the attention" of the students in this manner and after students have been introduced to a skill over a period of several units in a course, test items on a particular skill or strategy may be scattered throughout the entire test or tested in conjunction with other skills, while the separate skill sections of the test focus on additional newly introduced or elaborated thinking skills.

The number of test items on a special thinking skills section of a unit or major subject-matter test should vary according to the extent to which a skill has been a subject of instruction in the course. Six objective items may provide an adequate measure of proficiency in any single skill or strategy that has been newly introduced (or transferred or elaborated) and practiced a number of times during the preceding several weeks. These six items should require students to (1) define the skill, (2) identify an example of the skill in use, (3) execute the skill several times, and finally (4) explain to others how to execute the skill. Assessing more than a single newly introduced or elaborated skill will require a combination of items that require these operations for each skill to be assessed. Thus, a mid-semester or final exam testing three such skills, for example, may consist of fifteen to eighteen objective items relating specifically to these three skills.

Suppose an American history teacher who had introduced and provided guided practice in the skill of classifying data (as described in the preceding chapters) wished to assess student proficiency in the skill on the first unit exam in the course. Six objective test items on this skill could be added in a special section to the objective part of this unit exam. Figure 9.1 presents these items arranged as they would be on this test.

The first two questions on this sample test require students to define and identify an example of the skill. Question 1, requiring its definition, may be a multiple choice item if the teacher seeks only to measure recognition (as is done on this sample test) or a completion item if the teacher wishes to assess student recall of the skill definition. The latter type of question could simply ask students to "Define the skill of classifying. . . ." Question 2 calls for students to pick an example of the skill being used or a product of the skill's having been used. A variety of different questions could serve this function well, but the type of question on the sample test appears to be most useful. In this sample, students are asked to choose from three different options the one or ones that most likely show(s) data that have already been classified.

Question 3, 4, and 5 require the students to execute the skill and to show how they did it. Plenty of space is provided around each question so that students can mark the data directly with circles and lines to connect items in the same category or with different symbols to identify items related to one another. Students can also use the space under the data in each selection to list items in groups, labeling each group. The key to this type of item, of course, is the requirement to "show your work," to indicate or even explain how and why the skill was executed as it was. Questions 3, 4, and 5 also contain a "check-up" request for students to infer a generalization or two about the data that they have classified.

Three opportunities are provided to demonstrate competence in the skill because at times the information to which a skill is applied can affect adversely how a skill is executed. One must allow for the possibility of students' not being able to execute a skill because of misreading or not understanding the given data. Several opportunities should thus be provided for using the skill; a teacher could consider passable a student's getting two out of three questions correct. It should be noted here that no specific instructions are given with these items that could either "give away" how to do the skill or limit any specific techniques that the students could use in executing the skill. Because asking students to group or list these items would hint at what they could do to carry it out, such hints need to be avoided. At best, the skill label used in class should be the action word in questions or tasks of this type only in the initial tests assessing the skill.

Probably the most difficult question in this sequence, question 6, requires students to know the skill well enough to explain to others how to execute it. Students may write their directions in paragraph form, make a list of steps and rules to follow, or draw and label a flowchart or other type of diagram to present these directions. When students direct their explanation to those younger and thus presumably less competent in the

UNIT I—TEST FOR THE SKILL OF CLASSIFYING

1. Which of the following best defines the skill of *classifying*?

   a) to arrange things in the order in which they occurred.
   b) to put together things having a common characteristic
      or characteristics.
   c) to invent a theory.

2. Which of the following show(s) information that has been classified?

a) A   b) B   c) C

A

As the Indians approached, we put down our muskets and stood up. We recognized the one known as Red Feather clearly. As he came toward us he raised his right hand to salute. Captain Smythe returned the salute and held out the blue blanket. Red Feather smiled and clapped his hands together, shouting to his warriors. They lowered their bows and lances. We had made friendly contact!

B

The original colonies had different kinds of governments. Connecticut and Rhode Island, under charters, selected their own officials. Others, like Pennsylvania, Maryland, and New Jersey, had been granted to individuals known as proprietors. Some colonies, including New York and Georgia, were controlled by appointees of the King; these colonies were known as Royal colonies.

C

Spanish	*English*	*French*
Coronado	Cabot	de Champlain
Cabrillo	Hudson	Cartier
deSoto	Drake	Joliet
		LaSalle

Figure 9.1 A Model for Testing a Newly Introduced Thinking Skill or Strategy

3. The following words were commonly spoken by inhabitants of London, England, around the year 1750. Classify these words so you can identify what life was like for these Londoners at this time and *show all your work*. Then answer the question below.

customs house	journeyman	stock exchange
lottery ticket	workhouse	alehouse
malaria	milkmaid	mugger
apprentice	cesspool	pauper
almshouse	typhoid	gin
watchman	dockworker	poor house
coffee house	butcher	cow
weaver	smallpox	liquor
squire	debtors' prison	master
gambling house	wool-comber	night soil
chimney sweep	typhus	police court

Circle the letter preceding whichever of the following is/are probably true about life in London around 1750.

a) Most Londoners lived like rich people.
b) Life in London was unhealthy and unsafe for many people.
c) Farming was a way of life for most Londoners.

Figure 9.1 *(continued)*

4. The items listed below were recovered from a dried-up well near a place where people lived in late eighteenth century America. The place of origin of each item is indicated, where known. Classify these items in some way that would help tell you about the people who used these items. *Be sure to show how you classify these items.* Then answer the question at the bottom of the page.

1 iron candle chandelier (France)
3 pewter mugs (Germany)
18 copper buttons (America)

7 pewter spoons (America)
3 hand painted, porcelain plates (England)
1 pewter plate (Germany)
2 westerwald stoneware chamber pots (Germany)
1 porcelain teapot (China)
5 whiteware hand-painted plates (France)
3 bone-handled forks (England)

2 stoneware milk vessels (America)
1 pewter fork
8 liquor bottles (England)
3 soda glasses

1 horn-handled knife (America)
8 perfume bottles (France)
1 pocket knife, mother-of-pearl handle (England)
9 medicine bottles (England)
1 iron hoe (America)

11 wine decanters (France)
1 silk glove

3 bone-handled tooth brushes
3 hand-painted pearlware plates (China)

7 hand-painted porcelain tea cups (England)
3 porcelain cups (China)
2 printed silk cloths (China)
1 leather shoe (England)
2 bone-handled hair brushes

Circle the letter preceding the phrase that best completes this sentence:

The people who once used the items on the above list almost certainly

a) made a living as craftsmen.
b) lived on the western frontier.
c) were upper class, wealthy.

Figure 9.1 *(continued)*

5. Classify the information in the following paragraph to answer this question: What was the economy of the thirteen colonies like before the American Revolution? *Show all your work.*

By 1763 the thirteen colonies were sending many products overseas. Lumber, tar, fish, rum—a drink made from molasses—and furs went from Massachusetts, New Hampshire, Connecticut, and nearby colonies. Pennsylvania, New York, Delaware, and neighboring colonies shipped iron, iron kettles and tools, flour, lead, woolen cloth, and hats as well as furs and livestock. The Carolinas, Virginia, and neighboring colonies shipped tobacco, indigo—a plant from which a dye was made—rice, and farm products like grain, beans, pork, and horses.

Now, complete the following:

Based on how you processed the above items, write one sentence describing the economy of the thirteen American colonies just before the American Revolution. In another sentence explain why your first sentence is accurate, based on the data above.

1. _____

_____

2. _____

_____

Figure 9.1 *(continued)*

6. In the space under the data below, give *specific*, detailed directions that a fifth grader could follow to classify the *names* in order to answer this question: "What was colonial culture like by 1775?"

Name		Name	
Phyllis Wheatley	poet	Cotton Mather	minister/scientist
Benjamin Franklin	printer/inventor	John Copley	painter
Benjamin West	painter	Jonathan Edwards	minister/author
Sarah Kemble Knight	author	Roger Williams	minister
David Rittenhouse	astronomer	Anne Bradstreet	poet
John Peter Zenger	editor		

END OF TEST

Figure 9.1 *(continued)*

skill than are they, these directions will probably be in a clearer, more direct, simpler form than if addressed to the teacher or anyone else students suspect of knowing more about the skill than they do.

A cluster of test items like these suggested here offers many advantages in assessing student performance in thinking skills. In effect, this collection of items assesses three levels of proficiency. If a student answers questions 1 and 2 satisfactorily but cannot answer the remaining questions on this part of the exam, a teacher can reasonably assume that the student knows only a little about this skill and cannot do it well. For even if not familiar with the meaning of the data, a student could classify these words by first letters, by syllables, by number of letters, or by some other non-subject-matter criteria. A student who answers questions 1 through 5 but does not do well on item 6 shows a high degree of knowledge and proficiency in the skill in this type of context, but still not enough to be able to explain it satisfactorily to others. Any student who can complete the entire range of questions correctly may well have a very high proficiency in this particular skill, at least in this subject area and format.

In preparing such tests, teachers must give special attention to the kinds of data used with the questions and to the way these data are used. In devising items that require application of the skill to be assessed, teachers must especially guard against creating or selecting those that confuse or mix recall of subject matter or information with the thinking operations being tested. Figure 9.2 illustrates this problem. It presents two test items, both designed to assess student proficiency in the skill of comparing/contrasting.[5] Yet item 1 requires students to recall information before they can process it to answer the question. Item 2 provides virtually all the information needed to answer the question. Students who fail to answer question 1 correctly may fail because they cannot recall appropriate information as much as because they cannot compare it correctly. Inferring that the skill of comparing is at fault in such instances could hardly be justified. As a rule of thumb, items that call for a student to apply any given thinking skills should be those like item 2 in this figure, providing data needed to answer the stated skill-applying questions. Such data can be presented in lists, graphs, maps, paragraphs, scripts, narratives, illustrations, and other appropriate formats. The key to minimizing interference in skill assessing, caused by a need to recall information or use other skills, is to provide all the information needed to answer a thinking skill question as part of the question or item.

Furthermore, data used in skill application questions should be the same kinds of data and in the same format as those used in teaching the skill in class. But these data must *not* have been seen or used before in this form by the students. Students should be familiar with their meaning but should not have processed them in class exactly as they are to be pro-

1. In the late nineteenth century, western vigilantes and southern Ku Klux Klan (KKK) members were similiar in what way?

   A. Both took the law into their own hands.
   B. Both were concerned with jury trials.
   C. Both were against violence.
   D. Both found jobs for immigrants.

2. Population Growth in the United States and Canada

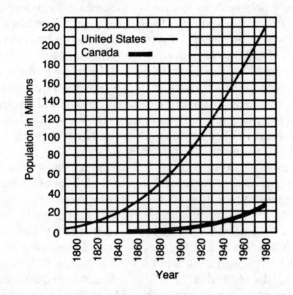

Which of the following statements is true concerning the population growth of the United States and Canada?

• Both the United States and Canada are growing at the same rate.
• The United States is growing in population more rapidly than Canada.
• People do not like living in Canada.
• There are more people living in Canada than in the United States.

Figure 9.2 Questions Calling for Comparing/Contrasting

cessed on the test. To include as data in a particular thinking skills question data that the students already have worked with in learning that skill in class can invalidate the test. Student answers to such items are less likely to evidence proficiency in the skill that the items seek to assess than they are skills of simple recall or recognition. For the most valid and reliable test results, data included in thinking skills test items must not be the same data that students have used in practicing the skill in their classes but must be similar in form and method of presentation of class-room data.

To provide on a test data of a kind or in a form with which students are completely unfamiliar—especially on a test given early in the course of learning a thinking operation—is likely to result more in a measure of a student's ability to transfer a skill on his or her own than it is to be a measure of skill competency at this point. Keeping the data the same as that used in instruction provides a fairer and more valid measure of skill competency. As teachers help students elaborate a thinking skill and learn how to apply it in various settings, then test questions can use data representative of the variety of settings in which it has been taught.

The amount of data provided with thinking skill test items should also be relatively small. A cluster of items such as those in the model test (Figure 9.1) will require much more than ten or fifteen minutes to complete; what time is allocated for the test must be devoted to processing data rather than simply reading it. Paragraphs, lists, and other types of data should, therefore, not be too long. What students do with the data is more important than how much data they process.

Teachers may wish to add more test items to these basic six. For example, a question asking for synonyms of a skill label or asking students to indicate a word that does *not* belong in a group of such synonyms might be suitable following question 1 on the model test. Two items requiring picking examples might be included instead of one, as on the model test here (question 2). In this case, the first of these two items could illustrate use of the skill in a data set identical to the data set used in introducing a skill; the second of the two could provide a data set in a form identical to that used in introducing the skill but the data could be from other parts of the subject-matter unit being tested.

Application items (like numbers 3, 4, and 5 on the model test) can also be modified in a number of ways. It may be advisable to add one or two multiple choice questions at the bottom of each page after each major question as checks on how students processed the data. For example, the following items could have been included under question 3 of the model test in Figure 9.1.

a) Which of the following might have been classified together?

   a) 1 and 2   c) 2, 3, and 4
   b) 1, 4, and 6   d) 2, 5, and 6

     1. police court   4. mugger
     2. chimney sweep   5. apprentice
     3. coffee house   6. watchman

b) What is it those items in your answer to the above question have in common?

In asking questions like these, teachers take some risk of limiting student options or of "giving away" certain categories. However, by giving only a few options, a teacher can steer students to provide a desired response and thus test knowledge. But such a question fails to allow students to truly generate their own categories. A more useful format for "check-up" items under questions like 3, 4, and 5 might thus be:

> For one of the categories of information you have identified, explain why you have developed it as you did.

Notice the sequence of the data and tasks in questions 3, 4, and 5. The task and data in question 3 are virtually identical to those used in introducing the skill in class. The task in question 4 requires classifying but with data that students may not be familiar with, at least as a result of study in class. However, the general context of the data in the question resembles closely the topics being studied in the course and the subject matter of the test itself. Question 5 presents familiar data but in a paragraph format rather than in a list; the "listing" of data is, in fact, embedded in the paragraph. Such a change in data format presumes that students had used data presented in this second format prior to the test (as is the assumed case here). A progression of application items moving from an item as much as possible like those done in the class introduction of the skill being tested to the most recent elaboration of the skill may be a useful question sequence. But whatever sequence is used, it should be remembered that formats and data sets ought to be like those used with the skill in class up to the point of the test.

The items on this sample test presume student understanding of the data used. There is, thus, a risk that inability to execute the skill may reflect ignorance of the data rather than of the skill. Research clearly indicates that competence in a skill is enhanced by knowledge of the context or field in which it is applied.[6] Since this set of sample items is to be on a unit test for which students are to have studied, it seem reasonable to presume that students will recall enough about the data in these items to demonstrate proficiency in the skill. This is quite appropriate, especially since using a category of "miscellaneous" is a useful emergency rule students should have learned regarding how to handle unfamiliar or fuzzy data.

Where student knowledge of the data may not be presumed, some definition or description of the data needs to be supplied, as in question 6. To minimize interference with the skill caused by failure to know all the data used here, question 6 includes for each individual a significant attribute that can be used as categories for arranging them. Of course, the names themselves reflect the sex of each individual, and students may also recommend use of this distinction as a basis of classifying.

In the initial stages of teaching a skill or strategy, testing should concentrate on assessing proficiency in the operation as it has been introduced. This means essentially that the data used in the test items must be of the same type as that in which the skill was introduced and initially practiced. While it is tempting to produce a test to assess transfer, it is patently unfair and unproductive to do so until students have received instruction and guided practice in elaborating the skill in a number of related contexts or with a number of different types of data. Students need experience and instruction in generalizing a skill to a variety of contexts before they can be reasonably expected to know enough to, or even voluntarily make, the transfer necessary to apply the skill successfully in a new context. Forcing students to make such a transfer before they have received appropriate instruction in how to do so and then giving students grades on the quality of the resulting performance may not only discourage students from further effort to learn the skill but merely confirm what we already know: transfer is not usually automatic. Results on such a test item would reveal more about the quality of instruction than about student proficiency in the skill being assessed.

As students receive more instruction and guided practice in applying a thinking skill or strategy in a variety of contexts and thus generalize it beyond the setting in which it was introduced, tests can more legitimately seek to assess proficiency at transfer. Tests for this purpose should not only provide "surmountable challenges" but also, according to educator Edys Quellmalz:

1. present tasks of significance,
2. require sustained thinking,
3. require integration of information used in a series of items, and
4. represent a range of generalized transfer tasks.[7]

Quellmalz recommends, for example, that test items for a particular skill include settings that are (1) life experience, (2) in subject-matter contexts and in (3) novel contexts. Thus, a test on classifying might present as items 3, 4, and 5 (1) a task involving classifying the items found in a garage or auto in an effort to identify something about the user of the garage or auto, (2) a task involving classifying a series of historical events (if the subject is history), and (3) a task involving classifying the ingredients of a structure found in the ruins of a "lost" civilization such as Atlantis or on Venus.

If each time this skill of classifying had been applied in class the teacher had been asking students to consider where this skill could be used in the context of their own school experiences, another application item could be added to the sample test presented here, an item that asks students to apply the skill with school-based data and "to show your work". For example, the following item might follow question 5 on the model test (Figure 9.1):

(6). Four high school students were comparing their class schedules for the new school year. Process the information they reported so you can tell something about the kind of school which students A, B, C, and D attend and/or something about these students themselves. *Be sure to show how you processed this data.* (See Figure 9.3.) Based on how you processed the data, write two sentences (1) describing the school attended by students A, B, C, and D or (2) describing the students themselves. Be sure to give a reason for what you say in each sentence.

This kind of item requires "transfer" of the thinking operation being assessed. Providing items using data typical of out-of-class contexts to which a skill can be legitimately applied should be done only if cues to these data have been previously introduced and used in class, at least in the early stages of teaching and testing a particular skill. On later tests additional items could require "transfer" to other data formats with clues similar to those discussed or used in class.

In sum, one specific format for a set of questions to assess proficiency in a newly introduced thinking skill or strategy (as with the skill of classifying used as an example here) consists of six items requiring, in sequence:

1. Definition of the skill
2. Identifying an example of the skill in use
3. Application of the skill
4. Application of the skill
5. Application of the skill
6. Explanation of how to execute the skill

If a teacher had already used this format to assess proficiency in this newly introduced skill and then, in the next teaching unit, had introduced a second thinking operation, the number of items on that unit test assessing *both* skills would have to increase. Such a format might then look like this:

Questions on
skill introduced earlier:

1. Identification of example of the skill
2. Application of the skill
3. Application of the skill
4. Explanation of how to execute the skill

	A	B	C	D
1st period	Geography	Creative Writing	English Literature	International Relations
2nd period	General Math	Trigonometry	Introd. Spanish	French Literature
3rd period	Study Center	U.S. History	Algebra	Creative Writing
4th period	English Grammar	Gym/Study	Geography	Calculus
Lunch A	x		x	
Lunch B		x		x
5th period	Gym/Study	Physics	Study Center	Physics
6th period	General Science	Physics Lab	Gym/Study	Physics Lab
7th period	Typing	Spanish III	Biology	Typing
8th period	Introd. French	Typing	Biology Lab	Gym/Study

Figure 9.3 High School Student Schedules

Questions on
more recently introduced skill

1. Definition
2. Identification of example of skill
3. Application of the skill
4. Application of the skill
5. Application of the skill
6. Explanation of how to do the skill

Subsequent skill tests will need fewer application items of skills introduced earlier in a course than application items for skills most recently introduced. Nor is it necessary to require definitions or identifications of examples of these skills. Yet, in order to get a reasonable measure of proficiency in them, some attention needs to be given these skills, especially in terms of picking out examples of them in use, applying them, and explaining them to others. As a rule of thumb, teachers might experiment on "cluster" skill tests with sets of four questions on skills introduced earlier and six questions for newly introduced skills.

One final point remains about test items of the type discussed here. Answering them requires considerably more time than is often allotted for conventional objective items designed to assess knowledge of subject matter alone. A six-item skill cluster like that described here may well require thirty minutes or so for many students. Thus, teachers may wish to administer this section of a unit test on a second day after students have completed the regular subject-matter segment of the test. But regardless of when it is administered, teachers should allow a reasonable time for students to complete it. At least on early administrations of items like these, time limits should not be restricting.

Formats for Testing Skills in Context

Thinking skills, of course, are rarely used singly or in isolation from one another. Thinking is a complex process involving a variety of skills and strategies. In order to resolve a problem, an individual may have to translate data, classify it and compare it to other data, and then infer a generalization about the unique feature(s) of a particular subject or phenomena. To assess student proficiencies in employing a variety of thinking skills or some combination of these skills, a teacher can construct multiple choice test items similar to those skill items used on major reading tests or on the Scholastic Aptitude Test. As in question 3, 4, and 5 in Figure 9.1, these items consist of a data set—a paragraph, map, chart, or table, for example—followed by a series of questions, each designed to elicit the use of a particular thinking skill. Figure 9.4 illustrates this type of test item:

Like the data used in question 3, 4, and 5 on the model skill test (Figure 9.1), the data in Figure 9.4 are used to answer the questions that follow it. But unlike questions 3, 4, and 5 in Figure 9.1, a number of

The Egbas and Yorubas were the main actors in these merciless conflicts. They also were the main sufferers from them. They were once the most peaceful and civilized tribes in the country, famous for their agriculture and trade. Fighting with their neighbors and with each other ruined them. When I arrived, many of the Egbas and Yorubas felt sick of war and the slave trade. They wanted peace and prosperity.

1. According to this excerpt, the Egbas and Yorubas were recently involved in:
   a) changing their religion.
   b) civil war.
   c) starting to trade with Europe.
   d) outbreaks of contagious diseases.

2. The excerpt suggests that the Egbas and Yoruba were:
   a) the only civilized people in the country.
   b) the most warlike of all people in the country.
   c) famous as fishermen and traders.
   d) two of several groups living in the region.

3. According to this excerpt, its author:
   a) fears the Egbas and Yorubas.
   b) is unfamiliar with the Egbas and Yorubas.
   c) sympathizes with the Egbas and Yorubas.
   d) dislikes the Egbas and Yorubas.

4. The best title for this excerpt is:
   a) Trade among the Egbas and Yorubas.
   b) From War to Peace.
   c) Egbas versus Yorubas.
   d) The Fruits of War.

Figure 9.4 Sample Question to Assess Thinking Skill Proficiency in Several Thinking Skills

different questions follow each set of data like this one. And each of these questions accompanying the data requires students to employ a different thinking skill. Question 1 here, for example, requires students to translate the data provided in the paragraph. Question 2 requires students to interpret the data, while question 3 assesses the reader's ability to analyze data to infer the author's frame of reference. And in question 4 respondents must synthesize what they have read to produce a generalization in the form of a title.

Questions such as these can be constructed for use in any subject area and be clustered at the end of a regular unit or other major subject-matter test to assess student proficiency in applying a variety of thinking operations that have been taught over the months preceding the test. A chemistry teacher, for instance, who has already taught skills of comparing, classifying, and generalizing may prepare five or six such items, each using different data sets followed by four questions. Of these questions, the first in each item could require translation, the second comparing, the next classifying, and the fourth generalizing. Thus, on such a test containing five, four-question items, five questions will assess proficiency on each of the four skills. From answers to these questions, teachers can infer students' proficiencies in each skill being assessed. Such inferences based on this type of test item are much less shaky than those based solely on conventional teacher tests.

An even more sophisticated format for a thinking skills test might resemble the Cornell Test of Critical Thinking developed by Robert Ennis and Jason Millman.[8] Such a test would include, as the data to be processed, a continuing narrative, a debate, a journal account, or an argument interspersed with questions, each requiring use of a particular thinking skill that has been taught. Questions can be keyed to a limited number of skills so that student proficiency in each can be assessed over several instances. Students answer the questions in a context of continuous thinking; they must apply many specific operations in order to resolve a problem, make a decision, clarify a argument, comprehend something, or develop a concept. Although extremely difficult to produce, such tests prove to be most intriguing to students and offer considerable internal motivation for completing them. The advent of the microcomputer and the possibilities of multiple branching based on student responses offer considerable potential for using tests like these for both teaching and assessing student proficiency in thinking.

Essay questions, too, produce some measure of student proficiencies in thinking skills and strategies. However, these essays must differ from traditional subject-matter essays and must be evaluated for the thinking they represent or report rather than solely for content accuracy or grammar. Several types of essay questions might be used for this purpose. Students can be asked to construct arguments to explain their evaluation of given statements or hypotheses, as for example:

> To what extent do you agree or disagree with the claim—"Wars do not solve old problems—they merely create new ones"?

In answering questions like this one, students are expected to build an argument containing all the evidence of a good argument including an assertion, evidence, and reasoning. Analysis of a student's argument in terms of reasoning skills could serve as a useful assessment of proficiency in these skills.

Another type of essay might be based on the critical thinking essay developed by Robert Ennis and Eric Weir.[9] Here, given a series of paragraphs on a topic, students are asked to respond in a series of paragraphs of their own. The given paragraphs illustrate basic reasoning or critical thinking principles or faults, and student responses either judge these given statements or respond to them. Again, however, evaluation of such student writing must focus on the thinking skills evidenced by the writing rather than on the nature of the writing itself.

Two additional types of essays may also be useful measures of student thinking. Students can be assigned regular subject-matter essay questions to answer and, after having written their answers, can write a paragraph or two explaining what they did in their heads to invent their answers. These latter essays require students to articulate what thinking decisions they made and the reasoning behind such decisions. "I think" writing exemplifies such writing. The second type of essay consists of having students write a narrative explaining to another student, younger and less well informed and skilled than they, how to employ a selected thinking operation to complete a specific task. Of course, none of these types of essays should be included on any tests until students have written such essays as class assignments and have had opportunities to discuss and revise what they have written; otherwise, unfamiliarity with the answer format may interfere with execution of the skill or strategy.

Where can teachers find test items of the kinds mentioned here? Unfortunately, few sources exist that can be consulted for this purpose. Yet there are a number of sources that teachers can consult that may provide useful models for some thinking skill test items. Benjamin Bloom's *Taxonomy of Educational Objectives* provides some sample questions on a limited number of thinking skills.[10] The most useful sources, however, are commercially available cognitive skills tests, developed and validated for use in measuring student proficiency in a number of thinking skills. Figure 9.5 lists some of the more widely used of these instruments and provides data about each instrument and the skills it seeks to assess. Teachers can use items on these tests as models for items they themselves will have to write for inclusion on their own tests, if they choose to make such tests. State education department tests of thinking skills may also provide useful sources of test items or models that teachers can use for developing their own items. California's State Education Department developed such a test of critical thinking in the mid-1980s,[11] and other states—including Connecticut, Michigan, and New York— apparently plan similar tests.

Instruments and questions such as those described here have both advantages and disadvantages. They suffer from the same problems of validity and reliability from which all teacher-made tests suffer. But their use will produce better assessment of student proficiency in thinking skills than most current practices do. The practice of clustering skill items on regular classroom tests—and discussion of these items when such

Objective Tests

Cognitive Abilities Test (1985) by Elizabeth Hagen and Robert L. Thorndike. Riverside Publishing Company, 8420 Bryn Mawr Ave., Chicago, IL 60631. For grades K–12. A research test of three twenty-five item sections, timed, on: *verbal* skills of detecting similarities, sentence sense, classification and analogies; *quantitative* skills of relating and seriating; *nonverbal* skills of figure classification, synthesis, and analogies.

Cornell Critical Thinking Test, Level X (1982) by Robert H. Ennis and Jason Millman. Midwest Publications, P.O. Box 448, Pacific Grove, CA 93950. Seventy-six items, timed, for grades 4–14; sections on induction, deduction, observation, determining credibility, meaning, and assumption identification.

Cornell Critical Thinking Test, Level Z (1982) by Robert H. Ennis and Jason Millman. Midwest Publications, P.O. Box 448, Pacific Grove, CA 93950. Fifty-two items, for advanced or gifted high school students, college students, and other adults; sections on induction, deduction, observation, credibility, defining, and assumption identification.

Kaufman Assessment Battery for Children by A. S. Kaufman and N. L. Kaufman. American Guidance Service, Publisher's Building, Circle Pines, MA 55014. An individually administered battery for grades 2–8 on three scales: *sequential processing*—hand movement, number recall, word order; *simultaneous processing*—partial visibility, face recognition, *Gestalt* closure, triangles, matrix analogies, spatial memory; and *acquired achievement*—expressive vocabulary, faces and places, arithmetic, riddles, reading-decoding, reading-understanding.

New Jersey Test of Reasoning Skills (1983) developed by Virginia Shipman. IAPC, Test Division, Montclair State College, Upper Montclair, NJ 07043. Fifty items, untimed, for grades 4–college; syllogistic reasoning, contradictions, causal relationships, assumption identification, induction, good reasons, and others.

Ross Test of Higher Cognitive Processes (1976) by John D. Ross and Catherine M. Ross. Academic Therapy Publications, 20 Commercial Blvd., Novato, CA 94947. One hundred five items, timed, for grades 4–college; sections on identifying analogies, deduction, identifying missing premises, abstract relations, sequencing, questioning, relevance in mathematics problems, and analysis of attributes.

Structure of the Intellect Learning Abilities Test by Mary and Robert Meeker. Western Psychological Services, 12031 Wilshire Blvd., Los Angeles, CA 90025. Grades K–12, assessing twenty-six cognitive abilities including recall, evaluation, convergent and divergent production; figural, symbolic, and sematic dimensions of content; and product dimensions of units, classes, relations, and systems.

Watson-Glaser Critical Thinking Appraisal (1980) (forms A and B) by Goodwin Watson and Edward Glaser. The Psychological Corporation, a subsidiary of Harcourt Brace Jovanovich, 7500 Old Oak Blvd., Cleveland, OH 44130. Eighty items; two forms, timed or untimed; for grades 9 through adult; sections on inference, assumption identification, deduction, conclusion-logically-following-beyond-a-reasonable-doubt (interpretation), and argument evaluation.

Whimbey Analytical Skills Inventory (1979) by Arthur Whimbey. Franklin Institute Press, Box 2266, Philadelphia, PA 19103. Thirty-eight items, untimed, for grades 4–12; sections include following directions, mathematical analogies, problem solving, analogical reasoning, trends and patterns, differences/similarities, sorting.

Figure 9.5 Thinking Skills Tests

Essay Test

The Ennis-Weir Critical Thinking Essay Test (1983) by Robert H. Ennis and Eric Weir. Midwest Publications, P.O. Box 448, Pacific Grove, CA 93950. For grades 7 through college. Students read a nine-paragraph "letter to the editor" and then have forty minutes to write a ten-paragraph letter in response critiquing paragraph by paragraph, with a summary paragraph, the quality of thinking in the original letter. This instrument seeks to measure the following critical thinking skills: getting the point, seeing the reasons and assumptions, stating one's point, offering good reasons, seeing other possibilities, and responding appropriately to or avoiding: equivocation, irrelevance, circularity, reversal of an if-then (or other conditional) relationship, the "strawperson" fallacy, overgeneralization, excessive skepticism, credibility questions, and the use of emotive language to persuade.

Figure 9.5 *(continued)*

tests are returned to students after having been graded—will confirm to students the value of learning the thinking skills taught in class. These tests will also provide valuable information about the degree of proficiency achieved in each skill assessed. For students who are assessed with items like these, the appearance of similar items on state, national, or other mandated tests will no longer be a shocking surprise. Of all the methods teachers can use to assess student proficiency in thinking, explicit testing—in depth—of the thinking operations being taught in the classroom can be the most useful and powerful. Not only does such an assessment provide a more reliable measure of student skill learning than do most methods commonly used by teachers, but it also provides a measure of instructional effectiveness. Even more so, explicit testing of the skills being taught can also motivate student learning of such skills. Consistent and in-depth classroom paper-and-pencil testing of thinking skills and strategies can improve both teaching and learning of these skills.

OBSERVATION OF STUDENT BEHAVIOR

Besides using various types of paper-and-pencil tests to assess student proficiency in specific thinking skills and strategies, teachers can also look for patterns of student behaviors indicative of skillful thinking. By recording specific incidences of such behaviors over a year or so, teachers can develop another measure of student thinking. Consulting both observational data and test data, teachers are likely to get a thorough and realistic appraisal of the thinking proficiencies of their students—and of their own proficiency at the teaching of thinking.

Paper-and-pencil tests customarily reveal whether students get right—correct—answers. Observation can be a useful tool for providing information about how they go about developing those answers. Indeed, some educators assert that the ultimate assessment of student thinking is to identify what students do when they *don't* know an answer.[12] In both instances, knowing the behavior indicative of skillful thinking is a prerequisite to effective use of observation for assessing student thinking.

Over the past several decades, researchers have identified a number of behaviors that characterize ineffective thinking.[13] Knowing these, teachers can then perhaps look for their behavioral opposites as indicators of more effective thinking. These thinking behaviors are primarily those indicative of the dispositions supportive of effective thinking outlined in the preceding chapter. Students good at thinking voluntarily cite evidence and reasons for claims they make and they ask others, including texts and other authorities, to do the same. They initiate questions, ones that ask why? how come? and so what? rather than simply calling for descriptive information. They deliberately seek out information in making decisions and constantly seem to want more of it before deciding. They deliberately generate many alternatives before judging or choosing any. They deliberately seek other points of view on a topic, issue, or question as a way of securing such information. They consult and cite reliable sources and insist that others do so, too. Consistent and persistent behaviors such as these can be interpreted as indicative of skillful thinking just as can be high scores on thinking skills tests.

Educator Arthur L. Costa has suggested a list of behaviors that he believes are indicative of an effective thinker. Such an individual, he writes:

1. Persists in a thinking task, applying alternative methods until a goal is achieved.
2. Deliberately plans how to execute a thinking task by clarifying goals, identifying givens, and carefully selecting methods and data.
3. Exhibits flexibility in thinking, approaching a task from a number of perspectives or angles.
4. Tells the steps engaged in when executing a thinking skill or strategy.
5. Identifies missing data in a problem-solving situation and how to locate it.
6. Goes over test answers, papers, and reports to check for accuracy, completeness, and clarity.
7. Recognizes discrepancies in the environment and raises questions about them.

8. Asks his/her own questions about causation, relationships, hypothetical situations, and stimuli.
9. Gives and requests evidence and reasoning in support of assertions.
10. Draws on past experience and knowledge and the accumulative knowledge of others.
11. Applies knowledge and skills learned in one context to another context.
12. Uses and insists on precise language.
13. Expresses enjoyment in thinking.
14. Expresses pride in the way in which he/she goes about thinking and the results he/she gets.[14]

Of course, additional behaviors could be included on this or any similar list based on research, but the behaviors noted here are sufficient to indicate the range and types of behavior that teachers can look for in attempting to assess student proficiency in thinking.

Recording student demonstrations of such behaviors can, however, be a challenging task. Cumulative impressions of the extent to which students exhibit such behaviors might be recorded on observation forms using Likert scales for each of a number of such behaviors. Figure 9.6 presents one such form that might serve this purpose for general thinking behaviors. Here the observer is asked to record on a four-point scale his or her observations regarding twelve student behaviors often considered to typify effective thinking. This same kind of device can be used to record observations of behaviors deemed illustrative of proficiency in a specific thinking skill or strategy, as well. Figure 9.7 presents such a scale for recording student behaviors typically associated with effective use of the skill of analysis. Teachers can prepare similar observation scales for virtually any thinking operation and may modify or elaborate such devices as the occasion warrants. When the behaviors or skills to be observed are keyed to specific skill teaching objectives, the use of observational instruments such as these may be one useful way of assessing, for both formative and summative purposes, student learning as well as classroom instruction.

As attractive as such an approach to assessing thinking may be, however, problems exist in devising and using these observation instruments. First, the validity of such instruments and procedures needs to be determined. Beyond establishing a significant correlation between these instruments and other validated measures of thinking, this involves developing a consensus among potential observers about the kinds of behaviors to be noted. Indeed, it involves agreement on the extent to which the behaviors listed actually are evidence of effective thinking or are essential ingredients in any specific thinking operation to be assessed.

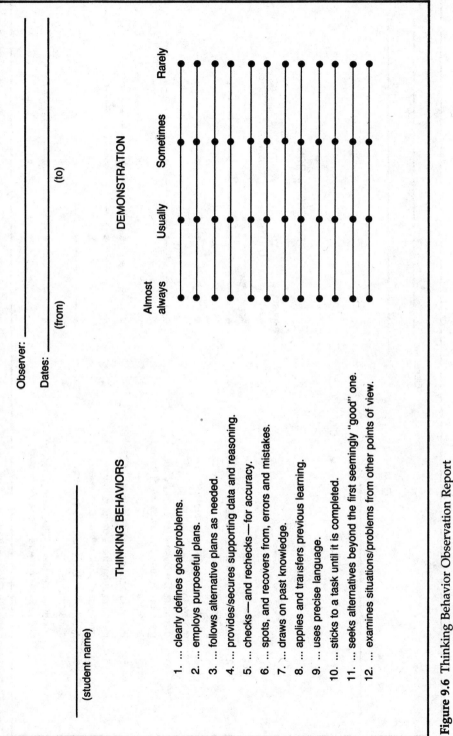

Figure 9.6 Thinking Behavior Observation Report

241

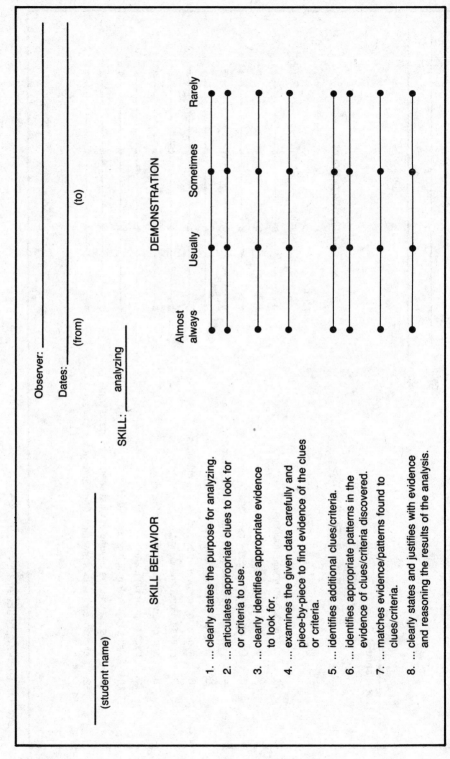

Figure 9.7 Thinking Skill Observation Report

242

It also requires attention to the degree of competence of the respondents in recognizing or recalling the use of such behaviors in the first place.

Furthermore, attending to student thinking behaviors requires more than merely noting the forms or content of such behaviors. It involves also noting the context of those behaviors—whether they are exhibited in familiar and previously experienced settings only or in novel and unfamiliar contexts as well. It is important to note also whether such behaviors are exhibited in response to teacher or other outside stimuli or are exhibited at the initiative of students themselves. Just as in paper-and-pencil testing, teachers employing observation to assess student thinking must look for patterns of voluntary thoughtful behavior in a variety of unfamiliar as well as familiar settings in order to judge the proficiency of student thinking.

Moreover, the logistics of using observation instruments, of virtually any kind, may well be overwhelming, especially if a single teacher is expected to complete one for each student he or she teaches or if an evaluation is sought from all teachers and other school officials for a large number of students in a school. Such an effort is likely to be rather forbidding, to say the least.

Finally, special efforts must be made to prevent abuses inherent in using observational devices such as these. Teachers must take care, for instance, *not* to reduce the points on the scales to numbers that can then be totaled and averaged across responses. They should make every effort to assure that student thinking behaviors are not put into the forms of numbers by which students can subsequently be classified and labeled. They must also be careful how they interpret data derived from such observations. At best, noting only patterns of behavior accumulated over time will be a valid interpretation. Data secured from a single observation will almost assuredly be inappropriate as a basis for describing or making judgments about a student's thinking or growth in thinking abilities.

In spite of serious problems in the use for summative purposes of observational instruments for assessment of thinking, these instruments may prove useful in other ways. They could be given directly to the students themselves, periodically, for self-assessment of their proficiency at thinking. Using the instruments in this way may serve instructional goals far better than assessment goals. Use of these instruments as a basis for student self-diagnosis early in a school year and periodically thereafter can alert students to the kinds of behaviors they *ought* to be exhibiting. Even if what they check on the accompanying scales remain suspect, the very fact that they know what the desired or expected behaviors are may motivate or otherwise lead them to adopt some of these behaviors. These instruments may also be provided periodically to parents so that they can note the behaviors of their children. And, even if parents choose not to use them, this may alert them to the school's goals in this aspect of the curriculum and thus serve a very useful public relations function. Indeed, allowing parents to contribute to the rating of student progress in thinking can educate parents about the kinds of thinking behavior they might reinforce at home and thus provide continuing support for such learning beyond the classroom.

SUMMARY

Without appropriate assessment we cannot know how skillful a student is at thinking or how effective a teacher is at teaching it. Nor can we know what needs to be attended to in order to improve either. By observing and testing directly the thinking behaviors and skills of students, teachers can sharply enhance both the teaching and learning of thinking. Making continuing and in-depth paper-and-pencil testing of these skills an integral part of each major subject-matter classroom test where thinking is being taught calls student attention to the importance of thinking as a legitimate learning and teaching objective. Such testing also provides diagnostic feedback about both the quality of student learning and teacher teaching. Without it, improvements in either are most difficult to come by.

Assessing student thinking is as essential a part of teaching of thinking as are the strategies and materials used in this teaching. Without it, the teaching and learning of thinking remain only half done. Unless teachers assess explicitly, continuously, and consistently the thinking skills they teach, the direct teaching of thinking is not likely to lead to the kinds of student proficiencies in thinking deemed most desirable today.

NOTES

1. Walter Doyle, "Academic Work" *Review of Educational Research* 53:2 (Summer 1983), pp. 185–186.

2. Richard W. Burns, "Objectives and Content Validity of Tests," *Educational Technology* (December 15, 1968), pp. 17–18; R.E. Stake and J.A. Easley, Jr., *Case Studies in Science Education: Report to the N.S.F.* (Urbana, Ill.: Committee on Culture and Cognition, University of Illinois, 1978), p. 11.

3. Edys S. Quellmalz, "Needed: Better Methods for Testing Higher-Order Thinking Skills," *Educational Leadership* 43:2 (October 1985), pp. 29–35.

4. Robert J. Sternberg and Joan B. Baron, "A Statewide Approach to Measuring Critical Thinking Skills," *Educational Leadership* 43:2 (October 1985), p. 43.

5. Peter Kneedler, "California's Assessment of the Critical Thinking Skills in History–Social Science." (Sample thinking skill questions distributed at The State of Thinking Conference, Detroit, Mich., October 28, 1985).

6. Alan Newell and Herbert Simon, *Human Problem Solving* (Englewood Cliffs, N.J.: Prentice-Hall, 1972); Doyle, "Academic Work," p. 168; Raymond S.

Nickerson, "Kinds of Thinking Taught in Current Programs," *Educational Leadership* 42:1 (September 1984), p. 27; Ibrahim Q. Saadeh, "The Teacher and the Development of Critical Thinking," *Journal of Research and Development in Education* 3:1 (Fall 1969), p. 87; Robert J. Sternberg, "Teaching Intellectual Skills: Looking for Smarts in All the Wrong Places" (Paper delivered at ASCD Wingspread Conference on the Teaching Thinking Skills, Racine (May 17–19, 1984), p. 16.

7. Quellmalz, "Needed."

8. Robert H. Ennis and Jason Millman, *Cornell Critical Thinking Test, Levels X and Z* (Pacific Grove, Calif.: Midwest Publications, 1985).

9. Robert Ennis and Eric Weir, *The Ennis-Weir Critical Thinking Test* (Pacific Grove, Calif.: Midwest Publications, 1985).

10. Benjamin Bloom et al., *Taxonomy of Educational Objectives—Handbook I: Cognitive Domain* (New York: David McKay, 1956).

11. *Assessment of the Critical Thinking Skills in History–Social Science* (Sacramento: California State Department of Education, 1985).

12. Arthur L. Costa, "Teaching for Intelligent Behavior," *Educational Leadership* 39:2 (October 1981), p. 31.

13. Benjamin Bloom and Lois Broder, *Problem-solving Processes of College Students* (Chicago: University of Chicago Press, 1950); Reuven Feuerstein, *Instrumental Enrichment* (Baltimore: University Park Press, 1980).

14. Arthur L. Costa, "Thinking: How Do We Know Students Are Getting Better at It?" *Roeper Review* 6:4 (April 1984), pp. 197–198.

Epilogue

Implications for Teaching

If there is one message that the preceding chapters seek to get across, it is that in the teaching of thinking, practice is *not* enough. Developing a high degree of proficiency in thinking requires more than simply making students think. It requires more than encouraging and exhorting, more than questioning and discussing, more than stimulating and challenging. While all these techniques may provide students opportunities to exercise their thinking, if they choose to partake of these opportunities, none provides actual instruction in how to execute the operations that constitute thinking any better than they can already do. To be successful, the teaching of thinking requires instruction as well as practice.

Teachers can provide this instruction by addressing directly the components of skillful thinking. These include the dispositions and metacognitive skills needed to provide conscious control and direction of thinking as well as the specific cognitive operations that constitute thinking. To be most effective, the teaching of thinking should provide continuing instruction in, and elaboration and reinforcement of, these components. Teachers must use classroom strategies and techniques that provide explicit instruction and guided practice as well as instruction in how to transfer thinking skills and strategies. Finally, teachers must test the thinking skills they teach in ways that enhance teaching as well as learning. Skillful thinking is best developed by continuing explicit attention to how to do it by teachers and students alike.

The preceding chapters have presented some ways to provide this kind of instruction. The direct teaching of thinking, as described herein, has many implications for schools and teachers alike. Of these, the following implications for curriculum, instructional materials, teaching and supervision seem particularly significant. All directly affect what goes on in classrooms regarding the teaching of thinking.

IMPLICATIONS FOR CURRICULUM

What is taught as thinking is as important as how it is taught. Because time is limited and curricula and courses are usually already bursting at the seams with many subjects, topics, and skills to be taught, it is not possible to teach all the aspects and operations of thinking or their related dispositions as thoroughly as some might wish. Yet, teachers can accomplish a great deal by implementing in the classroom a carefully sequenced curriculum of selected thinking operations. Among the aspects of such a curriculum that most directly affect classroom teaching are the following:

1. The Teaching of Thinking Is NOT an Either-Or Proposition

In the teaching of thinking what is taught should not simply be a matter of either critical thinking or problem solving, of either discrete skills or generalized dispositions and behaviors, of either grand thinking strategies or more specific, less complicated thinking operations. Nor should it be a matter of teaching either thinking or subject matter. Such dichotomies are false dichotomies. Improving student thinking requires attention to "all of the above." Any worthwhile thinking program provides instruction in general strategies such as decision making as well as in discrete operations such as recall, analysis, or identification of unstated assumptions. It requires instruction in analytical judgment making as well as in the subject matter about which such judgments are to be made. Instruction must develop general behaviors of effective thinking, such as always giving evidence and reasoning in support of a claim, as well as develop proficiency in specific cognitive operations such as synthesis. The teaching of thinking, to be most effective and successful in terms of student learning and subsequent performance, requires purposeful attention to the whole range of ingredients compromising skillful and effective thinking rather than to any one single dimension of thinking or content.

2. Thinking Should Be Taught

Thinking and its components take on meaning and significance when taught in at least two contexts. First, rather than teach thinking operations as isolated procedures and ends in themselves, teachers should introduce them and teach them for transfer and autonomous use as they are needed to execute major thinking operations such as decision making, problem solving, or major intellectual activities like argumentation or discussion. In other words, discrete thinking skills take on added meaning and function when taught in the context of major thinking strategies. One can, for example, introduce a problem-solving process and then, in moving students through the various steps in this process again and again throughout the year, teach directly the various processing, reasoning, and critical thinking skills used in selected steps of the process when needed. Providing instruction in a specific skill when it is needed to help students execute a purposeful thinking process enhances their motivation to learn both skill and process as they tie the skill to functions meaningful for them. Such instruction also casts skill teaching in a structure that facilitates learning and remembering rather than fragments it into a series of unconnected and unrelated episodes.

Content or subject matter provides a second context for the teaching of thinking. Thinking skills take on meaning and significance when they are needed and used to develop insights, knowledge, or other substantive products. Improving one's thinking is not the ultimate goal of the teaching of thinking. Rather, the major goal is to improve student abilities to develop knowledge more effectively, efficiently, and accurately than they are able or wont to do on their own. Teachers who provide direct instruction in major thinking operations when these operations are required to process data, to invent meaning, to resolve significant problems, to make decisions of personal or social import, or to achieve subject-matter goals give students added incentive to learn such meaningful operations. Thinking skill instruction in regular subject matter as well as in areas within the life experiences of students enhances student understanding of these subjects and experiences.

These two contexts for teaching thinking operations directly—subject matter and major thinking processes—are closely interrelated. It is difficult to do one without the other; thus, they are mutually reinforcing. Subject matter serves as a vehicle for thinking: students have to think about something. And thinking serves as a way of understanding and making meaning from subject matter. Indeed, the thinking skills to be taught move subject-matter learning through the topics to be studied in a course. For best results in the teaching of thinking—in terms both of subject matter and skill learning—the teaching of thinking should be an integral part of existing subject areas in a school's curriculum rather than an add-on or discrete, stand-alone course.

3. The Teaching of Thinking Should Permeate a Curriculum

Thinking should be a subject of instruction throughout a school's curriculum. A single teacher teaching thinking skills in one course or a single course devoted to teaching selected operations to all students will be for naught unless follow-up instruction is provided in how to use previously introduced skills in a variety of subsequent subject-matter courses and other contexts. Moreover, instruction in one version or model of a particular thinking skill will be less than satisfactory unless the skill attributes are elaborated and extended into the more sophisticated forms they take as students gain experience in using them.

IMPLICATIONS FOR INSTRUCTIONAL MATERIALS

Most teaching programs require the use of some type of instructional material. Of all the materials available to teachers, the textbook still remains the most common and most influential. Unfortunately, however, most texts, and indeed most other kinds of "skill teaching" materials (including computer software, workbooks, and blackline masters) in all subject areas and at all grade levels customarily give only the most superficial attention to the teaching of thinking skills, substituting as they do quantity of skills for quality of instruction and practice for teaching. Yet these instructional materials could contribute immensely to improving student thinking skills if they used the framework and strategies for direct instruction in thinking skills and strategies presented here. This framework and these teaching strategies can be incorporated into texts and other teaching materials as easily as they can be employed by a teacher in regular classroom teaching.

To be most useful in the teaching of thinking, commercially prepared instructional materials should follow a number of important principles. Of these, two principles are crucial. First, text programs and other instructional materials must clearly differentiate among three kinds of thinking skills and strategies: (1) those introduced and taught to a high degree of proficiency in a variety of contexts in earlier materials or grade levels; (2) those introduced in earlier texts, materials, or grade levels, but not yet transferred into, or elaborated in, the subject matter of the current material; and (3) those to be introduced and taught to some degree of proficiency in the materials at this grade level. The amount and type of attention given to each type of skill or strategy should vary.

Second, textbook programs and other instructional materials that seek to teach thinking should actually provide instruction in how to execute specified thinking operations appropriate to students' present understanding of, and experience in using, these operations. Previously introduced and mastered skills or strategies can generally be exercised or practiced through end-of-chapter activities or exercise worksheets, as is the common practice. To facilitate learning in this case, a review lesson or two focusing on these skills or strategies and using the guided practice strategy presented in Chapter 6 can be incorporated in an accompanying teaching guide or in an activity book. Skills requiring transfer to, or elaboration in, data or contexts included in a text require specific instruction in the text in how to make the transfer or how to employ the new dimensions of the skill, followed by a number of guided practice lessons, each using appropriate strategies. Skills of the third type—those to be newly introduced in the course—require a series of instructional lessons in the text, software, activity book, and/or blackline masters that provide a formal introduction, continuing guided practice and, eventually, opportunities for independent application. One-shot skill lessons or simple practice exercises in any kind of instructional material are simply not sufficient to "teach" any skill.

In addition to the above principles, textbook, computer, and other instructional programs that purport to *teach* thinking skills should:

1. Focus on a few thinking operations rather than on a multitude of them.
2. Set instruction in a thinking skill or strategy in a teaching framework that uses strategies appropriate to each stage of this framework, as outlined in this book.
3. Provide for transfer of a skill to and its elaboration in data sets, media, or contexts other than those in which it is introduced and practiced—but only after students have demonstrated proficiency in the introductory type of data, media, or context.
4. Relate the thinking operations emphasized in one text to those emphasized in preceding and subsequent courses in the same subject and to thinking operations in courses and materials in other major subjects at the same grade level.
5. Use the same terminology to describe the thinking operations it teaches as is used to describe these skills and strategies in materials in other subjects at the same and other grade levels. This can be easily done by publishers for their own publications. To accommodate materials of different publishers, a glossary of definitions and synonyms for selected thinking skills and operations can be in-

cluded in every text. Such a glossary might be modeled after that included in *Developing Minds*, a resource book on teaching thinking skills published by the Association for Supervision and Curriculum Development in 1985.[1]

6. Test the skills that receive continuing instructional attention. These tests should devote significant attention to assessing student proficiency in those thinking skills and strategies newly introduced, transferred, and elaborated in these materials.

If instructional materials, especially textbook materials and computer programs, are to provide the most effective instruction in thinking, they should incorporate the principles outlined above. By so doing, these materials can provide instructional models for teachers unaware of how best to teach a particular thinking skill or untrained in so doing while at the same time providing the instruction that students need to master thinking skills. Instructional materials accomplishing this goal prove much more valuable to teachers and students than do those that cover superficially dozens of skills with single exposures to each at a practice rather than instructional level. In considering instructional materials for adoption, schools and teachers should insist that their treatment of thinking honor the principles outlined above, if they are to be endorsed for adoption.

IMPLICATIONS FOR CLASSROOM TEACHING

The strategies and techniques of the direct teaching of thinking presented in the preceding chapters have significant implications for classroom teachers. Among the most important of these are the following:

1. Know the Skills and Strategies to Be Taught

It has become a truism that to be most effective as a teacher, one must know the subject being taught. In the teaching of thinking, the subject consists of the skills and strategies that constitute thinking, of knowledge related to these operations, and of dispositions that direct and support thinking. Teachers should know in some detail the various features of these dimensions of thinking. They must know especially the major attributes—the procedures, the rules, and the principles—that constitute the specific thinking operations to be taught. They must know, for example, if classifying is the skill being taught, how one classifies data, why certain procedures are more useful than others in classifying data, any rules or heuristics that prove useful, and any discipline-based knowledge that informs or shapes how this operation can be best executed.

A simple, one-sentence definition does not provide such information. Rather, descriptions like that in Figure 10.1 of the skill of classifying

Label: CLASSIFYING

Definition: putting things together that have the same feature(s); arranging into groups on the basis of (a) shared or common characteristic(s) or attribute(s)

Synonyms: grouping, sorting, categorizing

Steps:

Procedure A	Procedure B
1. Identify/state purpose for classifying.	1. Identify/state purpose for classifying.
2. Skim data to spot significant items/to get ideas.	2. Specify category labels to be used.
3. Focus on an item.	3. Search data item-by-item and place into appropriate categories.
4. Pick other item(s) just like focus item.	4. Modify category labels, if necessary.
5. State (as a label) unifying/ common attribute(s)	5. Combine or subdivide categories, as necessary.
6. Find other items just like focus item.	
7. Repeat procedure with other focus items until all items are classified and labeled.	
8. Combine or subdivide categories as necessary.	

Rules:

1. When to classify? When data
   - are unorganized,
   - are too much to manage easily,
   - don't make sense.
2. How to do it?
   - State identifying label as soon as match two items "alike".
   - Use label as search tool to identify other samples of it.
3. What to do ...?
   - if data in a category vary? Subdivide (reclassify) the category.
   - if same item fits into more than one category? Get new system of divisions or revise all categories.
   - if items are left over? Make a miscellaneous category (tentatively).
   - if begin to "run down"? Switch to working on a new category—don't press.
4. ... (others)

Knowledge Needed:

1. Potential category systems.
2. Information about the data or items to be classified.
3. How to compare and contrast.

Figure 10.1 A Model Skill Description

should be provided for all the major thinking skills and strategies teachers are to teach. The information in these detailed skill descriptions should be a part of the knowledge base that all teachers bring to their classroom teaching.

Such descriptions, it should be noted, represent not so much what is to be repeated by students but take-off points and targets of student learning. They represent the kind of knowledge of a subject that enables teachers to provide students with the most useful instruction, assistance, and opportunities for practice. Not knowing what it is that one is teaching severely handicaps both teaching and learning.

There are many ways to develop knowledge of thinking skills and strategies. These include surveying the literature on thinking, watching experts execute a skill or strategy, or self-reflection in how one actually executes the operation. The companion volume to this book describes and demonstrates some of these procedures in detail.* It also outlines some of the key ingredients of a number of major thinking skills and strategies, presenting them in developmental sequences of differing levels of complexity. As teachers study sources such as this, reflecting on what they are doing and how, their knowledge of thinking increases and deepens. Such essential knowledge is the basis for the effective teaching and learning of thinking.

The skills taught should be continuously refined, extended, and broadened in complexity and variations as students learn how to use them in different contexts for increasing more sophisticated purposes. The teaching of thinking should not be a "one-shot" effort but a continuing part of an entire curriculum, across all grade levels.

2. Practice the Strategies of Direct Instruction Repeatedly with Your Colleagues

Several heads really are better than one in learning a new teaching strategy.[2] Team planning of a lesson is likely to be more helpful and instructive than is individual planning. Taping a lesson for analysis later or inviting some colleagues who know something about the teaching strategies being used to observe one's use of these strategies in a class will certainly be helpful in developing proficiency in these teaching strategies. Review and analysis by a number of teachers of how a lesson was conducted will also be of use in gaining insights into the teaching methods being used as well as into the thinking skills being taught. Revising and reteaching a lesson following such a review also assists one in becoming more adept at using these strategies.

---

*Barry K. Beyer, *Developing a Thinking Skills Program* (Boston: Allyn and Bacon, 1988).

Teaching a jointly planned and revised lesson a number of times proves helpful in getting the feel of a new teaching strategy. Thus, it is very useful in learning a new strategy to teach a group-developed lesson to the group itself or to another small group of one's colleagues before trying to teach it to students. It also proves useful to "pilot-teach," using a new teaching strategy to a small group of four or five in an informal setting—whether teachers or students—before attempting to use it with a larger group. Finally, using the same teaching strategy in successive classes or with different skills provides opportunities to improve on identified weaknesses, fill in gaps in execution of a teaching strategy, or adapt a strategy to different groups of students. Although practicing a new strategy with self-analysis helps one to learn it, working with other colleagues to plan, execute, review, and revise a strategy provides the kind of coaching and support that develops teaching proficiency fastest.

3. Start Slowly!

In the initial stages of using the teaching strategies outlined in the preceding pages, it proves useful to introduce and teach to mastery only a limited number of skills, perhaps two or three a year in each grade level or subject area. Teachers should strive for some degree of proficiency in using these teaching strategies rather than for coverage or quantity of thinking skills. This means devoting enough time to deliberately using and reusing the teaching strategies appropriate to each stage of the skill teaching process, from introduction of a skill to its transfer and independent use. Because of the newness of these teaching strategies, more time may be required to use each at first than would normally be required in using them when experienced in so doing. It may even be advisable to repeat lessons when they have gone less well than desired, because of lack of familiarity with the teaching strategy being used. Under such circumstances, it is best to have time to try out and reteach rather than be under pressure to use these new teaching strategies to teach superficially a large number of thinking operations.

4. Keep Your Teaching Sights on the Target!

In teaching thinking—especially in initial lessons on any thinking skill, strategy or even disposition—the skill, strategy, or disposition is what is being taught. Teachers should eliminate or minimize interference with such teaching that may come from the content or subject matter or data being used, from other skills being employed, or from the environment in which the learning is being carried on.

The target in teaching thinking is learning a thinking skill; temptations to digress into explorations of content must be resisted, especially in the introduction of new skills. To keep focus on a skill, teachers should introduce it using only data or subject matter familiar to the students. They must continuously direct student attention to the attributes of the thinking skill or strategy being taught, gradually reducing such focus as students demonstrate increased proficiency in applying the skill on their own. Only after students have received instruction and guided practice in executing a skill should they be expected to execute it automatically while focusing on other skills and on the subject matter in which it is being applied.

5. Anticipate Teaching Problems

Learning a new skill, according to researcher Bruce Joyce, can be "an invitation to incompetence."[3] This is as true of learning the new strategies for the *teaching* of thinking presented here as it is of learning the thinking skills and strategies being taught. Individuals just beginning to learn and apply these teaching strategies should expect some difficulty initially in making them work efficiently and smoothly. It takes repeated guided practice, modeling, and analysis of such strategies for one to develop proficiency in their use.[4]

The reasons for any difficulty thus encountered are quite likely to be in the skill or in the process of skill learning rather than in the teacher or the teaching situation. Learning a new or systematic way of doing something very often requires unlearning an older way of doing the same thing. Moreover, it means consciously attending to certain prescribed procedures that may not be part of one's usual repertoire. On occasion, this leads to halting and rather awkward performance, but that is to be expected as part of learning. However, by careful planning and by sharing one's experience with colleagues as well as by watching and analyzing demonstrations and by repeated practice at trying these strategies, a teacher can turn a rather halting initial performance into finely tuned expertise. Modifications can be made as one takes ownership of and feels comfortable in using these teaching strategies.

6. Use a Common Language of Instruction

One of the major problems that students confront in learning thinking skills is that of the great variety of terms used to denote the same thinking operation or skill-using practice. For example, even in the same school building or subject areas different teachers may use the term *categorize* or *group* or *classify* to mean essentially the same cognitive operation. It is not unusual to see texts that define a given thinking operation in quite different ways.[5] Such variety confuses more than clarifies, especially for beginners. Using synonyms for a skill label in introducing a new thinking skill acknowledges this variety of terminology and broadens student awareness of the skill's meaning. Where possible, teachers should agree on a common set of skill labels and descriptions and use these consistently in classroom instruction. A number of sources of commonly accepted skill labels and definitions are available and should be consulted to assist teachers in selecting appropriate terms for this purpose.[6]

7. Model Skillful Thinking As Well As Teach It

In addition to using the teaching strategies presented here to help students learn specific thinking skills or behaviors, teachers can model the use of the thinking skills and behaviors they are teaching. This modeling can produce at least three beneficial results. First, it helps students learn the thinking skills and strategies being modeled by showing them exactly how these operations are supposed to work when well executed. Second, conscious modeling of thinking behaviors or skills can make teachers more aware of the intricacies of the cognitive skills involved and make them more sensitive to potential difficulties students may have in learning a skill. Moreover, by repeated use of skillful thinking and reflective analysis of such thinking, teachers can increase their own competencies at executing these operations.

Skill modeling by teachers should be a practice outside as well as inside classrooms. Thinking should not stop at the classroom door for teachers or students. A school environment that values and exhibits effective thinking in *all* aspects of group and individual activity provides the support necessary for effective teaching of these operations.

8. Continue to Investigate and Try Out Different Approaches and Materials for the Direct Teaching of Thinking

Many different teaching techniques may be used within the instructional framework and strategies presented in these pages. Teachers seeking to add to their repertoire of such teaching strategies can try out and analyze— and perhaps even adopt or adapt—materials and strategies from existing thinking skills programs, such as Edward de Bono's CoRT program, Arthur Whimbey's and Jack Lochhead's TAPPS (Thinking Aloud Paired Problem Solving), and Reuven Feuerstein's Instrumental Enrichment.[7] Studying and analyzing the articles and books listed in the Selected References that concludes this book can also contribute to the improved teaching of thinking. Continued study as well as classroom practice are essential to develop a high degree of proficiency in the teaching of thinking.

IMPLICATIONS FOR FACULTY DEVELOPMENT, SUPERVISION, AND EVALUATION

Classroom observations serve a number of purposes: providing feedback for faculty development, monitoring and assessing curriculum effectiveness, and evaluating teacher performance. Administrators and/or teachers who engage in such observations, however, will not find them useful in furthering or appraising the teaching of thinking, as presented in these pages, if they attend to conventionally accepted indicators of skill teaching. Such observers, instead, must look for activities that typify the various stages of teaching for thinking and skill learning described here. In order to judge the effectiveness of such teaching, an observer must do two things. First, he or she must ascertain the kind of lesson being taught—whether it is to introduce a new skill or strategy, provide guided practice, elaborate or transfer a skill, or provide opportunities for independent application of the skill. Second, the observer must look for the kinds of behaviors and conditions most useful in executing the kind of lesson being taught. Specially designed classroom observation forms may be required to guide these observations.

1. Observing Skill Introducing and Transfer Lessons

Figure 10.2 presents a general purpose classroom observation checklist for a lesson introducing a new thinking operation or transferring such an operation to a new context. Notice that this checklist does not focus on levels or techniques of teacher questioning, student discussion patterns, use of worksheets, or other techniques commonly associated with thinking skill instruction. As pointed out earlier, these techniques do not provide such instruction. Rather, this checklist focuses on the techniques that ought to be employed in executing the skill introducing and elaborating/transferring strategies presented in this book.

To facilitate use of lesson analysis, this checklist is divided into three sections: a *context* part (A) related to the subject of the lesson—the thinking operation being taught; a *conduct* part (B) relating to the actual execution of the lesson; and a *components* part (C) dealing with the lesson as a whole. Parts A and C can be completed after an observation has been conducted, preferably with added reference also to the course syllabus or curriculum guide and/or text. Completion of Part B, however, requires observation of the teacher and students as the lesson unfolds. The items in this part (items 2 through 10) refer to the essential components of introductory and transfer/elaboration strategies, including the introduction (item 3); modeling (4); discussion of the skill attributes (5); metacognition (7); data used (8); and student work with the skill (6, 9, 10). To have observed a good, indeed exemplary, introductory or transfer lesson, an

For Introducing or Transferring a Thinking Skill or Strategy

Teacher _____ Observer _____

Subject: _____ Date _____ Time start: _____ end: _____

	Yes	No
A. Context of the lesson		
1. The skill is		
1.1 of sufficient import to warrant detailed attention.	___	___
1.2 based on other prerequisite skills.	___	___
1.3 appropriate to the ability level(s) of the students.	___	___
1.4 introduced at a time it is needed to accomplish a content-related objective.	___	___
1.5 appropriate to the substantive function of the lesson.	___	___
B. Conduct of the lesson		
2. The purpose for attending to the skill at this point is:		
2.1 clearly stated.	___	___
2.2 appropriate.	___	___
3. The skill is clearly introduced by		
3.1 giving its label.	___	___
3.2 defining it.	___	___
3.3 giving synonyms for it.	___	___
3.4 giving appropriate examples of its use	___	___
• in everyday life.	___	___
• in previous coursework.	___	___
3.5 relating it to other skills.	___	___
4. The skill is modeled/demonstrated.	___	___
5. The major components of the skill are explained, or reviewed, including:		
5.1 key procedures for using it.	___	___
5.2 its key rules/principles.	___	___
5.3 knowledge needed to use it.	___	___
6. Students engage in the skill		
6.1 prior to its explanation or demonstration.	___	___
6.2 after having it explained or discussed.	___	___
7. Students explain/discuss what goes on in their heads while using the skill		
7.1 as they engage in the skill.	___	___
7.2 after they engage in the skill.	___	___
8. If there are several skill applications in this lesson, the data/media to which the students apply the skill are in the same form.	___	___
9. Students		
9.1 modify given skill components.	___	___
9.2 suggest major skill components.	___	___
10. In concluding the lesson, *students*		
10.1 define the skill.	___	___
10.2 give synonyms for it.	___	___

Figure 10.2 A Checklist for Introducing or Transferring a Thinking Skill or Strategy

	Yes	No
10.3 tell when/where it can be used.	—	—
10.4 articulate its key components.	=	=
10.5 relate it to other skills.	—	—
C. Components of the lesson		
11. The focus of the lesson was		
11.1 clearly on the skill.		
11.2 consistently on the skill.	—	—
	—	—
12. The teaching strategy used was		
12.1 inductive.		
12.2 directive.	—	—
12.3 other_____ .	=	=
	—	—
13. The teaching strategy used was appropriate to		
13.1 the complexity of the skill.		
13.2 the ability level of the students.	—	—
13.3 experience of the students.	=	=
13.4 the time available.	=	=
13.5 content goals sought.	—	—

Figure 10.2 (*continued*)

observer would want to have recorded a "yes" for virtually every one of the items on this checklist.

2. Observing a Guided Practice Lesson

Figure 10.3 presents a classroom checklist that can be used when observing any guided practice lesson in any thinking skill or strategy. This checklist contains the same three parts as the preceding checklist, focusing on the context, execution, and general conduct of the lesson, And, as in the preceding checklist, the items under *Conduct of the lesson* relate to the key components of strategies for guiding student application of a newly introduced skill. To have observed a most effective lesson of this type, an observer should have recorded a "yes" for virtually all the items in this part of the checklist as well as on the other two parts.

3. Observing Lessons in Using a Thinking Skill

While level of teacher questioning, teacher "wait-time," degree of student-to-student interaction, and similiar activities are not especially good indicators of effective teaching in the preceding kinds of lessons for

For Guiding Practice of a Thinking Skill or Strategy

Teacher _____ Observer _____

Subject: _____ Date _____ Time start _____ end _____

	Yes	No	Notes
A. Context of the lesson			
1. The skill lesson is			
1.1 on a skill of sufficient import to warrant this degree of attention.	___	___	
1.2 one of a series of similar lessons on this same skill.	___	___	
1.3 spaced appropriately after the most recent preceding lesson on this skill.	___	___	
1.4 appropriately tied to course content.	___	___	
B. Conduct of the lesson			
2. The purpose for using the skill at this point is			
2.1 clearly stated.	___	___	
2.2 appropriate.	___	___	
3. The skill is clearly introduced, by			
3.1 giving its label.	___	___	
3.2 defining it.	___	___	
3.3 giving synonyms for it.	___	___	
3.4 giving appropriate examples of its use	___	___	
• previously in class.	___	___	
• in everyday life.	___	___	
4. The major components of the skill are articulated *before* the skill is used including			
4.1 its key procedures.	___	___	
4.2 its rules/principles.	___	___	
4.3 the knowledge needed to use it.	___	___	
5. The skill is deliberately applied to relevant content.	___	___	
6. The major components of the skill are articulated and justified *after* the skill is used, including:			
6.1 its key procedures.	___	___	
6.2 its rules/principles.	___	___	
6.3 the knowledge needed to use it.	___	___	
7. Modifications and/or additions in the skill components are articulated, considered, made.	___	___	
8. Where and when the skill can be used is discussed.	___	___	
C. Components of the lesson			
9. The focus is clearly on the skill throughout the above portion of the lesson.	___	___	
10. The media/content form in which the skill is applied is similar to that in which it was initially presented (or extended).	___	___	
11. The components of the skill are reviewed *before* students discuss the content results of using the skill.	___	___	

Figure 10.3 A Checklist for Guiding Practice in a Thinking Skill or Strategy

teaching a thinking skill, these methods are appropriate in any lesson that seeks simply to allow students to execute one or more thinking operations on their own. No special checklist need be prepared for observation of such lessons. Most school systems have such instruments. If these are not available, however, anecdotal or informal notes may suffice; or observers may use observation forms designed for more conventional thinking skill instruction.

4. Using These Checklists for Teaching Improvement as Well as for Program or Teaching Evaluation

Use of the checklists presented here, at appropriate places in a sequence of lessons providing direct instruction in thinking, can serve several purposes. They may provide information that, when shared with teachers, can assist them in improving use of the teaching strategies and techniques most appropriate to the kinds of lessons that should be taught. Such information may also provide a basis for judging program effectiveness or teacher proficiency in executing appropriate teaching strategies.

These checklists prove useful in another way, too. Individual teachers can use them as guides for constructing or reviewing lesson plans *before* actually applying these plans in the classroom. By checking a lesson plan against the items on the appropriate checklist, a teacher can assure that the key steps in the strategy are included, that techniques pertinent to each step are also included and that the significant conditions related to that particular type of lesson are likely to be met. These checklists can guide teachers in planning appropriate lessons as well as in identifying omissions or flaws in lessons already planned. Teachers who use these checklists in planning assure that what they will do in class will be most helpful to students in learning thinking skills and strategies.

TOWARD THE TEACHING OF THINKING

James Bryce once observed that, to most people, nothing seems more troublesome than the effort of thinking.[8] To the extent that this is true, it may well be because most people have not received the kind of education that enabled them to develop fully the skills, strategies, and dispositions that constitute effecting thinking. By teaching these skills, strategies, and dispositions directly, as described in the preceding chapters, teachers can help youngsters and others inexperienced in thinking become more skilled at this process than they normally are likely to become. By working toward this goal, teachers can help these individuals develop the facilities and expertise at thinking that will enable them to say, with conviction, as did Descartes years ago, "I think, therefore I am."

NOTES

1. Arthur L. Costa and Barbara Presseisen, "A Glossary of Thinking Skills," in Arthur L. Costa, ed., *Developing Minds: A Resource Book for Teaching Thinking* (Alexandria, Va.: Association for Supervision and Curriculum Development, 1985), pp 309–313.

2. Bruce R. Joyce and Beverly Showers, *Power in Staff Development Through Research on Training* (Alexandria, Va.: Association for Supervision and Curriculum Development, 1983).

3. Bruce R. Joyce, Presentation at George Mason University, Fairfax, Va., April 25, 1986.

4. Joyce and Showers, *Power*.

5. Barry K. Beyer, "Improving Thinking Skills—Defining the Problem," *Phi Delta Kappan* 65:7 (March 1984), pp. 486–490.

6. Costa and Presseisen, "A Glossary."

7. Paul Chance, *Thinking in the Classroom* (New York: Teachers College Press, 1986); Raymond S. Nickerson, David N. Perkins, and Edward E. Smith, *The Teaching of Thinking* (Hillsdale, N.J.: Lawrence Erlbaum Associates, 1985).

8. Quoted in *Bartlett's Familiar Quotations*, 15th ed. (Boston: Little, Brown, 1980), p. 635.

Selected References

BOOKS

Anderson, Howard, ed. *Teaching Critical Thinking in Social Studies*. Washington: National Council for the Social Studies, 1942.

Baron, Joan B., and Robert J. Sternberg, eds. *Teaching Thinking Skills: Theory and Practice*. New York: W. H. Freeman, 1987.

Bloom, Benjamin, and Lois Broder. *Problem-solving Processes of College Students*. Chicago: University of Chicago Press, 1950.

Burton, William H, Roland B. Kimball, and Richard L. Wing. *Education for Effective Thinking*. New York: Appleton-Century-Crofts, 1960.

Chance, Paul. *Thinking in the Classroom: A Survey of Programs*. New York: Teachers College Press, 1986.

Charles, Randall, and Frank Lester. *Teaching Problem Solving: What, Why and How*. Palo Alto, Calif.: Dale Seymour Publications, 1982.

Copple, Carol, Irving E. Sigel, and Ruth Saunders. *Educating the Young Thinker: Classroom Strategies for Cognitive Growth*. Hillsdale, N.J.: Lawrence Erlbaum Associates, 1984.

Costa, Arthur L., ed. *Developing Minds: A Resource Book for Teaching Thinking*. Alexandria, Va.: Association for Supervision and Curriculum Development, 1985.

de Bono, Edward. *Teaching Thinking*. New York: Penguin Books, 1980.

Fair, Jean, and Fannie R, Shaftel, eds. *Effective Thinking in the Social Studies*. Washington: National Council for the Social Studies, 1967.

Feuerstein, Reuven. *Instrumental Enrichment*. Baltimore: University Park Press, 1980.

Furth, Hans, and Harry Wachs. *Thinking Goes to School*. New York: Oxford University Press, 1974.

Glaser, Robert, ed. *Advances in Instructional Psychology*. 2 vols. Hillsdale, N.J.: Lawrence Erlbaum Associates, 1978.

Hayes, John R. *The Complete Problem Solver*. Philadelphia: The Franklin Institute Press, 1981.

Hudgins, Bryce B. *Learning and Thinking*. Itasca, Ill.: F. E. Peacock Publishers, 1977.

Joyce, Bruce R, and Beverly Showers. *Power in Staff Development Through Research on Training*. Alexandria, Va.: Association for Supervision and Curriculum Development, 1983.

Kail, R., and Jerome Kagen. *Perspectives on the Development of Memory and Cognition*. Hillsdale, N.J.: Lawrence Erlbaum Associates, 1977.

Klahr, David, ed. *Cognition and Instruction*. Hillsdale, N.J.: Lawrence Erlbaum Associates, 1976.

Lipman, Matthew, A. Sharp, and F. Oscanyan. *Philosophy in the Classroom*. 2d ed. Philadelphia: Temple University Press, 1980.

Lochhead, Jack, and John Clement, eds. *Cognitive Process Instruction*. Philadelphia: The Franklin Institute Press, 1979.

Nickerson, Raymond S., David N. Perkins, and Edward E. Smith. *The Teaching of Thinking*. Hillsdale, N.J.: Lawrence Erlbaum Associates, 1985.

Perkins, David N. *Knowledge as Design*. Hillsdale, N.J.: Lawrence Erlbaum Associates, 1986.

Peters, R. S. ed. *The Concept of Education*. London: Routledge and Kegan Paul, 1967.

Raths, Louis, et al. *Teaching for Thinking: Theories, Strategies, and Activities*, 2d ed. New York: Teachers' College Press, 1986.

Segal, Judith W., Susan E. Chipman, and Robert Glaser, eds. *Thinking and Learning Skills*. 2 vols. Hillsdale, N.J.: Lawrence Erlbaum Associates, 1985.

Toulmin, Steven, Richard Rieke, and Allan Janik. *An Introduction to Reasoning*. 2nd ed. New York: Macmillan Publishing Company, 1984.

Whimbey, Arthur, and Jack Lochhead. *Problem Solving and Comprehension*. 3rd ed. Philadelphia: The Franklin Institute Press, 1982.

Whimbey, Arthur, and Linda Shaw Whimbey. *Intelligence Can Be Taught*. New York: E. P. Dutton, 1975.

ARTICLES IN JOURNALS AND CHAPTERS IN BOOKS

Bereiter, Carl. "How to Keep Thinking Skills From Going to Way of All Frills." *Educational Leadership* 42:1 (September 1984), pp. 75–78.

Beyer, Barry K. "Common Sense about Teaching Thinking Skills." *Educational Leadership* 41:3 (November 1983), pp. 44–49.

―――. "Improving Thinking Skills—Defining the Problem." *Phi Delta Kappan* 65:7 (March 1984), pp. 486–490.

―――. "Improving Thinking Skills—A Practical Approach." *Phi Delta Kappan* 65:8 (April 1984), pp. 556–560.

―――. "Teaching Critical Thinking: A Direct Approach." *Social Education* 49:4 (April 1985), pp. 297–303.

Beyer, Barry K., and Ronald E. Charlton. "Teaching Thinking Skills in Biology," *The American Biology Teacher* 48:4 (April 1986), pp. 207–212.

Bondy, Elizabeth. "Thinking About Thinking." *Childhood Education* 17:2 (March/April 1984), pp. 234–238.

Brown, Ann L., Joseph C. Campione, and Jeanne D. Day. "Learning to Learn: On Training Students to Learn from Texts." *Educational Researcher* 10:2 (February 1981), pp. 14–21.

Case, Robbie. "A Developmentally-Based Theory and Technology of Instruction." *Review of Educational Research* 48:3 (Summer 1978), pp. 439–463.

Cornbleth, Catherine. "Critical Thinking and Cognitive Process." In William B. Stanley, ed., *Review of Research in Social Studies Education, 1976–1983*. Washington: National Council for the Social Studies, 1985. Bulletin #75.

Costa, Arthur L. "Mediating the Metacognitive." *Educational Leadership* 42:3 (November 1984), pp. 58–62.

―――. "Teaching for Intelligent Behavior." *Educational Leadership* 39:2 (October 1981), pp. 29–32.

Doyle, Walter. "Academic Work." *Review of Educational Research* 53:2 (Summer 1983), pp. 159–199.

Ennis, Robert H. "A Concept of Cricital Thinking: A Proposed Basis for Research in the Teaching and Evaluation of Critical Thinking Ability." *Harvard Educational Review* 32:1 (Winter 1962), pp. 81–111.

Frederiksen, Norman. "Implications of Cognitive Theory for Instruction in Problem Solving." *Review of Educational Research* 54:3 (Fall 1984), pp. 363–407.

Gersten, Russell, and Douglas Carnine. "Direct Instruction In Reading Comprehension." *Educational Leadership* 43:7 (April 1986), pp. 70–78.

Giroux, Henry A. "Writing and Critical Thinking in the Social Studies." *Curriculum Inquiry* 8:4 (1978), pp. 291–311.

Henderson, Kenneth B. "The Teaching of Critical Thinking." *Educational Forum* 37:1 (November 1972), pp. 45–52.

Hunkins, Francis P. "Helping Students Ask Their Own Questions." *Social Education* 49:4 (April 1985), pp. 293–296.

O'Reilly, Kevin. "Teaching Critical Thinking in High School U.S. History." *Social Education* 49:4 (April 1985), pp. 281–284.

Posner, Michael I. and Steven W. Keele. "Skill Learning." In Robert M. W. Travers, ed., *Second Handbook of Research on Teaching*. Chicago: Rand McNally College Publishing Company, 1973, pp. 805–831.

Rosenshine, Barak V. "Synthesis of Research on Explicit Teaching." *Educational Leadership* 43:7 (April 1986), pp. 60–69.

―――. "Teaching Functions in Instructional Programs." *Elementary School Journal* 83:4 (March 1983), pp. 335–352.

Saadeh, Ibrahim Q. "The Teacher and the Development of Critical Thinking." *Journal of Research and Development in Education* 3:1 (Fall 1969), pp. 87–99.

Sigel, Irving E. "A Constructivist Perspective for Teaching Thinking." *Educational Leadership* 42:3 (November 1984), pp. 18–22.

Stallings, Jane. "Effective Strategies for Teaching Basic Skills." In Daisy G. Wallace, ed., *Developing Basic Skills Programs in Secondary Schools*. Alexandria, Va.: Association for Supervision and Curriculum Development, 1983, pp. 1–19.

Sternberg, Robert J. "Critical Thinking: Its Nature, Measurement and Improvement." Pp. 45–65 in Frances R. Link, ed., *Essays on the Intellect*. Washington: Association for Supervision and Curriculum Development, 1985.

———. "How Can We Teach Intelligence?" *Educational Leadership* 42:1 (September 1984), pp. 38–48.

———. "Teaching Critical Thinking, Part I: Are We Making Critical Mistakes?" *Phi Delta Kappan* (November 1985), pp. 194–198.

Taba, Hilda. "The Evaluation of Critical Thinking." In Howard Anderson, ed., *Teaching Critical Thinking in the Social Studies*. Washington: National Council for the Social Studies, 1942.

———. "The Teaching of Thinking." *Elementary English* 42 (May 1965), pp. 534–542.

Whimbey, Arthur. "Teaching Sequential Thought: The Cognitive Skills Approach." *Phi Delta Kappan* 59:4 (December 1977), pp. 255–259.

———. "The Key to Higher Order Thinking Is Precise Processing." *Educational Leadership* 42:1 (September 1984), pp. 66–70.

Index